Death Angel

Death Angel

*A Vietnam Memoir of a
Bearer of Death Messages
to Families*

Harry Spiller

McFarland & Company, Inc., Publishers
Jefferson, North Carolina, and London

The present work is a reprint of the library bound edition of Death Angel: A Vietnam Memoir of a Bearer of Death Messages to Families, *first published in 1992 by McFarland.*

LIBRARY OF CONGRESS CATALOGUING-IN-PUBLICATION DATA

Spiller, Harry, 1945–
   Death angel : a Vietnam memoir of a bearer of death messages to families / by Harry Spiller.
     p.   cm.
   Includes index.

   ISBN 978-0-7864-6741-9
   softcover : acid free paper ∞

   1. Vietnamese Conflict, 1961–1975—Personal narratives. American. 2. Vietnamese Conflict, 1961–1975—Casualties (Statistics, etc.) 3. United States, Marine Corps—Recruiting, enlistment, etc.
4. Death notices—United States. 5. Spiller, Harry, 1945– I Title.
DS559.5.S66 2012
959.704'38—dc20   92-53500

BRITISH LIBRARY CATALOGUING DATA ARE AVAILABLE

Cover images © 2012 Shutterstock

Manufactured in the United States of America

McFarland & Company, Inc., Publishers
Box 611, Jefferson, North Carolina 28640
www.mcfarlandpub.com

For Lisa

Acknowledgments

To Katherine Derbak who first listened to the tapes and said I should try. For their typing and comments Sheri King, Theresa Hurford, Maxine Pyle, Steve Falcone, Barbara Randolph, Marcia Hogan, Dotti Frank, and Keith Kelley. And for their support and understanding for the many hours I spent writing, my family Shirl and Lisa, but especially to Chad who often said, "Gosh Mom! Daddy's working on his 'B-putor' a-gain."

Table of Contents

Introduction

This is a personal story of what I saw in Vietnam, what I saw as a recruiter in Southeast Missouri and Southern Illinois while delivering death messages and organizing military funerals, and how these experiences affected me. The book is written in third person and the "he" in the story refers to me. It is important for the reader to understand that the story is mine alone. I do not pretend to speak for anyone else.

The dialogues and events all happened. The chronology and geography are correct to the best of my memory. While the content is accurate, the quotes may not be entirely accurate word for word. Time has passed since these events occurred.

The names, other than government officials' and my own, have been changed in order to preserve the privacy and anonymity of those involved.

I hope that this book will encourage other Vietnam veterans to tell their stories. People, especially the young, must know the truth about war. The public should understand the tragedies of sending the youth of a nation into senseless political conflicts.

For now we see through a glass darkly;
but then face to face
I Corinthians 13:12

1
Boot Camp, the Beginning

On June 3, 1963, at 10 P.M., TWA flight #530 landed at San Diego, California. When the plane had come to a stop, the ladder was moved to the side of the plane, and 100 Marine recruits departed.

As 17-year-old Harry Spiller made his way down the ladder, he noticed a sergeant standing on the runway nearby. The sergeant wore a tan-colored summer uniform, known in the Marine Corps as the tropical uniform. Smiling, he seemed friendly enough, as he welcomed the recruits to San Diego and instructed them to get on the buses parked in front of the airport terminal. Parked bumper to bumper were three gray buses with "U.S. Navy" written across the sides. The recruits talked among themselves as they boarded.

"What's your name?" Spiller asked the recruit sitting beside him.

"Richard. Richard Wilson. What's yours?"

"Harry Spiller. Where are you from, Richard?"

"Kansas City, Missouri."

"Oh, really. I'm from Southern Illinois. We're neighbors."

"Yeah," laughed Wilson. "Hey, what do you think we'll do tonight?"

"I don't think we'll do much. It's too late. We'll probably be assigned a bed for the night and start everything in the morning."

"Yeah," replied Wilson, "but they'll have to yell at us a little bit first."

"That's true, but we can handle it."

As the bus passed through the gates at the recruit depot, everyone's eyes were on the MPs at the gate.

"Boy, they look sharp," Wilson remarked as the peach fuzz on his chin seemed to wiggle with each movement of his mouth.

"They sure do. Look at the theatre and the parade stand down there. This all looks just like the movies I've seen," Spiller said excitedly.

"Yeah, this reminds me of 'Gomer Pyle, USMC.' I guess all of that was filmed right here," Wilson offered.

"*The Sands of Iwo Jima* had parts filmed here, too, but they had tents instead of those huts over there. Did you see that movie?" inquired Spiller.

"I sure did."

"Man, this is neat."

The bus stopped. Spiller looked out the window and saw three cruel-looking Marine sergeants wearing tropical uniforms. Standing side by side, each stared straight ahead. Attached to the front of their Smokey the Bear hats was a large Marine Corps emblem. Painted on the asphalt beside the trio were a lot of yellow footprints.

The door opened. The bus driver, along with the sergeant who had met the recruits at the airport, disappeared. One of the three sergeants boarded the bus.

Loudly and insistently he ordered. "Get off the bus. Hurry up! Move! Get off the bus. Put your feet on the yellow footprints."

Spiller and Wilson, anxious to obey, grabbed their bags. In their haste, Wilson stepped on Spiller's heel, causing them both to trip. Spiller tumbled into the aisle. Wilson was on top of him.

"Way to go," Spiller snapped as he pushed the lanky 17-year-old off of him.

"Damn! I didn't mean it," insisted Wilson.

"Shut your mouths, privates! You're at no picnic," snarled the sergeant.

"Yes, sir," replied Wilson and Spiller as they scrambled off the bus.

The recruits stood rigidly on the yellow footprints while the sergeant shouted. "The first thing I'm going to do is give you instructions for the position of attention. In the position of attention," he continued by demonstrating, "your hands will remain at your sides with your thumbs touching the seams of your trousers. Your feet at a 45-degree angle with your heels together. You will look straight ahead. The only things that may move are your eyes. They may open and close. You don't move your eyeballs left or right. You do not move your hands or feet for any reason whatsoever. Do I make myself clear?"

"Yes, sir!" yelled the recruits.

"All right, people, when I give you the word, I want all of you to turn left. Each row, beginning with the row next to me, will double time into the building in front of you. When you get inside that building, a sergeant will direct you where to stand. Is that clear?"

"Yes, sir!" yelled the recruits.

"I can't h-e-a-r y-o-u!"

"Yes, sir!" the recruits yelled again.

"All right, move out. Move! If that man in front of you isn't moving fast enough, step on him. Quickly! Move, move, move!"

Inside the building the recruits were lined up in front of barber chairs for half-minute haircuts. A recruit got out of a chair. Blood was running down the side of his head.

"My God! What happened to him?" Spiller thought.

When Spiller entered the chair, the barber instructed, "If you have any moles on your head, put your finger on them, or they'll come off with the hair."

"Yes, sir! I mean, no, sir! I don't have any moles," replied Spiller.

After their haircuts, the recruits were quickly assembled in front of a small stage at the far end of the room.

A drill instructor began, "I'm going to tell you what is expected of you and what you should expect while in receiving barracks. The treatment you're going to receive here is different from what you receive elsewhere. You're going to find yourself doing things you never thought you could do or would be doing. You're now going to get what we call the bucket issue. When you go through this line, you will be issued a mattress cover, known in the Marine Corps as a fart sack. You will take that fart sack, open it, and stand at attention in front of each table, as you move through the issue area. When you step up to the appropriate table, you will sound off your shoe size, such as nine-and-a-half, sir! You will add 'sir' at the end of it. Do you understand, girls?"

"Yes, sir," replied the recruits as they quickly scrambled.

After the issue the drill instructor spoke. "The first door on your left is the shower. Everyone will go in, take a shower, then you'll get back in here, unlock your locker, and get dressed in the uniform that was issued to you: white tennis shoes, wool socks, utility trousers, yellow sweat shirt, belt, and put your cap in your right rear pocket. All right, everybody, turn to and get that done," growled the drill instructor.

Spiller, looking forward to getting the hair off his neck and shoulders, hurried for the shower, only to be surprised by a stream of ice-cold water. Finally, Spiller, Wilson, and all the other recruits were finished with the bucket issue. They had experienced the dizzy world of receiving barracks and their first taste of boot camp discipline. Each was assigned a rack.

Spiller's last thought as he crawled into his bunk was the statement he'd made to Wilson: "It's too late to start anything tonight. We'll probably be assigned a bunk and start in the morning."

It was 4 A.M.

At 5 A.M. the lights came on in the barracks. The door swung open, and a sergeant ran into the squad bay, banging loudly on a garbage can lid.

"Get out of those racks, get dressed, and get downstairs. Hurry up! Move, move, move!" screamed the sergeant.

Spiller jumped out of his rack, put on his clothes as fast as he could, and ran down the stairs. As he and the others ran outside, a sergeant lined the recruits into formation. It was still dark outside. The recruits were in a state of mass confusion. Finally in formation, they were ready to meet their drill instructors for the first time.

"Good morning, Privates!"

"Good morning, sir!" replied the sleepy recruits.

"I'm Gunnery Sergeant Anderson, your platoon commander. Two other drill instructors, Sergeant Johnson and Sergeant Lewis, and I will be working with you. We'll tell you when to do everything. When to shower, when to shave, go to chow, go to church, write letters. We'll even get your mail for you. Everything that has to be done will be done by one of us. Do I make myself clear?" shouted the gunnery sergeant.

"Yes, sir!" yelled the recruits.

"Now, Privates, the first word out of your mouth, when you speak to a drill instructor, is the word 'sir.' To anyone, who is not a recruit, you will say 'sir.' Is that clear?" yelled Anderson.

"Yes, sir!" the recruits yelled.

"From now on you will keep your hands out of your pockets. You will not smoke, until you're told to smoke, and you will not chew gum. When you write home, don't exaggerate. Anytime you have any trouble or problems, you will see your drill instructor. Is that clear?"

"Yes, sir!" replied the recruits.

"I can't hear you, girls!"

"Yes, sir!"

"All right, everyone, turn to your left," Johnson ordered. When I give you the word, everyone will begin walking, starting with your left foot first. Is that clear?"

"Yes, sir!"

"All right, move!" Johnson snapped.

Soon the recruits were in front of the mess hall.

"All right, Privates, you're going in for morning chow. You will go through the line in column, starting with the right of the formation. As you go through the line, you will stand at attention with your eyeballs glued to the back of the head of the private in front of you. When you get to the chow line, you will remain at attention holding your tray level with your waist. You will then side step through the chow line, and Sergeant Lewis will show you which table to go to. Is that clear?"

"Yes, sir!"

"All right, move out!"

As Spiller passed through the chow line, two pieces of toast were thrown on his plate. Hitting the tray, the toast bounced, and the crust fell to the sides. A soup, made with hamburger meat, tomatoes, and onion, was poured over the toast. The recruits were directed to tables.

Sergeant Lewis stood at the end of the table and continued to instruct. "All right, girls, I'm sure all of you are used to eating junk food for breakfast, but this morning you are going to eat the United States Marine Corps' finest, shit on the shingle. You will love it, girls. Do you understand?"

"Yes, sir!" replied the privates.

"When I give you the word, you will sit down at attention and remain at attention, until I tell you to eat. Is that clear?"

"Yes, sir!"

"Ready, seats!" yelled Lewis.

The recruits sat quickly.

"Get up! That isn't fast enough, girls," said Lewis.

"Ready, seats!"

The recruits again sat quickly.

"Get up, girls. You don't seem to want to get on with the program, do you, girls?" Lewis yelled.

"Yes, sir!" yelled the hungry recruits.

"All right then. When I give you ready seats, you'd better move. Ready, seats!"

The privates moved quickly.

"All right, girls, you will eat while sitting at the position of attention. You will not talk, unless you are asking for the salt and pepper. You have ten minutes to eat. Is that clear?"

"Yes, sir!"

As his first forkful of Marine chow lay stagnant on his taste buds, Spiller thought, "The only thing good about this shit on the shingles is that it softens the toast as it soaks through. I sure wish I had some of Mom's pancakes."

When morning chow was finished, the recruits were marched to the medical center for a complete physical before starting training. Spiller stood at attention in front of the Navy corpsman to have a sample of blood drawn.

"All right, Private, hold your arm straight out," said the corpsman.

"Yes, sir!"

The corpsman stuck the needle into Spiller's arm. Unable to hit a vein, he pulled the needle out.

"I missed, Private," he said with a laugh. "I'll try again."

The corpsman stuck the needle into his arm again, and again he missed the vein. The corpsman wiggled the needle, causing Spiller to moan.

"What's the matter, Marine? Can't you take it?"

"Yes, sir, I can!"

The corpsman laughed.

"You don't have a blood vessel in that arm. We'll have to try the other one, Private. Put this arm down and give me the other one."

"Yes, sir," replied Spiller, lifting his left arm.

The needle entered Spiller's left arm. Still no blood. The corpsman wiggled the needle again.

"Come on, Marine, faint. Faint, Marine. Your drill instructor will love it," the corpsman said in a taunting manner.

"No, sir!"

Fortunately, the next time the corpsman hit a vein. When Spiller finished his blood test, both arms started to swell and turn black. As he walked through the process line, Sergeant Johnson saw his arms.

"What happened to your arms, Private?"

"The blood tests, sir. The corpsman missed my vein," Spiller explained.

"Get down and give me twenty push-ups, Private," said Johnson.

Spiller hit the floor and painfully pumped off the push-ups. To his surprise, he felt the soreness leave his arms.

The last stop before leaving the medical center was an interview with the base psychiatrist. Spiller stood at attention in front of the psychiatrist's desk.

"What do you think of the Marine Corps, Private?" the doctor asked.

"I think it's great, sir."

"Do you think your drill instructors are crazy?"

"No, sir!"

"Do you think you're crazy, Private?"

"No, sir!"

"Very well, Private, get out of here."

Spiller left the medical center thinking that if anyone knew what this was like before they got here, they would have to be crazy to volunteer.

After the medical exams, the recruits were taken to their platoon living quarters. The living quarters consisted of three metal buildings in a half-moon shape with small windows on all sides and a door in front and back. They were known as Quonset huts. Each hut housed 25 men. Between the rows of Quonset huts was a road, an asphalt strip about twice the width of a sidewalk. There was nothing but sand between the road and the huts.

For the next two hours each recruit was assigned a rack, issued a mattress, blankets, sheets, and a footlocker. The men were instructed on how to make the racks, using the hospital folds, and where to place all the gear they'd been issued. Every item was to be placed in a particular location in the footlocker. When that was finished, the recruits were called on the road.

"All right, Privates, your platoon number is Platoon 135. Before you leave boot camp, this will be the best platoon in the history of the United States Marine Corps. Is that clear?" yelled Gunnery Sergeant Anderson.

"Yes, sir!"

"I can't h-e-a-r you," said Anderson.

"Yes, sir!" the recruits replied.

"This area looks like something a bunch of civilians would live in. We are going to make this entire area shine like a diamond in a goat's ass. Do I make myself clear?" shouted Anderson.

"Yes, sir," replied the privates.

"All right, people, when I give the word, all of you will return to your Quonset hut, get the cleaning gear that was issued, and start cleaning. We are going to scrub the decks, the bulk heads, the over heads. We're going to scrub everything. Do you understand, girls?"

"Yes, sir!"

"When I dismiss the platoon, Private Wilson and Private Spiller will remain on the road. Dismissed!"

"Aye, aye, sir!" replied the privates as they ran into the huts.

Anderson approached Spiller and Wilson.

"Privates, do you see the grass around these Quonset huts?"

"Yes, sir," replied Spiller and Wilson with puzzled looks.

"I want both of you to take those buckets over there, fill them with water, and water the grass. Before you leave boot camp, I want that grass looking like a golf course, Privates. Do you understand?"

"Yes, sir," replied Spiller and Wilson.

"All right, turn to and get that done," demanded Anderson.

"Aye, aye, sir," replied Spiller and Wilson, grabbing the buckets.

Anderson went into his office, known as the duty hut. As Spiller and Wilson watered the grass, Spiller, on his hands and knees, ran his hand through the sand looking for grass.

As Wilson was doing the same, Spiller whispered, "Hey Wilson, there ain't any grass here."

"I can't find any either," said Wilson. "How are we supposed to make it grow, if there isn't any grass?"

"I don't know, but we'd better," Spiller replied.

As Spiller turned to reach for his bucket, he found himself staring at a pair of spit-shined shoes.

"Get on your feet!" yelled Anderson.

Spiller stood at attention, nose to nose with Anderson.

"Private Spiller, did I hear you say there wasn't any grass?"

"No, sir. I mean yes, sir!" replied Spiller.

"Did I tell you there was grass there?" yelled Anderson.

"Yes, sir."

"Then you're calling me a liar, aren't you, Private?"

"No, sir!"

"Then there is grass there!" yelled Anderson.

"Yes, sir, there is!"

"Then I suggest you make it grow."

"Aye, aye, sir!"

"Do it then, Private!"

After half a day of watering grass and scrubbing floors, Platoon 135 was called on the road and taken back to receiving barracks.

"All right, Privates, when I give you the word, you will go into the barracks, pick up your civilians clothes, and bring them back here. Do you understand?"

"Yes, sir!" replied the privates.

"All right, turn to and get that done," yelled Anderson.

Spiller ran up the stairs to the second floor to get his clothes. He couldn't find them. Looking around several other racks, still he found nothing. Spiller rushed back outside and requested to speak to the drill instructor.

"Sir, Private Spiller requests permission to speak to the drill instructor."

"Speak," snapped Anderson.

"Sir, my clothes are gone!"

"What do you mean, your clothes are gone?" mocked Anderson.

"Sir, I went to my rack, and they're gone."

"Private, you have exactly 15 seconds to get those clothes and get back down here, or I'm going to kill you," Anderson threatened.

"Yes, sir!" replied Spiller.

Spiller turned and ran up the stairs. With his feet hitting every fourth step, he thought only of what the drill instructor said. Spiller ran to the third floor instead of the second, and this time found his clothes. Back in formation, he was given a brown piece of 4' × 4' paper and a piece of tape to wrap his clothes. Spiller placed his clothes on the paper with his shoes on top and attempted to wrap the clothing. When he finally made his last fold, the paper ripped.

Anderson yelled, "Go get another piece of paper, Spiller. Hurry up! Move, move, move!"

Spiller's second attempt proved to be as futile as the first.

When Spiller approached the supply sergeant for the third time, the sergeant yelled, "You're going to break this man's Marine Corps, Private. Why don't you give those shoes to the Navy relief?"

"Yes, sir," Spiller replied.

He handed the shoes to the sergeant and then returned to his clothing. Spiller, on his hands and knees, tried nervously to wrap his clothes. Anderson was in front of him, Sergeant Lewis on one side of him, and Sergeant Johnson on the other.

All three were yelling. "Get them clothes wrapped. You're holding up the entire platoon, Private. Hurry up! Hurry up!"

Spiller finally finished wrapping his clothes, and returned to the platoon formation. He wondered, "What is the Navy relief? Those were my new shoes. The only time I ever wore them was to high school graduation."

Platoon 135 returned to the platoon area.

"All right, Privates, when I dismiss you, go inside and straighten up the area. Make sure your racks are tight and footlockers are in place. Do I make myself clear?" said Anderson.

"Yes, sir," replied the recruits.

"Dismissed."

"Aye, aye, sir," yelled the privates as they ran for the huts.

As the recruits tightened racks and shuffled footlockers, they talked among themselves.

"This isn't anything like I thought it would be," said Wilson.

"Me either," said Spiller. "They have us watering grass that isn't there. I gave my new shoes to the Navy relief, and I don't even know what it is. Do you?"

"No," replied Wilson, "besides, why should you have to give your shoes to the Navy? I thought we were in the Marine Corps."

Private Lindhurst spoke up. "If you think watering grass is bad, you should've seen Sergeant Johnson in here. See this floor?"

"Yeah," said Spiller and Wilson, "what about it?"

"What color is it?" asked Lindhurst.

"It's gray," replied Wilson.

"Sergeant Johnson said he wanted it white when we finished scrubbing it."

"White!" exclaimed Spiller.

"That's right, white," replied Lindhurst.

"How are you supposed to make it white?" asked Wilson.

"I don't know. I can tell you one thing," said Lindhurst.

"What's that?" asked Wilson and Spiller.

"This sure ain't like in the movies."

Spiller and Wilson agreed.

As they turned to check their racks one more time, Spiller whispered to Wilson. "I wish I was home."

"Me, too," Wilson agreed, "more than anything."

"Platoon 135, on the road," yelled Sergeant Anderson.

As the platoon formed, Anderson looked up and down the formation. He removed his Smokey the Bear hat and started talking.

"I don't often ask anything of privates, but I want to ask each and every one of you to do me a favor. I want you to pray for war." Tears swelled in his eyes. He continued, "I've been a staff sergeant for four years. I can't be promoted, unless the Marine Corps has openings for rank, and the only way for an opening to occur is through casualties of war. So, Privates, during your stay in boot camp, I'm asking that when taps are sounded at night, each and every one of you pray for war, so that I might be promoted."

The entire platoon area was quiet.

Spiller thought, "My God, is he crazy!"

Sunday morning was slack day in boot camp. It was a day to go to church, to write letters, and to have organized athletics. The privates had returned from church, and Spiller was writing a letter home.

Dear Mom,

How are you and everyone else doing? I sure do miss everyone. I guess I am a lot more homesick than I thought I would be.

Boot camp is a lot tougher than I thought it would be, too. We are constantly being yelled at. This is the end of our sixth week and the drill instructors seem to get tougher on us the longer we are here. We get up at 5 A.M., have roll call, and then do 30 minutes of exercise. We eat chow and then train, train, train. We have a lot of classes on the history and tradition of the Marine Corps. They have a real reputation for being fighters. No wonder though, all they train us for is war.

I still can't believe Sergeant Anderson isn't crazy. He has had me and Wilson watering sand for six weeks. He claims there is grass there, but we haven't been able to find any. Wilson told me the other day he wrote his Mom and asked her to put some grass seed in one of her letters. He is from Kansas City, Missouri, and says they have some kind of prairie grass that grows in the sand. Maybe we can get it to grow. Oh, yeah, please don't send me any cookies or cake for my birthday. The other day Lindhurst got a cake in the mail. Sergeant Johnson sat it out in the sun all day and made Lindhurst eat the whole thing without any water. Boy, he sure got sick.

We have been to the rifle range and all of us qualified with the rifles. You have to score 220 out of 250 to qualify as expert. I shot expert, how about that? Would you believe I can take my rifle apart and put it back together blindfolded?

I have lost some weight, but no wonder. We double time everywhere we go, and run three miles a day. Yesterday, we were on our three mile run, and about halfway through, Sergeant Johnson started laughing and halted the platoon. He said that in his last platoon he had a private that died right where we were standing. He quit laughing, got that cruel look on his face, and we started running again. I am not sure that he is sane, either. Also, we have been having a lot of drill, at least three hours a day. Sometimes more.

I guess we are lucky that we don't have to carry the field transport pack, while we are doing all of this. The field transport pack is everything that we would take into combat: a tent, entrenching tool, extra boots and clothing, the whole works. We sure would need those things, but the pack weighs about 60 pounds, and that doesn't count our cartridge belt with the canteens, bayonet, and extra clips of ammunition for our rifles.

I better go. We have to eat noon chow, and then we are going to have organized athletics this afternoon. I believe we are going to play football. I am halfway through. I can't wait to graduate and come home.

> Love,
> Harry

P.S. Tell everybody I said "Hi."

The next morning Sergeant Johnson called Platoon 135 on the road for a rifle inspection. A short time later the inspecting officer, Lieutenant Jenkins, arrived. Johnson called the platoon to attention.

Jenkins stepped in front of the first man, and as he took the rifle, he began asking questions. "What is your serial number, Private?"

"Sir, my serial number is 2043565, sir," replied Lindhurst.

"Private, you have dust around the trigger guard."

"Yes, sir."

The lieutenant stepped to the next man. "Private, what does *semper fidelis* mean?"

"Always faithful, sir," replied Wilson.

"Always faithful to whom?"

"To God, country, and the Marine Corps, sir!" yelled Wilson.

"In that order, Private?"

"Yes, sir!"

The lieutenant handed Wilson's rifle back and stepped in front of Spiller. Examining Spiller's rifle, he asked, "What kind of rifle is this?"

"Sir, an M-14 rifle, sir."

"Tell me what you know about the rifle, Private."

"Sir, the M-14 rifle is a semi-automatic, gas-operated rifle. The rifle weighs 9.34 pounds unloaded, and 11.34 pounds fully combat loaded. The rifle fires a 7.62 mm shell and holds a clip rate of fire of 8 to 10 rounds per second and a rapid fire of 200 to 300 rounds per second, sir."

"Very well, Private," said Jenkins.

When the lieutenant finally finished inspection, he left the area.

"All right, girls, there were a few discrepancies, were there not?" yelled Johnson.

"Yes, sir," replied the privates.

"We are not going to have any discrepancies, are we, girls?"

"No, sir!"

"All right, when I give you the word, you have 15 seconds to put those rifles away and fall out on the road for exercise," yelled Johnson. "Dismissed."

"Aye, aye, sir," replied Platoon 135, scrambling for the quonset huts.

When the platoon was back on the road, Johnson began, "You're all going to die, if we go to war. Do you know why, girls? Because your rifles are dirty, and when your rifles are dirty, they do not fire, do they, Privates?"

"No, sir!"

"We have a saying here, girls. The more you sweat in peace, the less you bleed in war. And girls, when we finish with our exercise, there won't be a drop shed from this platoon. Is that clear?" yelled Johnson.

"Yes, sir!"

"Right face, forward march, double time, march, march."

That afternoon the platoon was put through the final phase of bayonet training. Each private was given a football helmet with a face mask. The platoon, divided in half, gathered for instruction.

"All right, people, this is a pugil stick. On each end we have two bags. One has a red ring around it. What do you suppose that means?" asked Johnson.

"That is the bayonet," replied the recruits.

"That's right. The platoon will be divided. Half of you will line up over there; the other half will line up here," instructed Johnson.

The recruits lined up in two lines, approximately ten feet apart.

"When I blow the whistle, I want you to run at each other and fight like the other private is the enemy. No mercy shown. Is that clear?" asked Johnson.

"Yes, sir!"

"All right."

Johnson blew the whistle.

Gunnery Sergeant Anderson whispered to Spiller as he waited his turn. "When you get up there, run right at that private and throw your left arm straight forward with your bayonet aimed at his head. Do you understand?"

"Yes, sir."

The whistle blew, and Spiller followed instructions. He was so successful he almost took the other private's head off. When it was his turn again, the results were the same. The third time Spiller was instructed to do the same. He threw his arm forward, but this time the other private ducked and swung his pugil stick, catching Spiller square in the face. Spiller, lying flat on his back, was out cold. The next thing he remembered was looking up with Anderson staring down at him.

"How do you feel, Spiller?" Anderson asked.

"Uh, I'm, uh, fine, sir."

"No you're not. You dumb shit, you're dead," replied Anderson.

Back in the platoon area, Spiller and Wilson were watering the grass.

"Private Spiller! Private Wilson! Report to the duty hut."

Spiller and Wilson ran to the door and knocked loudly with their fists.

"Sir, Private Wilson requests permission to enter the duty hut."

"I can't hear you," said Anderson.

Both knocked again and even more loudly requested to enter the duty hut.

"Come in," Anderson said.

Spiller and Wilson approached his desk.

"Sir, Private Spiller reporting as ordered."

"Sir, Private Wilson reporting as ordered."

"What are you reporting for, Spiller?" said Anderson.

"You called for me, sir," yelled Spiller.

"Ewe? What is a ewe? What is a ewe?"

"A ewe is a sheep, sir," replied Spiller.

"Am I a sheep? Do I have horns like a sheep?"

"No, sir."

"Then what am I?"

"A drill instructor?"

"Are you sure?"

"Yes, sir!"

"Why are you sure? Because you think so or because I say so?"

"Because I think so, sir!"

"Why did you join the Marine Corps, Private?"

"Because I think I need discipline, sir."

"Are you getting it?"

"Yes, sir!"

"Do you like it?"

"Yes, sir!"

"You're going to get a lot more?"

"Yes, sir!"

"How does your head feel?" asked Anderson.

"Fine, sir!"

"You're sure?" asked Anderson.

"Yes, sir."

"If you'd been in combat, you would've been dead, wouldn't you?"

"Yes, sir!"

"Wilson, you and Spiller have both been watering my grass for six weeks, and the grass doesn't look any better than it did when you got here. Why?"

"I don't know, sir!"

"It had better look like a golf course, or you'll both be here forever, Privates. Do you understand?"

"Yes, sir!"

"All right, get out of here," said Anderson.

"Aye, aye, sir," said Spiller and Wilson as they left the duty hut.

Once again it was Sunday, boot camp slack day, and Spiller was writing home.

Dear Mom,

Well, boot camp is finally coming to an end. We graduate next week, and I can hardly wait. I guess the best news besides graduation is that we got our duty station assignments. Guess where Wilson and I got stationed? Hawaii! Do you believe it? We both about flipped, when we heard. We are being assigned to the Fourth Marine Regiment in the First Marine Brigade. That will really be a great duty station.

A marine at 17. This picture of Harry Spiller was taken shortly after boot camp in 1963.

Wilson's mom sent him some grass seed in one of his letters, and we planted it. I didn't think it would do any good, but Mom, some of it is sprouting! Wilson said it was prairie grass and that it would grow. I guess he knew what he was talking about. I don't know what Gunnery Sergeant Anderson will say.

I still can't believe that boot camp is almost over. All the yelling, obstacle courses, drill, and bayonet training, and classes are behind us. I sure wish you could be here to see me graduate.

We get base liberty after graduation, so I will get to call. Well, I better go now, got to shine my shoes for graduation. Talk to you next week.

Love
Harry

All the members of Platoon 135 had waited for August 31, 1963 – graduation day. The fear gone, graduation was a day of self-respect and gratitude toward other Marines. Chills ran down the backs of Spiller and Wilson, as they marched to the front of the depot theatre, where the Marine Corps hymn was being played by the base band. As the platoon halted, the drill instructors were ordered to dismiss their platoon. Gunnery Sergeant Anderson did an about face.

Hesitating for a moment, he yelled, "Platoon 135, dismissed!"

The members of Platoon 135 screamed, "Aye, aye, sir!"

Amidst the hugs and the handshakes, hats were thrown wildly into the air. As things settled down, Spiller and Wilson made their way to shake hands with Anderson.

When they approached, Anderson looked half cruel and half puzzled.

"Wilson, Spiller, do you know anything about that grass growing in front of the quonset huts?"

Wilson replied, "No, sir."

Anderson, his eyes squinted slightly, looked at Spiller and then at Wilson. He shook hands with both and said, "All right, get out of here."

As Spiller and Wilson walked away, Wilson asked, "Hey, Spiller, did he have tears in his eyes?"

"Hell, no."

"He really looked like he was going to cry."

"I don't think so. Not Gunnery Sergeant Anderson. That is, well, maybe if he was wanting us to pray for war!"

2

Rumors of War

On December 11, 1963, the USS *William A. Mann* crept to the side of Pier 4 at Pearl Harbor. Wilson and Spiller, on the port side of the ship, gazed across the harbor at the monument of the USS *Arizona*. Two of its gun mounts protruded through the water. Tourists stood in silence as they read the names of the men who died and whose bodies were still aboard the ship.

"It's hard to believe there are still two thousand men on the ship," said Spiller.

"Yeah," said Wilson in a low voice. "It reminds you of World War II all over."

"Sure does. I guess they left them down there to remind us," said Spiller.

"Yeah, let's get out of here."

Wilson, Spiller, and 35 other Marines boarded a bus that transported them across the island of Oahu. As the bus moved across the island, Wilson and Spiller admired the beautiful scenery. The Pali was its most impressive site. Its mountain region stretched across the middle of the island. A white cloud lingered softly across the top of the dark green, odd-shaped mountains.

"Everything's so green," said Spiller.

"Yeah," said Wilson. "This place sure has the palm trees."

"You know the first place I wanna go on liberty?"

"Where?" asked Wilson smiling.

"Waikiki Beach."

"To get a tan or to look at the girls?"

"Both," laughed Spiller. "How about you?"

"Sounds good to me."

Late that afternoon the bus arrived at Kaniowi Air Station, the home of the First Marine Brigade. The Brigade consisted of a Marine fighter squadron and the Fourth Marine Infantry Regiment. A lance corporal met the bus and led the Marines to a supply building, where they were issued rifles, field packs, cartridge belts, and canteens. The group of Marines was split up; half went to the Second Battalion, Fourth Marines, and the other half, to the Third Battalion, Fourth Marines. Afterwards, they were all taken to battalion headquarters.

Having turned in personal records, both Wilson and Spiller were assigned to Lima Company, First Platoon and sent to the barracks. They walked into the squad bay area, laid their gear on the floor, and watched the men of the First Platoon. On the floor in the middle of the squad bay, three Marines were holding another Marine, who had no shirt on. A fourth Marine was hitting the pinned Marine on the back of the arms and hand slapping his stomach. The victim was yelling and cursing. Another Marine, jumping up and down on his bunk, cheered the men on, but stopped and smiled at Spiller and Wilson.

"That's initiation for new guys. Hey, new guys! You'll get your turn," he laughed.

He continued to jump up and down, cheering the Marines on. Two other guys, wrestling on one of the lower bunks, were biting at each other.

Spiller looked at Wilson, "These guys are a bunch of animals!"

At that moment a corporal walked up to Spiller and Wilson.

"Welcome aboard," said a smiling Corporal Denis. "Come on down here, and I'll show you where your bunks and wall lockers are."

"Yes, sir, Corporal," replied Spiller and Wilson as they picked up their gear.

"Listen, you two. You're not in boot camp any more," said Denis. "You call me Corporal Denis, not sir. I'm not an officer, understand?"

"Yes, sir," replied Spiller and Wilson, "I mean Corporal."

Smith showed Spiller and Wilson to their bunks and then introduced them to Private First Class Jim Orr.

"All right, the three of you make up the first fire team of the first squad. I'm responsible to the squad leader for your entire performance. We have a personal and rifle inspection every morning at 0730. I want you to put your gear away, clean your rifles, and get a uniform ready for tomorrow morning. I want to see your rifles before taps, got that?" instructed Denis.

"Yes, sir," replied Spiller and Wilson as they continued to watch the other Marines in the barracks.

Denis laughed, "You'll get used to these guys. As a matter of fact, it won't be long till you're doing the same thing."

Denis continued laughing as he walked away.

Orr helped Spiller and Wilson put their gear away.

Spiller asked, "What's this place like?"

"Not bad," replied Orr. "We get up at 0530, eat chow, clean the barracks, and fall into formation for inspection at 0730. That takes about half an hour. Then we drill for another hour. After that we have training classes then we PT around 1500."

"How far do we run?" asked Wilson.

"Usually three miles."

"What about liberty?" inquired Spiller.

"Liberty call is at 1600 hours most of the time, and we usually get liberty on the weekends. About the only time we don't get liberty is when we go to the field. We're going to Molokai next month for 30 days. We'll get dungaree liberty over there. Only one town, not much to do but drink," said Orr.

"How is liberty here?" asked Spiller.

"It's okay, but it's awfully expensive. You can lay on the beach for nothing down at Waikiki, but that's about it. The people around the hotels are either tourists or owners. The place is a tourist trap."

"Yeah," said Wilson, "Seventy-eight dollars a month won't go very far."

"That's right," replied Orr. "Not here, anyway."

For the next two months, Spiller, Wilson, and the rest of Lima Company trained. There was drill, classes on nuclear war, history, germ warfare, and other conventional warfare, physical training, personnel and equipment inspections.

Lima Company was given word that they were to be part of the troops to be filmed by Warner Bros. for a World War II movie, *In Harm's Way*, starring John Wayne and Kirk Douglas. Everyone joked about being movie stars. Both Spiller and Wilson wrote home telling their families about the movie. Finally, the day had arrived and Lima Company was aboard ship, preparing for the landing. At 0600 hours the troops, lined on the port side, waited for word to go down the nets. Lima Company, in full transport packs, went down the beach landing. Spiller looked down at the Mike boat, as he lowered himself on the nets.

One second the Mike boat seemed to be under his feet, and the next, 15 feet under him. Lima Company, aboard the boats, circled.

To Spiller the ride in the Mike boat seemd much rougher than the ride on the ship. Some Marines even got seasick.

"Wilson, you look green," said Spiller.

"No, shit," said Wilson, "I'm sick as hell."

"I'm starting to feel a little, a little. . . ." Spiller threw up.

"What's the matter Harry, you sick?"

"Fuck you, Wilson! These damned diesel fumes are enough to kill anybody."

Some of the other Marines, all landing for the first time, became ill, too. Meanwhile, the Mike boats, in line, headed for the beach.

"You two okay?" asked Corporal Denis.

"Sure we're okay, Corporal," replied Spiller and Wilson.

"You two are going to make real movie stars," laughed Denis.

Spiller looked at Wilson.

"I wasn't seasick, Wilson. It was the fumes. And, what the hell were you so green for, Richard?"

"I wasn't."

"All right, you two straighten up and get ready. We're gonna hit the beach shortly. Wait until the ramp is secure before you run off. Be careful on the ramp. It's slick. You'll bust your ass if you aren't careful," yelled Denis. "Everybody look sharp. We're gonna be on camera."

The Mike boats landed and the ramp went down.

"All right, let's hit it!"

The troops dashed off the boat and up the sandy beach about ten yards then hit the dirt. The Marines, weapons loaded with blank ammo, fired from the prone position.

"That was neat," thought Spiller as he took the prone position.

Two large palm trees lay smoldering on the ground. They had been set on fire for special effects. One tree had been broken in half. Its upper portion was hanging parallel to the trunk, making it appear as though artillery had hit it.

When the exercise was over, Lima Company was lined up.

The producer came over to talk with the Marines. "I want to thank each and every one of you for your cooperation and for the fine landing you made. Each of you will receive a check for your performance. When the film is finished, we'll have a premiere for you."

Six months later, each of the men received a check for $7.95, and word came from the movie producer that *In Harm's Way* was coming to Hawaii.

Spiller, Wilson, and Orr joked again about being movie stars as they walked to the theater. Inside, the producer appeared on stage. Once again, he thanked the Marines for their cooperation and said he hoped they'd enjoy the movie.

The Marines waited anxiously to see if they could recognize themselves in the beach landing.

"I wonder where John Wayne and Kirk Douglas were when they filmed this?" asked Orr.

"I don't know," replied Spiller. "They were here though. Some of the other guys said they saw Douglas down at Waikiki Beach," added Spiller.

"That's right," said Wilson. "I heard them talking about it."

"John Wayne was on the base, too," said Spiller.

"Hey, here we go. There are the Mike boats," said Orr.

"Which one was ours?" Spiller inquired.

"I don't know," said Wilson.

"Me either," said Orr.

"That was me!" exclaimed Wilson.

"No it wasn't," said Spiller. "That face wasn't green enough!"

"Fuck you, Harry. You're the one that was barfing all over the place," said Wilson.

"I wasn't seasick. It was the fumes."

"Sure!"

Orr was laughing at both of them.

"Hey guys, let's watch the movie."

"All right," agreed Spiller and Wilson.

The three left the theater boasting about their parts in the film.

"I know I saw myself," said Wilson.

"Me, too," replied Orr.

"Yeah, I guess we could say we were all part of World War II, huh," said Spiller.

"Like hell you were," came a loud voice from behind.

The three turned. A sergeant major stared them right in the eyes.

"I was in World War II, youngsters! You were only a part of a fictitious war," snapped the sergeant major.

He turned and walked away. Orr, Spiller, and Wilson continued.

"Damn, he didn't have to take it so personally," said Spiller.

"Yeah, he's probably just jealous because he wasn't in the movie," said Orr.

"That's right," said Wilson. "Besides that, it couldn't have been all that bad in World War II. Did you see all the medals he was wearing?"

On Monday, July 19, 1964, at 0600, Spiller, Wilson, and Orr were making their bunks. Corporal Denis walked in.

"Spiller, Wilson, you forgot the inspection this morning. You both have to be at battalion headquarters at 0730."

"What for?" asked Spiller.

"I don't know," answered Denis, "but you have to report to Gunnery Sergeant Watson in the S-2 office."

"That's the intelligence section, isn't it?" asked Wilson.

"That's right," replied Denis.

Puzzled, Wilson and Spiller looked at each other.

At 0730 Wilson and Spiller reported to the S-2 office. Gunnery Sergeant Watson introduced himself and asked both Wilson and Spiller to be seated.

"Men, I have reviewed both of your records. Your records indicate that since you've been with Lima Company, your performance as infantrymen has been outstanding."

"Thank you, sir."

"Do you think you'd be interested in working for the intelligence office?" asked Watson.

"Well, sir," replied Spiller, "I think I would, sir."

Wilson spoke up. "What would we be doing, sir?"

"Both of you would be battalion scouts. There will be five for the battalion. It would be your responsibility to gather intelligence information concerning enemy activity in a combat situation."

"Five of us?" asked Spiller.

"That's right," answered Watson. "There are five. You may be required to sneak right into the enemy's backyard, so there can't be too many. There's a lot of extensive training ahead of you, if you think you want the job."

"What type of training, sir?" asked Wilson.

"Sniper school, jungle warfare, a survival course, and extensive PT."

Wilson and Spiller smiled at each other.

"I'd like to be a scout," said Spiller.

"Me, too," said Wilson.

"Good, I'll expect your performances to remain as excellent as they've been in Lima Company.

"Yes, sir," replied Wilson and Spiller.

"I'll put in for your transfers this week. Your orders should be ready by the first of next week."

"Thank you, sir," Spiller and Wilson replied as they left the office.

When they stepped outside the building, Spiller let out a yell and threw his cap into the air. Wilson ran up to Spiller and hugged him.

"We did it, Harry. We did it!" said Wilson.

"You're damned right we did it," replied Spiller. "Man, could you imagine if we went to war, Rich? We'd be right out there in the middle of things."

"That's right," said Wilson, "being part of a crack scout team in a war. Boy, we'd really rack up the medals."

"That's right," said Spiller. "I can see us walking down the street back home right now. Yeah, we did it, man. We really did it."

A week later Spiller and Wilson reported to the Third Battalion Headquarters and Service Company Scout Section.

"Good morning, Sergeant, I'm Harry Spiller. This is Richard Wilson."

"Good morning, I'm Sergeant Gray, your scout leader. Come on back to the squad bay. I'll show you where your bunks are and introduce you to the other members of the scout section."

Spiller and Wilson picked up their gear and walked into the squad bay with Gray.

"This is Lance Corporal Smith and Lance Corporal Stilley," said Gray.

"Good morning," Spiller and Wilson replied as they both shook hands with Smith and Stilley.

"All right, put your gear away and make up your bunks. When you get finished, I want to see all four of you in my office."

"Very well," replied Spiller and Wilson as they put their gear away.

Spiller, Wilson, Smith, and Stilley reported to Gray's office. Gray looked very serious at Spiller and Wilson momentarily then spoke. "Men, we five have a very important job. We're the enemy intelligence finders for the battalion. We may find ourselves separated from the battalion by as much as 10 or 15 miles, right in the backyard of the enemy. That means that any one person that screws up may get the rest of us killed. It's very important that we all work together closely. We'll eat, sleep, live, and train together. Each of us must know the strengths and weaknesses of the others. Spiller, Wilson, before I'm finished with you, you'll be able to sneak right into the C.O.'s desk drawer with him sitting there, and he'll never know you've been within five miles of him."

Spiller and Wilson smiled.

"All right, you have the rest of the day to get ready," said Gray as the scouts left the office.

"Yes, sir."

At 0600 the next morning, the five scouts boarded a six-by truck that transported them to the jungle training area on the north side of Oahu. Immediately upon arrival, Gray led the scouts down a path and into the jungle.

"Boy, a person could get lost in here," said Spiller.

"Yeah," said Wilson, "this sure is thick. We'd better watch for snakes."

Gray spoke up. "There aren't any snakes in this jungle. As a matter of fact, there are no snakes in Hawaii, period. That's one plus for all of us. If we were in the jungle in the Orient, there'd be plenty and the most poisonous."

"That's nice to know," Spiller laughed. "I'd just as soon be here."

About half a mile into the jungle, the scouts came to a clearing. In the middle of the clearing was a small set of bleachers, and in front of them, an instructor's podium.

"All right, men, take your packs off and sit down. We'll go over our schedule for the next two weeks. Today we're going to have classes on signaling techniques in both guerrilla warfare and ambushing. If you'll recall, I told you that we might be as much as 10 to 15 miles from the entire battalion, right in the enemy's back pocket. Therefore, we don't want to be carrying on any conversations. As a matter of fact, we don't talk at all. We use signals only. We'll go over the signals and ambushing today. Then, for the next three days, we'll set up ambushes and practice our signaling. On day four, we'll be going down the slide for life. In case you aren't aware of what the slide for life is, we have a rope that is connected to a 200-foot cliff on one end and stretches across a pond to the ground on the other end. The rope length is 700 feet. You'll be using sticks, shaped like wishbones, to slide down."

"Damn!" said Wilson.

"You'll have more than that to say the first time you go down," said Gray. "On day five, we'll be repelling from helicopters. The rest of the time will be spent training in signaling and ambushes, except for the last three days. They're reserved for the survival course. No C-rations, men. We'll live off the land. Does anyone have any questions?"

"You mean we aren't going to have anything at all to eat?" asked Spiller.

"If you get hungry enough, you'll find something," said Gray with a laugh.

The rest of the day the scouts learned the signals in guerrilla warfare: when to listen, when to move out, when to halt, when and where the enemy has been spotted by the lead man, when boobie traps are obstacles – all the necessary signals to effectively communicate for miles without saying a word. Next came the ambushes: the line ambush and the L-shaped ambush. Each type of ambush was set off by one man who opened fire when the enemy unit came well within the kill zone. The ambush, triggered properly, allowed no one to escape, all would be killed. The time period from the start of the ambush until all enemy soldiers were dead was 30 seconds.

For the next three days the scouts practiced signals and ambushes over and over.

Then came day four and the slide for life. The five scouts were at the top of the cliff. They listened carefully as Gray gave instructions. "Now, men, it's 200 feet straight down, so it's important that you do this right. Place your wishbone over the rope and stand with your legs stiff, then take a small hop, and you'll slide right to the bottom. Any questions?"

There was no reply.

"All right, I'll go first. Now watch closely."

Gray placed his stick over the rope, and with legs stiff, made a small hop, and down he went.

"That doesn't look hard," said Spiller.

Next went Smith, then Stilley. Spiller looked at Wilson.

"You scared?"

"Hell, no," replied Wilson.

"Sure. Getting ready to jump off a 200-foot cliff with a wishbone stick, and you're not scared. I was always told never to volunteer for anything. You wanted us to be scouts," scoffed Spiller.

"It was your idea," argued Wilson. "Besides that, you're scared yourself, or you wouldn't have said anything."

"I'm not scared, Wilson."

"You can go first then!"

Spiller placed the stick over the rope, stiffened his legs, took a deep breath, and hopped.

"Oh, shit!" said Spiller as he slid down the rope.

In a matter of seconds, he was on the other side.

"How'd you like that, Spiller?" asked Gray.

"That was fun. It isn't half as bad as I thought it would be, now that I've done it."

"Good," replied Gray. "We're going back up there to do it again."

Wilson came down right behind Spiller, and the unit climbed back to the top of the cliff.

"That wasn't bad, hey, Rich?"

"Not bad at all," grinned Wilson. "Not bad at all."

For the next eight days the dirty, unshaved scouts moved silently through the jungle, practicing over and over the tactics of guerrilla warfare. With only three days of training exercises remaining, it was time for the survival course. The scouts rested for a shirt while before starting their search for food.

"Spiller, you stink," said Wilson.

"You don't smell like a rose garden yourself."

"Why don't we split up and see what we can come up with to eat?" said Smith.

"What do we look for?" asked Spiller.

"There are a lot of guavas around," said Stilley.

"What's a guava?" asked Wilson.

"It looks like an apple, but they're pretty tasty," said Stilley.

"Anything else?" asked Wilson.

"There are red berries, too," said Stilley.

"Let's go," said Gray. We'll meet back here in an hour.

Spiller and Wilson left together. A few hundred yards into the jungle area they spotted some guavas. Spiller took his shirt off. Both he and Wilson picked until the shirt was full, and returned to the meeting area. Stilley had found guavas, Smith had red berries, and Gray had a cap full of snails.

Wilson looked at Spiller then turned to Gray. "Sergeant Gray, what are you gonna do with those snails?"

Gray grinned at Wilson, reached into the cap, and grabbed a snail.

"Eat 'em," said Gray. "They have a lot of protein."

He then put the shell to his lips and sucked its contents into his mouth.

"Oh, my God," said Wilson.

Squeamishly, Spiller watched Gray. Stilley and Smith were both laughing.

"What's the matter?" asked Smith. "They're tasty."

He reached for one and sucked it down. Stilley did the same.

Spiller spoke up. "I'm not eating them damned things!"

"Me either," said Wilson.

"If you get hungry enough, you will, said Gray.

"Guavas are good enough for me," said Wilson.

"We'll see," replied Gray.

Two days passed and both Spiller and Wilson had eaten only guavas and berries.

"I've got diarrhea," said Wilson.

"It's a wonder I don't," replied Spiller. "Nothing but fruit for two days."

"That's right," said Gray. "If all you can find is fruit, then that's what you have to survive on, but if there are other foods available, you need to eat them too. That brings us to the snails."

Wilson and Spiller looked at each other.

"That's right, men, snails! You're gonna try them now."

"But Sergeant Gray!"

"No buts!"

Hesitating for a moment, Spiller grabbed a snail, quickly put it to his mouth, and sucked it down. He looked at Wilson then at Gray.

"That wasn't bad," said Spiller sheepishly.

Wilson sucked one down. He looked at Spiller. "You're right. They aren't too bad."

"They'd better not be too bad. Snails, worms, lizards, or anything of that nature can mean the difference between life and death. You should try some more before the day is over," urged Sergeant Gray.

"Okay, Sarge," said Wilson.

The next morning the scouts marched some two miles out of the training area to a pick-up point located near a four-lane highway to return to Kanowi Air Station. The Marines sat in the muddy dungarees they'd worn for two weeks.

"We still have three hours before the trucks are due to pick us up," said Gray.

"Damn!" said Smith. "I'm starved to death."

"Me, too," said Wilson.

"There's a pizza parlor about a half mile down the road," said Stilley.

"Really?" asked Spiller.

"Has anybody got any money?" asked Smith.

Everyone fumbled, looking for money.

"Here," said Wilson, "I have two dollars."

"I've got one," offered Spiller.

"We have six dollars. That should be enough," said Smith.

"All right now, listen," said Gray. "You get caught down there in those dungarees, and the MPs will pick you up, so be careful."

"Okay, Sarge," replied Spiller as he, Wilson, and Smith left.

The three scouts knelt behind a tree in a small park in front of the parlor.

"We'll make a break and run for the parlor," said Smith. "It's about 50 yards. Do you see any MPs coming either way?"

"No," said Spiller. "I thought I saw a paddy wagon, but it was a bread truck. I know this though."

"What's that?" asked Wilson.

"If we don't get in and out, somebody's gonna have an accident. Did you see the guy that passed awhile ago? He was looking at us and ran up on the curb."

"All right, let's go," said Smith.

The three scouts ran for the parlor. As they entered, they slammed the door behind them. Standing behind the counter, at the far end of the parlor, was a young woman about 20 years old.

Her eyes grew larger and with hands to both cheeks, she exclaimed, "Oh, my God! Oh, my God! What in the world are you doing in here?"

"We wanna order a pizza, ma'am," grinned Spiller.

"If the MPs see you in here, they'll pick you up," the woman replied. "They come by here all the time."

"Will we get you in trouble?" asked Smith.

"I don't know, my Dad's in the Air Force. I might. He might. I don't know! Come hide behind the counter while I fix the pizza."

The scouts, grinning at each other, scrambled for the counter. As the woman prepared the pizza, she looked down and smiled at the Marines kneeling behind the counter.

"Where in the world have you been?" she asked.

"Jungle training for two weeks, ma'am," replied Spiller.

"We sure do appreciate this too, ma'am. We haven't had too much to eat. We're starved," said Wilson.

"Yeah, and no bath for two weeks either," said Spiller.

"That part you didn't have to tell me," laughed the woman.

With pizza in hand, the Marines left the parlor and ran across the street. A woman, getting out of her car, looked up and screamed.

"It's okay, ma'am," Spiller said as he ran past her. "We're on your side."

When the Marines returned with the pizza, the five hungry scouts ate as though they'd never eaten before.

"Boy, this is good," said Wilson.

"Yeah," said Spiller with his mouth full.

Smith grinned at Stilley, and Stilley looked at Gray. Gray looked at Wilson and Spiller.

"Sure beats the snails, huh, men?"

Spiller and Wilson quit chewing just long enough to laugh.

"It sure does, Sarge. It sure does," said Spiller.

As months went by the scouts continued to train in warfare techniques, physical exercise and survival, but most important, they learned to work as a team. One Saturday in December 1964, Spiller was sitting on his bunk writing a letter home. Wilson ran into the squad bay carrying a newspaper.

"Hey, Harry, read this!"

"Since when did you care about the news?" asked Spiller.

"Read this, damn it! We're going to war!"

Spiller looked at Wilson, grabbed a paper, and opened it. The headlines read: "Eight U.S. soldiers dead and 107 wounded in Vietnam."

"Damn!" said Spiller. "Things must be getting serious in 'Nam, but you never hear that much about it."

"Yeah," said Wilson, "but we will now. We're going to be right in the middle of that war before long."

"I don't know, Rich, the paper says the Vietcong mortared

Da Nang base to knock out aircraft, not to hit U.S. soldiers. Besides you know how the United States is. The government will let them run over us again and again before they'll react."

"They can't let the damned commies get by with that," snapped Wilson.

Smith and Stilley walked up. "That's right. We can't let them get by with that. We'll be over there in no time," smiled Stilley.

"You're right," said Smith.

"Look at the medals we can win," said Wilson.

"You know something," said Spiller, "I didn't know we had that many men in Vietnam. You never hear that much about the place."

"They're advisors," said Stilley.

"How many advisors do you need?" snapped Spiller.

"Why are you always being so technical?" asked Wilson.

"I'm not being technical, I just asked."

"Why? You afraid to go?" asked Wilson.

"No, I'm not afraid to go! I'll come out of there with more medals than you will, Wilson."

"Sure," said Wilson. "I'll have to lead you around by the hand."

"Like hell! You're the one that turned green in the Mike boat and the one that was afraid to go down the slide for life," snapped Spiller.

Smith smiled at Stilley. "There they go again."

"Yeah," replied Stilley. "Okay, guys, settle down."

"Yeah, okay," said Spiller. "Hey, Rich, we still gonna go to Waikiki on New Year's Eve?"

"Sure. Let's have a blast," said Wilson.

"Okay," smiled Spiller.

Smith and Stilley left. Spiller stood up.

"Hey, Rich, we may get the chance to get back home with all those medals after all, huh?"

"Yeah, man, they'll be proud of us, won't they?" said Wilson.

"They sure will, man. It'll be neat," replied Spiller.

Two weeks later on New Year's Eve, 1964, Spiller and Wilson walked to the bus depot. Except for the color of their shirts, they were dressed alike. Spiller wore a red-and-white Hawaiian shirt, bermuda shorts, white tennis shoes, and a straw hat that looked like something a fisherman would wear. Wilson's shirt was blue and white. The two Marines boarded the bus and headed for Waikiki Beach.

"We'll have to go to Fort Durussy to drink any beer," said Wilson.

"Isn't it something," commented Spiller, "we can fight the wars, but we're too young to drink."

"Boy, that's the truth," replied Wilson. "Maybe we can slip into one of the clubs after we've had a few beers at Durussy."

"Yeah, if they don't check IDs," said Spiller.

"Right. But they'll be crowded. And besides, since we only lack about six months being 20, they may give us a break," said Wilson.

"Likely story," said Spiller. "I wonder why the drinking age is only 20 in Hawaii, but 21 mainside?"

"There you are, getting technical again," said Wilson.

"I'm not getting technical, damn it! I just asked!"

"I don't know, Harry. The important thing is to get into the club."

Spiller and Wilson walked into the club at Fort Durussy. Most of the tables were full of servicemen.

"Rich, I'll hold a table for us. You get the beers."

"You're gonna do it again, aren't you?" asked Wilson.

"Do what?"

"Jew me out of the beer," said Wilson.

"No. You wanna stand in the corner and drink? I'm gonna hold us a table. Here, buy us a beer," snapped Spiller as he handed Wilson a dollar.

"Okay," smiled Wilson.

"You can complain over nothing, Wilson," said Spiller as he and Wilson sat sipping their beers.

"What do you mean by that?"

"I mean over a lousy beer. Twenty cents for a beer, and you think I'm conning you."

"You were," said Wilson. "You're always conning me out of beer."

"Bullshit! I bought, didn't I?" said Spiller, smiling.

"Yeah," said Wilson, returning the smile. "Boy, that tastes good. Let's get another one."

"Okay. I'm gonna get two each so we don't have to stand in line."

"Good idea."

When Spiller returned to the table with the beer, he asked, "Hey, Wilson, do my shorts and shirt go together?"

"As much as mine do," laughed Wilson. "Why?"

"That asshole bartender up there wanted to know where I got my outfit. I thought, maybe, I wasn't dressed right or something."

"You look fine to me."

"I hope so," laughed Spiller. "We're dressed alike. Boy, this beer sure is good."

"You can say that again," said Wilson. "Let's have two or three more then try to hit the clubs."

Five beers later, Wilson and Spiller headed for the clubs to see if they could slip in. Up one side of the strip and down the other, each club turned them down.

"Do you believe this, Rich? We've hit every club in town, and they've all checked IDs. There has to be some place that'll let us in."

"What about some of these hotels? They have some pretty fancy bars."

"Come on, we aren't gonna get into any hotels. These are classy joints."

"We can try, can't we?"

"Why not?"

Spiller and Wilson stood across the street from Waikiki Hotel, just two blocks off the main strip of Waikiki. A large, green, half-circle canopy hung over the door. A red carpet covered the sidewalk in front. A doorman, dressed in a black tux and white shirt with ruffles, greeted patrons as they entered the hotel.

"Look at the dresses those women are wearing," said Spiller.

"Those are more like formals than dresses, and all the men are wearing tuxes. We can't go in there," said Wilson.

"No, we'll never get by the doorman."

Spiller and Wilson smiled at each other.

"You thinking what I'm thinking?" asked Spiller.

"Yeah. Let's see if there's another entrance."

Wilson and Spiller crossed the street and entered a side door to the elevator.

"Let's get off at the third floor. Maybe they have a stairway," said Spiller.

They got off at the third floor.

"We went up too far," said Spiller. "Let's get off at the second floor."

They got off at the second floor.

"Hey, over there!"

"Yeah," said Wilson, "a stairway!"

They approached the stairway and were astonished by what they saw as they peeked through the wrought-iron gate. The back of the bar was covered with mirrors that reached to the ceiling. Champagne glasses were stacked in pyramids in front of the shining mirrors. Thick, plush, red carpet covered the floor, and soft music flowed from the violins.

"Damn!" said Spiller. "The damned gate's locked, too."

"We could climb over."

"Bullshit! There's a cop standing on the corner outside. Let's go, maybe we can find another hotel."

They got on the elevator and left the hotel.

"Hey, look. The doorman's gone."

"There's a woman there. You wanna try it?"

"Let's go. All they can do is say no."

Both sauntered to the entrance. The woman, wearing a red satin, full-length dress, smiled graciously at them.

"Happy New Year, gentlemen."

"Happy New Year, ma'am, but we still have three hours to go. Could we join your party?" asked Spiller.

"You sure may. Come right in."

"Thank you, ma'am," replied Spiller and Wilson. They entered the hotel and headed for the barroom.

"Have a good time, gentlemen," the lady said as she softly giggled.

The two entered the barroom and sat at a table on the far side of the room. No one seemed to pay any attention. Most of the customers were either talking among themselves at their tables or dancing.

"I wonder if they'll check our IDs, Rich."

"I don't know. I hope not, or we're out of this place."

"I guess we'll have to ask for a drink. I don't think the bartender's coming over."

"You go," said Wilson.

"Thanks, Rich. Thanks."

Spiller approached the bar. Three bartenders, dressed in white jackets, were busy mixing drinks.

"Sir," said Spiller.

The bartender, wide-eyed with disbelief, stared for a moment. A moment later his lips widened into a full smile.

"I'd like two vodka collins, please."

The bartender, still smiling strangely, hesitated for a moment. "Okay, just a minute, sir."

"Thank you," said Spiller.

Spiller paid the bartender and returned to the table.

"Damn, Rich, we won't be able to drink very long in here."

"Why not?"

"These two drinks cost five dollars."

"Five dollars! Damn! We'd better drink a little slower. Boy, this place sure has class."

"You can say that again. Hey, what's going on with the bartenders?"

"I don't know. I've got my back to them," said Wilson.

"Why, they were in a huddle talking a minute ago, then they turned and looked over here. That one guy is laughing so hard he has tears running down his face. The others are laughing, too."

"You think they're laughing at us?"

"Maybe, but I don't know why, unless it's your hat," Spiller teased.

"What's wrong with my hat?" snapped Wilson.

"Well, look at it. With that damned bill flipped up in front, you look like Gabby Hayes," said Spiller.

"Bullshit. I like it this way."

"Why don't you get us another drink?" asked Spiller.

"Okay, but we'd better slow down, or we won't have enough money to last until the New Year comes in."

Wilson returned with the drinks. He had just sat down when one of the bartenders approached the table.

"Well, that's the end of the party," thought Spiller as the bartender examined their IDs.

"Thank you, gentlemen," the bartender said laughing. "The drinks will be on the house from now until New Year's."

"Well, thank you, sir," replied Spiller as Wilson sat with his mouth open.

"What was that all about?" asked Wilson.

"I don't know, Rich. I thought for sure they'd throw us out of here."

The bartender returned with two drinks. He smiled and walked back to the bar.

"I don't know what's going on, but let's enjoy it," said Spiller.

"Yeah, let's see if we can get some of these ladies to dance."

Both were well on their way to being drunk. They rose unsteadily from their seats and approached a nearby table.

"Would you care to dance, ma'am?" asked Spiller.

"No thank you," one lady snobbily replied.

Wilson did the same and was turned down. Disappointed, they both returned to their table.

"Damned women! Sure are snotty, aren't they?" said Spiller.

"They sure are. Hey! They brought us another drink."

"Sure nice of them, but I'd still like to know what's so funny. If that one guy doesn't quit laughing so much, somebody's going to have to carry him out of here. He goes to pieces every ten minutes."

"He's probably laughing at your knobby knees," Wilson said.

"Sure, you birdleg fucker, you. Hey, we only have 30 minutes before 1965 is here. You got any New Year's resolutions or wishes?" asked Spiller.

"Yeah, if we go to Vietnam, I want to take home more medals than you do, Harry."

Spiller laughed, "Bet me, buddy!"

At midnight the orchestra played "Auld Lang Syne." Spiller and Wilson, arms across each other's shoulders, sang along with everyone else and shouted, "Happy New Year."

The party over, Spiller and Wilson headed for the door.

"Quit walking so crooked, Wilson."

"I'm walking straight. You're walking crooked."

They were surprised by the re-appearance of the doorman, who upon sight of the uncomely duo, gaped in total astonishment. Obviously quite upset, he spouted, "Oh, my God! Oh, my God! How did you get in here?"

"Through that door, sir," said Spiller as he hiccupped.

"I'm going to get the police. Oh, my God. Look at the way you're dressed. Look at the way you're dressed."

"Mister?" said Wilson.

"Hey look, the lady at the door let us in. The party's over and we're leaving, okay. So don't get excited and call the police," said Spiller.

"Okay, okay, Just get out of here."

"Okay, sir," replied Spiller as he and Wilson left the hotel. Shoulder to shoulder, Spiller and Wilson made their way to the bus stop.

"That doorman sure got excited," said Wilson.

"He sure did."

"Those people sure were snooty, weren't they?"

"Yeah, Rich, you know why?"

"Why?"

"They don't know real class, when they see it," laughed Spiller. Wilson laughed too. "You're right, Harry. You're right."

In mid–January 1965, Headquarters and Service Company was called for company formation. The company commander informed them that until further notice, they were on alert. No other information was given, and the company was dismissed. Wilson and Spiller made their way back to the barracks.

"I told you we'd be going to Nam," said Wilson.

"Yeah, I guess so," replied Spiller. "They didn't tell us that though."

"Then why are we on alert?" asked Wilson.

"I don't know. You're probably right, Rich. We're probably on alert for Vietnam, but it would be nice to know for sure if that's the reason. Let's pack our gear."

"Okay, we might as well get it over with."

In mid–February, Spiller was sitting on his bunk writing a letter home.

Dear Mom,

Things sure have changed around here. We have been on alert for a month now. We have all our clothes packed in sea bags and our combat equipment ready. It's pure hell living out of sea bags. The rumors are flying all over the place about going to Vietnam, but to be truthful, I'm not sure anybody knows what's going on. One day, we're going, and the next day, we're going to be taken off alert. I know one thing, I wish somebody would make up their minds about what we're going to do, so that we could either go or empty our sea bags. When we're on liberty, we have to call in every hour to see if we are going to move out.

I'll try to keep you informed of what is going on, as I find out anything. Here comes Rich with a grin on his face, so I know he wants something. I'll write soon. Take care.

Love,
Harry

"Hey, wanna go to the theater tonight?" asked Wilson.

"I guess so. What's on?" asked Spiller.

"*The Sands of Iwo Jima* is showing," grinned Wilson.

"Sure, why not?" Spiller said, licking the seal on the envelope.

Spiller and Wilson went inside the theater. "We should've come a little earlier," said Wilson.

"That's for sure. This place is packed," said Spiller.

The movie came on, and the place went into an uproar.

"This sure is a neat movie," said Spiller. "This is the third time I've seen it."

"Yeah, man, this is the second time for me. And you're right, it's a hell of a neat flick."

"Look at them hit that beach," Spiller said excitedly.

"Yeah, they're giving the Japs hell."

As the movie came to a close, and the Marines raised the flag on Iwo Jima, the Marine Corps hymn began to play. The theater went into another uproar. Marines stood, screaming and tossing their caps wildly into the air.

"Let's go get them Vietcong!" yelled Wilson.

"Yeah, let's give those bastards hell!" screamed Spiller.

After leaving the theater, Spiller and Wilson returned to the barracks.

"We'll give them the same thing in 'Nam that the Marines gave the Japs on Iwo," said Spiller.

"I hope so," replied Wilson. "I hope so."

"Think I'll hit the sack, I'm tired."

"Me, too. We may need a good night's sleep."

"Maybe," said Spiller.

The word came at noon the next day. The First Marine Brigade was moving out. Moving where? West was the only word given to the troops. The Marines, in full combat gear, formed outside the barracks and moved to locations for boarding the busses.

"I didn't know the Marine Corps had this many busses," said Wilson.

"Me either," said Spiller. "Can you see the end of the line?"

"No."

As the Marines looked on, lines of tanks, 155 howitzer guns, and trucks were everywhere. There were troops boarding busses and loading trucks. Wives and children of Marines stood on the curbs, watching. Many wives were crying.

One little boy looked up at his mother, and asked, "Mommy? Mommy? Where's Daddy going?"

His question went unanswered.

Wilson and Spiller, both spellbound, looked out the bus window. "Rich, I didn't realize we were this big, did you?" asked Spiller. "No," Wilson responded, "I really didn't."

By 3 A.M. the next morning, the troops and equipment were aboard ship and ready to move out. The Marines remained silent.

As Spiller lay in his bunk, the events of the day before flowed through his mind. When the word to move out was given the day before, he couldn't believe it. He remembered the look in that mother's eyes when her little boy asked her where his daddy was going. He didn't know, but his mother knew, and so did his dad. We all knew what west meant. In the back of his mind, Spiller never really thought they'd ever go to war, not really. All the talking and training about war didn't seem real.

3
The Landing

It was midnight, April 12, 1965, and somewhere off the coast of Vietnam, the battalion scouts met Sergeant Gray below deck of the USS *Vancouver* to receive the intelligence report for the next morning's landing in Hue, Vietnam.

The scouts listened attentively as Gray instructed. "We will be just outside the village of Phu Bai, where we'll set up battalion headquarters. Our mission is to protect the airfield at Phu Bai. Intelligence reports indicate that there are 800 Vietcong in the surrounding area."

The scouts all looked at each other. Wilson asked, "What should we expect when we hit the beach?"

"We don't expect a lot of resistance, at most, sniper fire," said Gray.

"But what about the 800 VC, Sarge? No resistance?" asked Spiller.

"The intelligence indicates only light resistance. That's all I can tell you," said Gray. "We'll be up at 0400, receive ammunition at 0445, and board ship at 0530. Is that clear?"

No one spoke.

"Very well, men, hit the sack. We have a long day ahead of us."

Spiller lay in his bunk and stared at the overhead above him.

"Hey, Rich, you awake?"

"Yeah."

"You scared?"

"I guess a little nervous."

"Yeah, me too. It sure is hard to believe this is the real thing, isn't it?"

"Yeah, you know the thing that bothers me is that intelligence report."

"What about it?" asked Spiller.

"Well, we're told that there are 800 VC in the area, yet we're only expecting light resistance. I wonder how they know that?"

"I don't know."

"Exactly! That's what I mean. I don't think they know either."

"Doesn't make much sense, does it?"

"It sure doesn't," replied Wilson.

"Well, we'll know for sure in a few hours."

At 4 A.M. Spiller, Wilson, and the rest of the Marines prepared for the landing.

"Hey, Rich, did you get any sleep at all?" asked Spiller.

"Not a bit."

"Me either."

"Bullshit," scoffed Wilson. "Do you snore, when you're awake?"

"No. I don't snore at all."

"I guess I was just hearing things, huh?"

"I wasn't asleep," snapped Spiller.

"All right, you two," said Smith, "we'll have enough fighting to do without you two fighting. Knock it off, okay?"

"All right," replied Wilson and Spiller.

At 4:45 A.M. the scouts went topside to receive ammunition. They were all given 100 rounds of ammo for their rifles and four hand grenades. As they loaded their clips, Spiller looked at Wilson.

"I never really thought we'd be doing this, did you?"

"No, not really."

"It's hard to believe we're actually going to war, but I don't know of anything that could make it more realistic than what we're doing right now."

The Marines, loaded with field transport packs, boarded the Mike boats at 5:30 A.M. The Mike boat circled as the sun broke the horizon.

"I guess we're fortunate, hey Wilson?" Spiller remarked.

"Why's that?"

"Look over there. We have the battalion chaplain on board with us."

"Yeah, I guess we're fortunate," said Wilson. "Where are we going to land, Sarge?"

"That area of land over there doesn't look like a good place to land.

We're going down the river to land in the city of Hue," said Gray.

"Oh, I see. Sarge, what's going on? We're the only boat out. There should have been more out by now."

"I don't know, but you're right. There should've been two or three boats circling with us by now," said Gray, sounding concerned.

About that time a Mike boat backed out the open doors of the *Vancouver.*

"Here comes one," said Smith.

"Sure took 'em long enough," remarked Stilley.

"Yeah, how long we been circling?" asked Spiller.

"Almost an hour," replied Gray.

"At this rate, we'll never get to shore," said Wilson.

"Okay, men, calm down," said Gray. "There's always a little confusion during a landing."

Three hours later the Mike boats were still circling.

"When we gonna hit the beach, Sarge?" asked Wilson.

"Should be soon," said Gray. "They should have only one more boat to unload. Here it comes now."

"Finally," snapped Spiller. "This is getting old. I feel like I've been riding a bucking bronco for the past four hours."

"Me, too," said Wilson, "but I never thought I'd have to with full combat gear on."

The Mike boats formed into a single line and headed for the Perfume River. The rough ride was forgotten by the time the Marines approached the mouth of the river.

Spiller spoke up. "Sarge, can we put a round in the chamber now?"

"No. Orders are to keep clips in our rifles, but no rounds in the chamber."

"But, Sarge, what if they start shooting at us?" asked Wilson.

"If they start shooting, we'll put a round in the chamber and go from there," snapped Gray. "Just keep a sharp look out and stay down. Understand?"

The Mike boats, in a single line, entered the mouth of the river. Spiller, Wilson, and the others peered over the edge of the boat at the two-foot mud banks. Beyond the banks lay nothing but dense jungle.

"What was that?" yelled Wilson.

"What did you see?" snapped Gray.

"I don't know. I saw something move in the trees."

"Me, too," said Spiller. "There! There!"

"Damn!" said Wilson. "A damned monkey!"

"Shit, my heart is about to come through my chest over a damned monkey," sighed Spiller.

"You're keeping a sharp eye out," Gray remarked. "Keep it up."

"Hey, Sarge, look up there on the right. There's a clearing."

"What the hell," said the sergeant. "There are people all over the place."

"It's a village, Sarge. There's one on this side, too," said Spiller.

"All right, men, keep an eye out."

The boats moved to a position parallel with the villages. The Marines were absolutely astonished by the behavior of the Vietnamese men, women, and children who laughed and waved at the new arrivals.

"I don't believe this," said Spiller.

"Me either," said Wilson.

"I thought we were going to war," snapped Smith.

"Get down! Get down!" yelled Spiller.

"What is it, Harry?" asked Wilson.

"I saw a VC!"

"Where? Where?" snapped Gray.

"Up there, Sarge. He's in the middle of those women. He has black shorts on, and he's carrying a grease gun."

"He's laughing and waving," said Wilson.

"That isn't a VC," snapped Gray.

"What is he then?" asked Spiller.

"Popular Forces, probably," said Gray.

"Probably!" snapped Smith.

"He isn't shooting at us, is he?" quipped Gray.

"No, Sarge, he isn't. But how are we supposed to know when they're VC or Popular Forces?" asked Smith.

Gray paused for a moment. "All right, everyone, stay down and keep a sharp eye out. It won't be long before we'll be at Hue."

The Mike boats approached the shore in Hue. Women, children, and even soldiers from the Army of the Republic of Vietnam (ARVN) laughed and waved at the Marines. As the Marines came ashore a South Vietnamese army band, missing every other note, played the Marine Corps hymn.

"Hey, what's the matter with this boat?" yelled Smith.

"Damn! We're taking on water," said Wilson.

"No shit!" said Spiller. "Hurry up and get us to shore!"

Three feet from the shore line, in about a foot of water, the Mike boat sank. The Marines rushed ashore.

"Just our luck, hey, Rich," said Spiller.

"No shit."

"Hey Sarge, I thought we were supposed to be at war," stated Smith.

"We are," snapped Gray.

"Sure looks like it," teased Smith.

"Vietnamese children ran up to the Marines, shook hands, laughed, and then ran back into the crowd. Women whispered, laughed, and giggled.

"Hey, Sarge, where do we go?" asked Spiller.

"I don't know, yet," said Gray. "Probably up by those trucks."

Spiller looked in the direction that the sergeant had pointed. About 200 yards behind the crowd of Vietnamese was a line of six-by trucks lined bumper-to-bumper in the street.

"Go up there, and wait for me," ordered Gray. "And stay together."

As the Marines headed for the trucks, Spiller spoke. "I wish that damned band would quit playing. We did better than that when I was in grade school."

The Marines stood by the trucks and looked on at the landing. Spiller shook his head.

"What's the matter, Harry?" asked Wilson.

"Look at this. We're supposed to have 800 VC in the area, receive light resistance, and everyone is walking around in mass confusion. No one knows where we're supposed to be. There are women and children all over the place, and Vietnamese troops, both in and out of uniform, carrying guns. How are we supposed to know who the VC are?"

"I don't know," said Wilson. "I guess it's like Sergeant Gray said, 'When they shoot at us, we'll know.'"

"Doesn't give us much of an edge, does it?"

"Hey, what's going on?" asked Smith. "Here comes Sergeant Gray, running like hell." The sergeant pushed his way through a crowd of villagers as he came towards their truck.

"All right, men, we have information. There's a kid running around here with a grenade," Gray blurted out.

"A kid!" yelled Spiller.

"That's right, a kid. Take off your packs, and leave 'em here. We have to mingle through the crowd until we get all the trucks loaded."

"What if we find the kid?" asked Wilson.

"We'll do what we have to do," snapped Gray. "Let's go."

The scouts took their packs off and moved cautiously through the crowd. The "glad to see you" look had disappeared from the faces of the friendly Vietnamese. Some looked scared; others just stared, but all were silent as the Marines passed them. Vietnamese soldiers passed through the crowd on the opposite side. One shot rang out, then another. Screams came from the crowd.

"That was ARVN," yelled Smith.

"Right, let's get over there," Spiller shouted.

The scouts rushed through the crowd to find three ARVN soldiers surrounding a body. Spiller pushed through and looked down. Lying on the ground was the lifeless body of a little Vietnamese girl. Blood trickled from the mouth of the child, who Spiller guessed to be about six years old. Everyone stared in total silence.

"Oh, my God! Oh, my God!" said Spiller as he turned and grabbed an ARVN soldier by the arm. "Why did you kill her?"

The soldier mumbled something in Vietnamese.

"I can't understand a fucking thing you're saying, you bastard! Why did you kill her?" he shouted as he continued to shake the ARVN soldier.

Wilson grabbed Spiller, "Hey, man, take it easy. We can get in trouble."

Another ARVN, mumbling in Vietnamese, reached down to turn the girl over. Spiller and Wilson watched as the ARVN raised the girl's black silk top. A cartridge belt with "US" stamped on its side was wrapped tightly around her. Attached to the belt was an old World War II pineapple grenade. A piece of bamboo stuck out of the top of the grenade with a string that protruded from inside the bamboo. The ARVN soldier pointed and rattled something in Vietnamese.

"That's why, Harry. That's why they shot her," said Wilson.

"All right, all of you get back up to the trucks. Now!" snapped Gray.

The Marines returned to the trucks.

"You okay, Harry?" asked Wilson.

"Yeah, I'm okay."

"God damn!" yelled Smith.

"What's wrong?" asked Wilson.

"Somebody took my whole fucking pack."

"Take it easy," said Wilson. "It's around here somewhere."

"Like hell. I had it laying right here. It's gone."

Gray came up. "Now what's wrong?"

"They stole my pack," said Smith.

"You sure?"

"Yeah, I'm sure. It was laying right here."

"We've looked, Sergeant Gray. It's gone," said Wilson.

"Damn!" said Gray. "All right, everyone, get on the trucks."

"What am I supposed to do about my clothes and boots, Sarge?" asked Smith.

"Don't worry about it, Smith. We'll get you some more. Now all of you get on the fucking truck and shut up."

The trucks moved through the streets of Hue. Signs draped across buildings read: "Welcome U.S. Marines." People stood along the curb waving and clapping. The battalion scouts looked on in silence.

The Marines unloaded in the middle of an open field just north of Phu Bai. To the east was the airfield they had been sent to protect. To the west, about five miles out, were vast areas of dark green hills and gullies. One particularly large hill, later known to the Marines as Hill 221, protruded above the cluster of hills. Through the tree line to the north, a few huts from the village of Phu Bai could be seen. Directly south was an army communications center. Mobile homes, clustered in the center, were surrounded by a double roll of consentina wire. Planted between the rolls were land mines.

"All right, men, we're going to set up a perimeter tonight. Two-man foxholes. Let's spread out and get digging," ordered Gray.

Wilson and Spiller began to dig.

"What's the matter with you, Harry. You haven't said a word since we got on the trucks?" asked Wilson.

"That little girl, Rich. That little girl. I can't get her off my mind. How could anybody use a little kid like that? I mean, just let her blow herself up," said Spiller.

"They'd have to be sick to do something like that, but you know how these commies are. Life doesn't mean a thing to them."

"I bet she didn't even know that pulling that string would kill her. No telling what they told her," said Spiller.

"You remember reading about these commies and the tricks they use in war."

Spiller stopped digging and looked Wilson straight in the eye. "Yeah, Rich, but I always thought this was something you read about, not something you would see for real."

"Yeah, you're right. Hey, man, come on, let's get this foxhole dug so we can take a break."

As the sun began to set, Gray met with the scouts.

"All right, men, we're going to be on perimeter all night. You can take turns sleeping, but whatever you do, don't fall asleep if you're on watch. The VC will crawl right into your foxhole with you and slit your throat. If it's your turn to watch, and you feel like you're going to fall asleep, wake up your partner. Now I want to emphasize this one more time. The VC are very good at moving undetected. They'll crawl right up to your foxhole without you seeing them, so stay alert."

"Sarge, can we put a round in the chamber?" asked Wilson.

"No. You leave your clip in the rifle, but no round in the chamber. If you spot a VC or think you have, pass the word along the perimeter for the line officer. We'll come to verify whether they're VC and then give you orders."

"What do we do if the VC just start shooting? Shoot back?" asked Spiller.

"No, the orders are the same. The line officer has to verify that they're VC."

"Damn, Sarge. If they're shooting at us, what the hell. Who in the hell else is going to be shooting at us?" asked Smith.

"I don't believe this," said Stilley. "I don't believe it!"

"Me either," snapped Wilson.

"Look, just follow orders," Gray insisted. "Now get on the perimeter and do what you're told."

As darkness fell Wilson and Spiller watched intently from the edge of their foxholes.

"Hey, Harry," whispered Wilson.

"What?"

"Listen to them damned mosquitoes. They sound like a wave of prop airplanes flying around."

"Boy, you can say that again," whispered Spiller. "I don't have any mosquito repellent, do you?"

"No, maybe we can get some tomorrow."

"That's great. What about tonight?"

Hours passed.

"Hey, Rich, you wanna get some sleep?"

"Hell, I can't sleep. I'm too nervous. Besides, I've seen that bush move three times."

"That's what I mean. I'm seeing things move, too. It's because we're tired," said Spiller.

"You go ahead and get some sleep."

"I guess I could try, but the mosquitoes won't let me," whispered Spiller.

"Yeah, who needs to worry about VC? At the rate we're going, these bloodsuckers will have eaten us alive before morning."

"Rich, I'm gonna try to get some sleep, okay?"

"Sure. I'll wake you up, if you start snoring," chuckled Wilson.

Spiller sat in his foxhole and leaned his head back. He touched his helmet against the side of the foxhole and closed his eyes. Before long fragments of the day's events invaded his sleep. . . .

"I wish they'd quit playing that music. We did better than that in grade school." The boat's sinking. Get us to shore. The blood trickling from her mouth. "Why did you kill her? Why did you kill her!" The little girl sat up and smiled at Spiller. Large dark eyes . . . the blood still trickling down the side of her mouth. She started laughing, "I had a grenade, I had a grenade. I was going to blow you up."

"Harry, Harry, wake up!" said Wilson.

"Huh, huh. What's the matter. What's the matter?"

"Man, you were moaning. You're soaking wet. You're having a nightmare."

"No, no. I'm all right. Why don't you try to get some sleep?" said Spiller. "I'll watch for a while."

"Okay, will do. It won't be long until daylight anyway, about another hour."

Spiller peered over the edge of the foxhole, and watched carefully in the darkness for movement.

"Hey, Harry."

"Yeah."

"Is the little girl what's bothering you?"

"It's nothing, Rich. It's nothing," said Spiller as he stared into the darkness.

When the sun broke the horizon, Wilson joined Spiller.

"Did you get any sleep?" asked Spiller.

"Hell, no. How are we supposed to sleep with these mosquitoes?"

"Yeah, look at my hands. They're swollen," said Spiller.

"So is your face."

"Yours, too."

"We definitely have to get some mosquito repellent today," snapped Wilson, "or we aren't going to have to worry about the VC."

"You're right. Hey, here comes Sergeant Gray."

"All right, men, we've been assigned to ride shotgun on trucks going into Hue to pick up ammo. Let's go."

Spiller and Wilson walked to the trucks and boarded. Smith and Stilley, already aboard, sat at the front. Smith turned and yelled back to Spiller and Wilson.

"How did you like the mosquitoes?"

"They were great, the fucking bloodsuckers!" said Wilson.

"Yeah, they got plenty of meat last night," yelled Spiller.

"Hang on, Harry, here we go."

The trucks pulled onto Route 1 and headed for Hue. Vietnamese women and children walked along the road. They were carrying honey buckets, buckets of human waste. A long flexible pole hung over one shoulder was balanced by buckets hanging from each end. Others, with pant legs rolled above their knees, stood in a foot or so of water. Some busily worked in the rice paddies. Most wore silk tops and bottoms, similar to pajamas, and cone-shaped straw hats. Few wore shoes.

"There's another one," yelled Wilson.

"What?"

"Look back there."

Spiller turned to look behind him. A barefooted Vietnamese man, wearing black silk shorts and no shirt, walked along the side of the road. A rifle was draped over his shoulder.

"Do you believe this? How in the fuck are we supposed to tell the VC from the ARVN. Everyone's running around with guns," snapped Spiller.

"I'm not sure it really matters," Wilson yelled. "We can't load our guns anyway. This whole damned place is crazy."

"You can say that again," said Spiller.

The trucks arrived at the landing area. Mike boats, loaded with ammunition, were docked against the bank.

"Look at those crates," said Wilson.

"No shit," said Spiller. "They've just thrown those damned boxes on those boats any way they can."

"We're going to have to unload that damned stuff by hand. We really need this in this heat. It must be 120 degrees," complained Wilson.

For the rest of the day, the Marines loaded trucks, rode shotgun, and unloaded supplies in the battalion headquarters. By afternoon the Marines had finished for the day and had returned to their foxholes on the perimeter. Spiller sat reading the labels on his C-ration cans.

"I wonder why these rations are so old," said Spiller. "Mine are dated 1947."

"Mine, too," muttered Wilson.

"Maybe that makes them taste good," laughed Spiller.

"I'll tell you one thing. I never thought water would taste so good."

"Me either. I bet we sweat off 30 pounds."

Soon darkness set in, and again, Wilson and Spiller stood side by side, keeping watch in the darkness.

"Oh, shit," said Wilson, "here come those waves of bombers again."

"Yeah, and we didn't get any repellent," replied Spiller.

Day after day for the next two weeks, the Marines rode shotgun, loaded and unloaded trucks, and sat on the perimeter at night. The battalion was low on water, and although the Marines were working in heat well over 100 degrees, they were rationed to one canteen of water a day. Orders were, they would shave each day. The Marines slept very little, averaging about two or three hours a night. The mosquitoes remained a real problem. There were no showers for two weeks, and everyone was beginning to stink. Clean clothes were unheard of. Socks were aired out, but after two weeks the air wasn't doing much good. Many Marines got heat rash and gall, meanwhile, the mosquitoes continued their feast. To prevent falling asleep while on watch, the Marines could stand in the middle of the foxhole, then if they fell asleep, they'd awaken as they fell against the side of the foxhole. After two weeks, all the supplies and communications were at the battalion area. Construction activities were ongoing at that location in order to provide better facilities for the Marines.

The scouts erected squad tents large enough to house 13 men. The tents looked like something from a circus. There were two large poles, one at each end of the tent to hold up the roof. The five-foot high flaps on each side of the tent acted as walls. The temperature was so high that the Marines pulled the side flaps out to a 45-degree angle and attached them to smaller poles at the same angle in the opposite direction in order to leave a two-foot clearance for air to flow through. Spiller and Wilson dug a trench two feet wide and three feet deep around the tent to catch water, if it rained.

"You know something?" asked Spiller one day.

"What's that?" replied Wilson.

"Money doesn't mean a thing, not a thing."

"What do you mean?"

"We've been here for a little over two weeks, and I'd give every penny I have just for one bottle of cold Coke and a shower, but I can't buy it. I mean, back home money is everything, or it's supposed to be. If you have money, you can buy anything you want. What I mean, Rich, is the important things in life, you can't buy at all. I guess I'd never have realized that if I hadn't come here."

"Yeah, I guess anybody takes things for granted, especially something as simple as a shower or a quarter bottle of Coke."

"A quarter bottle of Coke," Spiller laughed, "the price has gone up!"

"What do you mean?"

"It's a million dollar Coke now. Here comes Sergeant Gray. I wonder what's with the big smile."

"Men grab your towels. The showers are hooked up."

"All right!" yelled Wilson.

"Ha, ha!" yelled Spiller as he ran for his pack.

Soap and towels in hand, the Marines swarmed to the open field where the showers were located. They went laughing and shouting into the showers. The water, both cool and invigorating, fell briskly on their hot, dry skin. The soap smelled sweet. What a nice sensation to be clean again.

Three weeks later the morale was much higher. The men of the Third Battalion, Fourth Marines had settled in at Phu Bai. With a fresh water supply and mosquito repellent, the Marines slept much more comfortably. Protecting the airfield had been a success. The only casualty had been the little Vietnamese girl. It was obvious by now that the intelligence reports, concerning the 800 VC, must have been wrong. Not a single VC had been spotted.

4
Death of a Friend

By the middle of May 1965, Phu Bai had become very boring for the Marines. The only sign of Vietcong was just outside the perimeter. Several trip grenades had been missing from the area. Each night just before dark, they set booby traps, hand grenades with trip wires. Each morning they were gone. Night after night, they sat on the perimeter carefully watching. Yet no one had seen or heard anything.

During the day it was too hot to sleep. The temperature climbed as high as 120 and 130 degrees. With little to do, they cleaned their rifles, played cards, and talked about home.

Lying on his cot, Spiller gazed across at the engineering tent wondering why their flaps were down.

Kaboom!

The sides of the tent flapped. Dust rolled in all directions from underneath the tent, then silence. Spiller leaped to his feet.

"Oh shit! Someone must have pulled the pin on a grenade. We'd better get over there."

Spiller, Wilson, Smith, and Stilley ran for the tent. The corpsmen ran from sick bay with stretchers. Spiller opened the small flap.

"I can't see anything. The dust is too thick!"

"Let's go in," snapped a corpsman, pushing his way through.

The Marines entered, expecting to find bodies everywhere. But as the dust settled, they saw no bodies.

"Over here!" yelled the corpsman.

The Marines ran for the water trench at the left side of the tent. Three Marines were lying face down. The corpsman reached down to feel the side of one Marine's neck. As he did, the Marine looked up and rising to his feet, said "I'm okay!"

The other two Marines did the same. To the right of the tent, three other Marines crawled out of the trenches.

"No one's hurt? Is this all of you?" asked the corpsman.

"We're okay."

"What the hell happened?" asked the corpsman.

"Well, we kinda had this bet," said one of the Marines.

In stormed the first sergeant. "How many dead? How many dead?"

"Everyone's okay, Top," said the corpsman.

"What happened? What happened?" yelled the first sergeant.

"Well, sir, we were just kind of sitting around, bored like, and we made this bet."

"And just what did you bet, Marine?"

"Well, sir, we had a half-pound block of TNT, and we put a fuse in it. Then we lit it and started passing it around. The first one to chicken out and clip the fuse had to pay $100."

The first sergeant glared.

"Well, sir, when they handed it to me, I tried to clip the fuse, but I couldn't get the thing to go out. So I threw it down, and we dove for the trenches."

The first sergeant was flabbergasted. In an arduous effort to hide their laughter at what now seemed a humorous situation, the Marines turned their heads from the sight of the fuming first sergeant.

"You crazy, fucking kids. You're crazy. You almost blew the whole, fucking battalion off the map, because you were bored," the first sergeant screamed. "Get your entrenching tools. Get your entrenching tools. You won't be bored anymore. You're going to dig latrines for the entire, fucking battalion! Hurry up!"

Spiller and Wilson laughed about the incident as they grabbed their rifles and headed for the perimeter.

"Did you see the look on the first sergeant's face when that engineer was telling him what happened?" laughed Spiller.

"Yeah, man. He was foaming at the mouth. He was so mad," said Wilson.

Spiller and Wilson, sitting in their foxhole, looked around.

"I don't like this location," said Wilson.

"Me either," said Spiller. "That light from the communications center in back of us sure makes us sitting ducks."

"Yeah, but I'm beginning to wonder if any of this matters. We have yet to see any VC," said Wilson.

"Yeah, we're supposed to protect the airfield, but it didn't look like it needed much protection to me."

"Yeah, it looked like everything was running pretty smooth when we got here. I wish you'd get down here in the foxhole, or at least put your helmet and flack jacket on."

"Oh, bullshit. I'll get in the hole before the line officer comes around."

"That' not what I'm talking about. If the VC start taking pot shots, you're a prime target."

"What VC?" laughed Spiller.

Zing! Zing!

"Oh, shit!" Spiller said as he dived for the foxhole. "That hit right in front of us." He quickly grabbed his helmet and flack jacket.

"I told you, damn it. Where in the fuck is the major going?"

"I don't know. He's running toward the tanks."

"Get those tanks out of there now. Get those VC. Hurry up. Move," yelled the major.

The crews scrambled to the tanks and started beyond the perimeter. One tank nose-dived into a gully and sat, spinning its tracks. The others made it through the gulley and fired wildly into the night.

"My God," said Wilson, "there must be a million of them out there."

"No shit!" said Spiller. "We'd better watch. Some might get by the tanks."

Spiller and Wilson, rifles to their shoulders, watched for the VC to attack. One hour went by, yet there were no VC in sight. The tanks stopped firing and returned inside the perimeter.

"You see anything?" asked Wilson.

"No! Do you?"

"Hell, no. Hey, look at that tank. Those dumb shits are still spinning in their tracks. You'd think they'd know by now they're not going any place. Here comes the major again."

"All right. You four men get out there and cover the tank crew 'til you can get them back inside the perimeter."

"Yes, sir," replied Spiller and Wilson as they headed for the tank.

"All right, get out of there, and let's get back inside the perimeter," yelled Wilson to the crew.

Scrambling out of the tank, the crew jumped to the ground and with the scouts rushed back to the perimeter. The other tank crews had already grouped together.

"How many did you get?" asked Wilson.

"We didn't get any. There wasn't anything out there. We didn't see a thing," replied a tankman.

"Well, what were you shooting at?" asked Spiller.

"Hell, the way the major was acting, we figured we'd better do something, so we just started shooting. I'm telling you, there wasn't anybody there."

Spiller and Wilson returned to their foxhole.

"There must have been VC out there," said Spiller. "They shot at us."

"That's right, but doesn't it seem a little ridiculous to send six tanks after one sniper."

"Yeah, and besides that, they don't seem to be able to maneuver very well in this terrain," said Spiller.

"You know something? This is the craziest place I've ever seen. I don't believe anyone really knows what's going on."

Spiller peeked over the top of the foxhole at the tank left in front of the perimeter. "You're right, Rich, this sure is a crazy war."

The next morning as the scouts returned to their tent, they were met by Sergeant Gray, who gave them news of an inspection by the commandant. Gray smiled as the scouts entered.

"You had a little action last night, huh, men?"

"First time I've ever been shot at," said Spiller. "I didn't know I could get that close to the ground."

Gray laughed. "All right, men, the commandant will be here tomorrow to inspect our security. The battalion commander will be around this afternoon to hold an inspection. We have to lay out all our gear and tear the rifles down for inspection. I'll help make one display on the cot, so all of you can set your displays accordingly. Got to shine those boots and put on clean uniforms."

"But, Sarge," said Wilson, "you mean in all this dust and dirt, we have to stand inspection in shined boots? It won't do any good to shine them. They'll have dust all over them in five minutes."

"Yeah, Sarge, our rifles, too," added Smith.

"We're in the middle of a war zone, Sarge," said Stilley.

"All right, all right! I don't agree either, but that's orders," said Gray. "So let's get started."

The scouts grumbled as they prepared for inspection.

"This is crazy," said Spiller.

"The Marine Corps can find more ways to fuck with us than anything. Maybe that's why we never see any VC," said Stilley.

"What are you talking about?" asked Smith.

"Well, the VC are bound to be watching us. If they see us trying to stand inspection in shined boots and with our rifles torn down in the middle of a war zone in all this dust, they'll probably think we're too crazy to mess with."

At 3:00 P.M. the scouts stood at attention in front of their bunks. The major walked in, Sergeant Gray behind him. The battalion commander looked at Stilley's rifle, then at his ammo clips.

"Marine, this rifle is dirty. It has dust all over the barrel."

"Yes, sir."

"Get it cleaned, Marine, understand?"

The battalion commander stepped in front of Spiller.

"You the man that was fired at last night?"

"Yes, sir."

"Were you scared?"

"Yes, sir!"

"You should have got him, Spiller," said the major. "We need some VC bodies."

"Yes, sir," said Spiller, as he wondered how he was supposed to kill VC with an unloaded rifle.

"Your boots are dusty, Marine. Did you run out of polish?"

"No, sir," said Spiller.

"Get them cleaned up. I want everyone to look sharp when the commandant gets here."

"Yes, sir," replied Spiller. He thought how dumb the major must be. They weren't standing on a parade field. They were in a combat zone. And besides if all the commandant is worried about is dust on their boots, then they were all in trouble.

Before leaving the tent, the major turned back. "Look sharp tomorrow, men. We want to impress the commandant."

The next morning the Marines lined up in front of their foxholes. Each Marine was required to have shined boots and a long-sleeved shirt with buttoned sleeves. The commandant landed in a helicopter, and the battalion commander showed him the structure of the perimeter. As they walked, two F-4 fighters flew a mile in front of the perimeter and set a smoke screen. The Marines watched, as the battalion commander explained the entire operation to the commandant.

"How phony," thought Spiller. "He sure is putting on a show. You would think the commandant would know that we wouldn't be on perimeter in shined boots and long-sleeved shirts in 120-degree weather. They did get the tank out of the gully after last night's fuck up. And the plane, why show a smoke screen? We haven't seen any VC and can't even load our rifles. Could the commandant be so stupid that he can't see through all of this phony mess?"

At nightfall Spiller and Wilson sat on the perimeter once again.

"I think this mosquito repellent attracts these damned things instead of driving them away," said Spiller as he swatted mosquitoes.

"Yeah, I swear they have jet engines," replied Wilson.

Kaboom!

Spiller and Wilson ducked into their foxhole.

"That was a grenade," said Wilson.

"Yeah, it was a mile or so in front of the perimeter."

Automatic weapons were fired. Spiller and Wilson rose slowly and watched the fire fight from the perimeter. They could see the muzzle flashes as the weapons fired. Another grenade went off. Ten minutes went by, and the firing stopped. Everything was quiet.

"That must've been the recon unit," whispered Spiller.

"Yeah, I wonder how many VC they got?"

"I don't know, but I don't think they were allowed to load their weapons, either. I sure hope the VC didn't get the jump on 'em."

Anxiously, the men awaited daybreak. Morning came and along with it word that there had been no radio contact since the fire fight. Sergeant Gray entered the tent.

"We're going out on a chopper to see what happened. Orders are we can all carry loaded weapons. Grab your gear. We have a chopper coming 15 minutes from now."

"This may be our first action," said Wilson.

"I don't know if there were VC in the area or not. I'm sure, if they were, they're gone by now," replied Spiller.

The scouts boarded the helicopter and headed for the area of the fire fight.

"Men, when we get in the area, leave the chopper quickly, and hit the dirt. We don't know what we'll be facing," said Gray.

The chopper landed. The scouts jumped out, ran about 20 feet, and formed a semicircle as they hit the dirt. The men lay quietly for about five minutes, watching and listening for movement.

"Smith, see if you can raise them on the radio."

"Delta One, Delta One, this is Yank One. Over."

Silence.

"Delta One, Delta One, this is Yankee One. Over."

"Yank One, this is Delta One. We saw you land. We're located 100 yards due west of your location. We have one dead, one wounded, and one missing. We're having trouble transmitting. Over."

"Delta One, this is Yank One. We read you. Are there still VC in the area? Over."

"That's negative. Over."

"We'll get to you in a few minutes. Over."

The Marines, working their way through the elephant grass, headed for the recon unit. When they arrived, they found the sergeant from the recon unit had been wounded in the shoulder and had a pressure bandage wrapped around both his arm and shoulder. The dead Marine, covered with a poncho, was lying on the ground.

"Sergeant Miller, do you have any idea where your other man might be?" asked Sergeant Gray.

"He has to be somewhere between here and 400 yards due east. After we were hit last night, we attempted to move our location. We didn't know how many VC were around us. We only saw five, and I think we got two of them, but there could have been a lot more. Everything happened so fast. I can tell you this much, we're loading our weapons from now on, orders or not," said Miller. "My man might not be dead if we had been loaded when we got hit."

"Orders came down this morning that we're to carry loaded weapons," said Gray. "Right now, we've got to find your other man."

"He was hit. I don't know how bad."

Spiller looked across the field of elephant grass and thought of the saying "looking for a needle in a haystack." Only they were trying to find a missing Marine.

"Smith, get hold of base. Tell them we're located 100 yards due west of our drop-off location. Tell them the missing man is presumed somewhere between us and 400 yards due east. Ask them to have the chopper fly around to see if they can spot him. Also, tell them we're moving the recon unit back to our drop-off location for pick-up."

Smith called the base and relayed the message.

"Sergeant Gray, base wants to know if the chopper can pick them up here?"

"Hell, no! They can't land in ten feet of elephant grass."

Smith responded to base. "Sergeant Gray, they're on the way."

"Okay."

Sergeant Miller looked at Gray.

"I'm not going back until we find my man."

"I understand," said Gray.

The recon unit picked up the dead Marine and headed for the pick-up point. Meanwhile the scouts stalked their way through the elephant grass.

"Boy, it's like an oven in here," said Spiller.

"You can say that again," said Smith.

"All right, men stay fairly close together. It'll be easy to get separated," ordered Gray.

For two hours the chopper flew over, while the Marines searched on foot. Still nothing.

"Call base and ask them if the chopper's seen anything," ordered gray.

"Yank, this is Yank One. Over," said Smith.

"Yank, this is Yank. Go ahead."

"Yank, has the chopper spotted anything at all? Over."

"Yank One, the pilot indicates he can only spot you from time to time. The foliage is too thick. Over."

"Yank one, out. Sergeant Gray, the base said . . ."

"I heard them! All right men, we're going to spread out a little further and swing back through again. Watch closely. We don't want anyone else missing."

The Marines continued their search. Another hour went by.

"Over here, over here!" yelled Spiller. "I found him! He's alive, Sergeant Gray!"

Sergeant Miller and the other scouts ran over. The Marine, wounded in the arm and leg, had lost a lot of blood. He was unconscious, but still alive.

"All right, Smith, contact base. Tell 'em we found him, and we're heading for the pick-up point. It'll probably take us about an hour to get there."

As the Marines headed for the pick-up point, Spiller saw Sergeant Miller walk up to Sergeant Gray.

Teary-eyed, he whispered to Gray, "Thank God we found him. Thank God he's alive."

The reality of war was beginning to make itself known. The Marines had been shot at, and in addition to the child's death on the day of the landing, there'd been the casualties with the recon unit. Yet no one had seen any VC. They were like invisible men. The men knew they were there, but they just couldn't see them. Then a really crazy thing happened.

Two weeks had passed.

"Hey, Rich," said Spiller, "wanna go down to the barber shop and get a haircut?"

"Yeah," replied Rich, "let's see how well these new barbers cut hair."

Wilson and Spiller walked to a newly structured tent that was used as a barber shop. They stepped inside. Vietnamese barbers stood behind each of the four barber chairs. In front of each chair sat an MP. The Vietnamese were cutting hair.

Wilson walked over to one of the MPs and asked, "What are you doing here?"

"We have to guard the barbers. None of them have a clearance, yet."

"You mean they might be VC?" asked Wilson.

"You got it," replied the MP.

Wilson laughed and walked back to where Spiller was standing.

"Hey, Harry, want your hair cut by a VC?"

Spiller laughed, "Sure, Rich, sure."

Spiller and Wilson took seats next to each other. The Vietnamese barbers were friendly, and in spite of the hand-operated clippers they used, did a good job. Spiller remembered the haircuts his father gave him when he was a kid. Using hand-operated clippers, Harry's father had always managed to pull his hair. These barbers, however, operated them as smoothly as if they were electric clippers. When they were finished with the haircuts, the barbers gave Spiller and Wilson a shave then popped their necks. Wilson and Spiller thanked them for their service.

"That was pretty good, hey, Rich?"

"Yeah, they're good."

"I'm gonna get the same barber next week."

"Me, too," replied Wilson, "me, too."

The next morning was payday. Everyone looked forward to payday. The Marines didn't have much to spend their money on, so they always sent some home. Previously, everyone had been paid in cash. This payday was different. The men were paid in monopoly money, or funny money, as they called it. It was a weird feeling to go through the pay line and get $150 in monopoly money. It seemed almost as if they weren't being paid at all.

Spiller and Wilson walked to the postal tent to get money orders to send home. Wilson asked for $100 in funny money and left. Outside Wilson looked at Spiller and took a deep breath.

"What's the matter?" asked Spiller.

Wilson grinned, "I wasn't sure they'd accept this as real money."

Spiller laughed, "I know the feeling. It sure is different, isn't it? Man, I'm telling you, this is the craziest place I've ever seen."

A week later Spiller returned to the barber. Spiller noticed that the barber he'd seen last week was missing.

He walked up to the MP and asked, "What happened to the barbers that were here last week?"

"They didn't pass security," said the MP.

"What's that mean?" asked Spiller.

"They were VC, Marine. They were VC."

Dumbfounded, Spiller looked at the MP.

"You're shitting me."

"You don't see them here, do you?"

Spiller just stood there.

"I'm telling you, they were VC!"

Spiller, stunned, left the barber shop and returned to the squad tent.

"I don't believe this. We've been here almost two months. We've been shot at, but no VC. We've had one killed and two wounded, still no VC. But I get a haircut and shave from a VC. Nobody will ever believe this. Nobody!"

Spiller entered the tent.

Wilson looked up, "What's the matter with you. You look like you've seen a ghost."

"I saw two VC, Rich."

"Where, where? Somebody finally get one? Where they at?"

Spiller just stood there.

"You're not joking, are you? You're not joking! Damn! Those sons-of-a-bitches shaved our necks. Damn! How could that happen? What's the matter with this place?" yelled Wilson. "You never see any VC. You sit on the perimeter to protect this fucking place from VC, and they let them in here to give us haircuts! I don't believe it."

Spiller looked at Wilson. "You know something else? Nobody back home would ever believe this either. Nobody."

In the dark Spiller sat in his foxhole alone watching for VC. The night was long without Wilson's company. Wilson had been assigned to lead a patrol on the outskirts of Phu Bai. Bushes danced back and forth in front of Spiller's eyes as he looked into the black night.

The sun peaked over the horizon with an orange glow. Spiller returned to the squad tent. He plopped down on his cot. Suddenly Smith popped into the tent. He stood stiff and silent, then tears begin to swell in his eyes.

Spiller looked up in silence for a moment then asked, "What's wrong?"

"The patrol got hit last night," he mumbled in a broken voice.

Spiller's heart begin to pound hard against his chest, "Yeah. Anybody hurt?"

Smith took a deep breath, "Rich is dead," he blurted out.

Spiller's body became weak. "What happened?"

"Got ambushed, he got hit with a grenade."

Spiller sat lifeless, his face in his hands.

"Oh God," Smith mumbled as he began to cry.

The two Marines sat silently whimpering. "Where they gonna take him?" asked Spiller.

"Back to sick bay, Harry," replied Smith.

"I want to see Sergeant Gray. I want to see Sergeant Gray, Smith. Would you go get him?" asked Spiller.

"Sure, Harry, sure."

Smith left the tent and returned shortly with Sergeant Gray. Sergeant Gray stepped into the tent and put his arm around Spiller's shoulder.

"Harry, I know you were close to Wilson, but we all hate to lose him."

Spiller looked at Gray. "What are they gonna do with him?"

"They'll send him to Da Nang in the morning, and from there, home."

"I want to go to the airport with him, Sarge. It's important to me okay, Sarge? Please?"

"Sure, Harry, sure. I'll see to it. I'll see to it."

Spiller walked into sick bay and sat down beside a cot where a black body bag lay. A tag dangled from the zipper lock. Lance Corporal Richard Wilson, 2044445, 3rd FMF, Phu Bai. Spiller looked up and down the entire length of the cot in silence. Deep in sorrow, he began to reminisce.

"What's your name?"

"Richard, Richard Wilson. What's yours?"

"Harry Spiller. Where are you from, Richard?"

"Kansas City, Missouri."

"Oh, really. I'm from Southern Illinois. We're neighbors...."

"Hey, Wilson, have you found any grass?"

"Hell, no! There isn't any grass here."

"I can't find any either. How are we supposed to make it grow?..."

"Corporal, Corporal Spiller?"

"Yes," Spiller said as he looked up at the Navy corpsman.

"The truck will be here in about five minutes."

"Yes, sir," replied Spiller with tear-filled eyes.

"Platoon 135 on the road.... I don't often ask anything of privates. I want to ask each and every one of you to do me a favor. I want you to pray for war...."

"Corporal Spiller, it's time," said the corpsman.

"Yes, sir," replied Spiller as he followed the corpsman from sick bay and boarded the truck.

"I'd like to be a scout," said Spiller.

"Me, too," said Wilson.

As they stepped outside the building, Spiller let out a yell and threw his cap into the air. Wilson ran up and hugged Spiller.

"We did it, Harry. We did it."

"You damned right, we did it. Man, could you imagine, if we went to war, Rich? We'd be right out there in the middle of things."

"That's right. Being a part of a crack scout team in a war. Boy, we'd really rack up the medals."

"...I can see us walking down the streets back home right now...."

Propellers buzzed as the plane came to a stop and turned. Spiller looked up at the plane, then back at the bag holding his friend's body.

"...Hey, we only have 30 minutes before 1965 is here. You got any New Year's resolutions or wishes?"

"Yeah. If we go to Vietnam. I want to take home more medals than you do, Harry." ...

Spiller stood somberly at the end of the truck and watched the corpsman place Wilson's body aboard the plane. The engines grew louder as the plane moved forward.

"...Hey, Harry, want to go to the theater tonight?"

"...What's showing?"

"The Sands of Iwo Jima."

"Sure, why not."

As the movie came to a close and the Marines raised the flag on Iwo Jima, the Marine Corps hymn began to play. The theater went into another uproar. Marines stood, screaming and throwing caps.

"Let's go get them Vietcong!" yelled Wilson.

"Yeah," said Spiller, "let's give those bastards hell."

As the plane lifted into the air, tears streamed down Spiller's face.

"Good bye, Rich. I'm going to miss you, old buddy. I'm really going to miss you."

5

Personal Mayhem

The second week in June, the Marines were sent to Hill 221. The hill was now a forward observation post for the battalion, and rightfully so, since the visibility with the aid of binoculars and scopes was as high as ten miles to the north, south, and west. Looking in all directions, the land was a blend of dark and light green. The streams reflected a bluish tint. Looking at all this beauty, it was hard to believe the country had been at war for so many years. Usually, one platoon of 42 to 45 men manned the perimeter, which consisted of foxholes and bunkers lined with sand bags. Consertina wire was strewn across the front of the perimeter. Every 100 yards, 55 gallon barrels of napalm were placed. In case of ground attack, the barrels would be released and rolled down the sides of the hill then the Marines would fire at the barrels, exploding the napalm.

On a few occasions, artillery and air strikes had been called to Hill 221 on possible sightings of VC, but there had been no casualties. Patrols and ambushes were now being conducted from Hill 221, but at this point, there'd been no contact with the enemy. Around the battalion the standard joke about Hill 221 had emerged from an incident that occurred when a lieutenant called in for artillery. He claimed to have seen a VC guiding three elephants loaded with ammunition and guns on their backs. Of course, the artillery unit did not respond.

Spiller, Smith, and Stilley sat in a bunker enjoying the scenery.

"Hey, Smith," said Spiller, "what time does the fight come on?"

"About another 30 minutes."

"You sure you can get the station all right?" asked Spiller.

"Sure. The Armed Forces Network always comes in without any problem."

"Anybody wanna make bets," grinned Stilley.

"Sure," replied Spiller. "I'll put ten dollars on Liston. He's going to kill Clay."

"You're on," replied Stilley.

"Wanna bet another ten on Liston? Clay has a big mouth. He's going to get it caved in before the night's over," replied Smith.

"That's right," replied Spiller.

"We'll see about that," replied Stilley.

Smith tuned into the Armed Forces Network. The scouts waited anxiously for the fight to begin. Finally, the bell rang and the two fighters met in the center of the ring. The announcer was excited, almost yelling. Stilley laughed.

"What happened? What happened?" asked Spiller.

"Clay knocked Liston out in one punch," replied Stilley.

"Shit!" said Spiller.

"Damn!" said Smith. "Get ready for a big fight, and the damned thing is over in one punch."

"Yeah, we lost our ten dollars, too."

"That's right. Pay up, guys. Pay up," said Stilley.

Kaboom! Kaboom!

The ground shook. Spiller grabbed for his helmet, and the scouts dove for the floor of the bunker.

"Incoming," yelled a Marine on the perimeter.

The ground shook again. For the next 30 minutes, volley after volley hit Hill 221. Dust, smoke, and chunks of dirt filled the air. The scouts, hugging the ground, crawled under their helmets . . . then silence.

"It's over!" yelled Spiller. "Let's get out and watch the perimeter, guys. They may hit us with a ground attack."

The scouts hopped up to keep a close eye out for further VC activity near the perimeter. Thirty minutes passed and nothing. Sergeant Gray charged into the bunker.

"Everyone okay?"

"Sure," replied Spiller. "How many casualties did we get, Sarge."

"None," replied Gray. "They never did hit inside the perimeter."

"Really?" said Smith. "It sounded like they were right on top of us."

"Lucky for us, they must've just estimated when they fired their mortar," said Gray. "Keep an eye out, we may get hit tonight."

For the remainder of the night, the scouts kept watch in the darkness, but no VC.

Just as the sun broke the horizon, Gray entered the bunker.

"Okay, men, we're going on patrol today. Soft caps and cartridge belts. Make sure you have plenty of water. Take all four grenades and check your ammo. We'll be leaving in one hour. Everyone understand?"

"We got it, Sarge."

"Okay, get ready."

The four scouts, along with a squad of 13 men from the Lima Company, made their way down the side of Hill 221. The temperature had climbed to over 110 degrees. The Marines struggled to get through the thick, green foliage. The clear blue waters of the streams were now muddy.

The Marines, having patrolled for hours, found no signs of VC activity. They were now ten miles from Hill 221 and low on water. The patrol was ready to head back to the observation post when a shot rang out. Another shot was fired. Then came automatic fire. The Marines hit the dirt.

"Anybody see anything?" yelled Gray.

"The shots came from the left front, Sarge, but I didn't see anybody," replied Smith.

"Hey, Sarge, there they are. They're running. There are three of 'em," yelled Spiller.

"Smith, get on the radio. Tell base we've had contact with three VC. We're going after them," yelled Gray. "Come on. Don't let them get out of sight."

The Marines went after the VC.

"They've split up, Sarge. There are two still together, and one's gone the other direction," replied Stilley.

"Sarge, base says to capture them, if possible, not to kill them," said Smith.

"Great," replied Gray. "All right, Spiller, Stilley, take four men and go after the one that split off. The rest of us will go after the other two."

Spiller, Stilley, and the other four Marines ran in the direction that the VC had taken.

"There he is!" yelled Stilley. "He's ditched his weapon."

The VC stopped in the middle of the chase. The Marines were dumbfounded. The VC smiled at Stilley and Spiller, who approached him cautiously.

"Me tough VC, Marines. Me tough VC."

"You're tough, huh," snapped Spiller.

"Me tough VC."

"I'll show you what tough is," snarled Spiller. He raised his rifle and knocked the VC to the ground.

"Take it easy, Harry," said Stilley as he knelt and tied the VC's hands behind his back.

"I'll kill that little son-of-a-bitch. They killed Rich!"

"Take it easy. Orders are we're to bring him back alive."

Slyly, Spiller grinned as he and Stilley each took the VC by the arm and started up the path.

Gray beamed when the Marines approached with their prisoner. "You had better luck than we did. The other two got away."

"He ditched his weapon, Sarge," said Stilley.

"At least we got one of 'em," said Gray. "Get on the radio and tell them we're en route, and that we've captured one VC," ordered Gray. "All right, men, we'll take a five-minute breather, then we're going to head back."

The VC, wearing camouflage shorts, sat on the ground legs crossed, his hands still tied behind his back. He sat silently. A large knot protruded above his left eye. Spiller glared intently at the prisoner.

Spiller kept thinking of Wilson. He hated gooks.

"Let's move out," said Gray. "Spiller, Stilley, get him on his feet."

They grabbed the VC under the arms and lifted him. The VC wouldn't stand.

"Get up, damn it," said Spiller.

"Get up, you gookfucker," said Stilley. "He won't stand, Sarge."

"Then we'll carry him. Stilley, you take him first."

"Okay, Sarge," said Stilley as he placed the VC over his shoulder.

After walking a mile, Gray ordered the patrol to stop and told Private First Class Levering from Lima Company to carry the VC for a while. Levering was a weight lifter, who spoke with a slight lisp. No one made fun of him, however, except his close friends. Levering took the VC from Stilley and started to walk.

"God damn!" yelled Levering. He reached back with his left arm, grabbed the VC by the head, and with his right arm wrapped around the VC's thighs, flexed and squeezed.

"What are you doing, Levering?" yelled Gray when he heard a bone pop. "You're gonna kill him."

"That little son-of-a-bitch bit me on the back," yelled Levering.

"Put him down, put him down, Levering. We'll gag him."

"Okay, Sarge, I'll put him down."

Levering turned the VC's head loose and threw him over his shoulder. The VC hit the ground flat on his back, his head bouncing as he hit the ground.

"Gag him, Stilley. Use your pressure bandage."

"Okay, Sarge."

Stilley knelt, attempting to put the pressure bandage in his mouth.

"I can't get his mouth open, Sarge."

"I'll get it open," yelled Levering.

Levering walked over to the VC and with the heel of his boot, stomped him in the mouth. Blood gushed from the VC's mouth. Levering kicked him again. Blood poured. The VC turned his head as he gagged and spit blood and broken teeth from his mouth. The Marines laughed. Stilley knelt and tightened the pressure bandage in the prisoner's mouth. The patrol was on its way once more. This time, Spiller carried the VC. An hour passed and Gray stopped the patrol.

"All right, who wants him now?"

A Marine from Lima Company spoke up.

Spiller threw the VC off his shoulder. Again, the VC landed on his back with a loud thud. His head rebounded as it touched the ground. As Spiller started to walk off, the VC jumped up and ran. The Marines chased him. It was Stilley who finally tackled him.

"You little son-of-a-bitch," yelled Stilley. He grabbed the VC by the hair, lifted him, and then struck the VC in the face with his fist.

By then, two other Marines were kicking and stomping the VC.

"Knock it off!" yelled Gray. "Tie his feet, and let's get going."

Finally, the Marines reached the top of Hill 221. They dropped the VC on the ground. An officer, smiling broadly, hurried to the VC. As he came close enough to get a good look at him, the smile changed to a frown. The VC's eyes were swollen shut, the large knot protruded above his left eye, his teeth were broken, both lips bleeding and swollen, his nose broken, and his right shoulder dislocated. The VC lay bound, gagged, and motionless.

"My God, what happened to him?"

Gray grinned, "He tried to escape, sir."

The scouts were in their bunker eating C-rations when Gray walked in.

"All right, men, we're going on patrol again in the morning. We'll take the same gear, so be prepared."

"Maybe we'll find more VC," Spiller said eagerly.

"Maybe," said Gray, "but we're going to have to take it easy if we capture any more."

"Why?" asked Stilley.

"That VC we captured today died before we got any information from him."

The scouts laughed.

"I guess we'll have to take it easy. Poor little VC," mocked Spiller.

As daylight broke the scouts once again made their way down the side of Hill 221. The men had been on patrol for two hours and had formed back into their column after taking a 15-minute breather. Smith, some 25 yards in the lead of the rest, was the point man. As he approached the crest of a hill, he stopped quickly, knelt, and signaled for the rest of the patrol to take cover. Gray quietly crawled to Smith's location then returned to the rest of the patrol. He signaled for the Marines to move to the crest of the hill on line. Each of the scouts moved slowly and deliberately into position. Spiller peered down over the crest. A stream, some six feet wide, lay at the bottom of the hill. Approximately two feet from the bank, dense foliage and bushes grew out over the water.

Bamm! Bamm! Zing! Zing!

"Those shots came from the foliage," Spiller thought as he ducked.

The Marines opened fire and tossed grenades into the foliage below them. Only three or four shots were returned. Spiller took the empty clip from his rifle, replaced it, and fired again.

"Hey, Smith, they're like sitting ducks, huh!" laughed Spiller.

"Keep firing, Spiller, or we might be sitting ducks," yelled Gray.

"Okay, Sarge," replied Spiller as he instinctively pulled a pin on a grenade and threw it into the foliage.

Thirty minutes passed. The water had turned red. Bodies floated from beneath the foliage.

"Hold your fire," yelled Gray. "Hold your fire."

Spiller grinned at Stilley and Smith.

"All right, men, we're gonna move down to the stream," yelled Gray. "Watch yourselves. There might still be some hidden."

"Sergeant Gray, the battalion commander's on the radio. He wants a body count," yelped Smith.

"Tell him we're moving in. It'll be a while," replied Gray. "All right, men, move out."

The Marines moved down the side of the hill and approached what was left of the foliage. Bodies were mangled within the foliage. Some were missing an arm or a leg.

"All right, men, let's get the bodies up here on the bank. We need to get a body count and have them ready to load on the choppers. The C.O. will want them hauled in," said Gray.

The Marines started pulling the bodies from the water. One body was partially out of the water. The head and arm lay on the bank. Smith grabbed the VC by the arm, pulled, and fell backward.

"What the fuck," yelled Smith as he fell flat on his back. In both his hands was the arm of the VC.

"U-g-h!" Smith groaned. He threw the arm down, jumped up, and ran.

The others laughed as Smith threw up.

"Get back down there and get that body out of the water, Smith," yelled Gray.

"Fuck you, Sarge. Get him yourself!"

"Spiller, Stilley, get that body out of there," yelled Gray.

"Okay, Sarge," replied Spiller.

"There goes one," screamed Smith, "over there."

"Catch him, catch him," yelled Gray as two Marines chased the VC.

Spiller was amazed that anyone could have survived the barrage of grenades and automatic weapons fire. When the bodies were finally laid out and the VC captured, Gray ordered Smith to get on the radio and call battalion.

"Give them a body count. Tell them to send the choppers out. We need body bags."

"Okay, Sarge," replied Smith. "Yank, this is Yank One. Over."

"Yank One, this is Yank," replied battalion.

"Yank, we have 48 dead VC, one captured. Friendly troops, two slightly wounded. We need choppers and some body bags. Over."

"Yank One, this is Yank. The choppers are on the way. Over."

The choppers arrived and the Marines loaded the bodies. Spiller, Smith, and Stilley were assigned to ride back to Phu Bai Airport with the prisoners and six of the bodies. Two VC were in body bags and four others lay stiff with arms and legs missing. The captured VC, looking terrified, sat, arms bound behind him. The chopper landed. Some Vietnamese were departing a civilian airliner that had arrived at the airport moments earlier. Spiller and Smith hopped to the ground, and with Stilley's assistance, pulled the VC bodies off the chopper. Stilley then left with the captured VC. Soon two other choppers arrived and more bodies were dumped on the runway. The Marines loaded the VC bodies into two six-by trucks. As Spiller and Smith each grabbed the end of one body bag and ran for the truck, blood oozed from beneath. Both Spiller and Smith laughed and yelled along with the rest of the Marines. One Marine, with a camera, took pictures of the entire incident. Spiller looked across the runway as the truck pulled away. The passengers from the civilian airline lined the edge of the airfield and watched the Marines. Men, women, and children stared in silence. The look of fear showed on their faces.

The two six-bys pulled up to a Vietnamese cemetery just outside Phu Bai village. A Vietnamese, sitting on a backhoe, was parked beside a large hole, soon to be a mass grave for the VC. About 100 villagers stood around the gravesite. The trucks stopped and the motors were turned off. There was silence. Spiller and Smith stood at the back of the truck.

"Let's take this one first. He has an arm missing," laughed Spiller.

"Okay. Hey, let's see how high we can throw him."

Smith grabbed the arm. Spiller grabbed the legs. Back and forth they swung the body.

"Are you ready?" asked Spiller. "Here we go. One, two, three!"

At the sound of three, the body was tossed into the air. The body hit with a thud. Both men laughed and reached for another body. Two Marines in another truck yelled at Spiller. They wanted to make a bet to see who could throw a body the highest, Smith and Spiller or themselves.

"We'll bet you ten dollars," said Spiller.

"Okay," replied the Marine, "you're on!"

For the next 30 minutes the Marines took turns throwing VC into the air. Each duo claimed to have thrown their body the highest. As the trucks pulled away, Spiller became aware of the villagers. Again he saw that look of fear. Children stood silently, tears rolling down their innocent faces.

Some time later the trucks arrived back at the airfield. Smith and Spiller left the truck and went to the hangar bay where Stilley stood watch over the captured VC. Still bound with his hands behind his back, the VC sat looking as though his death was imminent.

"Get them buried?" asked Stilley.

"Yeah," replied Spiller. "What are we gonna do with him?"

"The lieutenant from intelligence will be over in a few minutes."

"They're gonna interrogate him?" asked Smith.

"Oh, shit!" Stilley exclaimed.

"What's the matter?" asked Smith.

"Here comes that damned Navy corpsman again. He thinks I'm being cruel because I won't untie the VC and give him any water."

The corpsman walked up. "Stilley, I'm going to give him some water."

"Okay."

The corpsman poured water into a canteen cup and held it to the VC's mouth. The VC took a drink, nodded to the corpsman, and said something in Vietnamese. The corpsman took a pack of cigarettes from his pocket, showed them to the VC, and asked if he wanted one. The VC nodded. The corpsman took the cigarette from the pack, lit it, and put it in the VC's mouth. The VC puffed a couple of times.

Stilley grinned, "I'd better take that so he doesn't drop it. Want another puff?"

The VC nodded.

Stilley quickly turned the cigarette and stuck the lighted end to the VC's mouth. The VC turned his mouth away, yelled, and spit. The cigarette fell to the floor.

The corpsman screamed at Stilley. "You fucking animals! All of you fucking Marines are animals!"

Spiller, Smith, and Stilley laughed.

"That's right, sailor boy, we are," replied Stilley, "but then again, you weren't out there when this gookfucker was trying to kill us, were you?"

The corpsman looked angrily at Stilley then turned quickly and walked way. The Marines continued to laugh.

"Bye, bye, sailor boy. Bye, bye."

Spiller reached down and picked the cigarette up off the ground. "Hey, VC, want a cigarette, huh? You gookfucker, want a cigarette?"

6

Blunders

In August 1965, the battalion began sending the Marines on patrols into the villages that surrounded Phu Bai. It was their responsibility to gather information concerning VC activity from the villagers.

The scouts were cleaning rifles in their squad tent at battalion headquarters when Sergeant Gray walked in.

"Okay, men, you have to go over to the airfield. One of the patrols is bringing in some VC suspects. They'll be coming in anytime."

"Nice they gave us notice," snapped Smith.

"Spiller, you're in charge of the detail. Hurry up and get over there."

The scouts grabbed rifles and cartridge belts and headed for the airfield. They arrived in the open field beside the air strip, where a holding area had been constructed out of consentina wire. The wire was strewn into a square with one small opening for entry.

"Here they come," said Stilley, pointing to the west.

"Damn! There are four choppers. I wonder how many they have," said Spiller.

"I don't know, but if all four choppers are full, the holding area isn't enough."

The choppers landed, and a first sergeant from the recon patrol jumped out. He waved the villagers off the plane. The first villager was a pregnant woman, followed by another, then several children. Two villagers carried an old man, probably 90 years old or so. They were all crying and looked terrified. Several young boys, suffering from air sickness, were throwing up.

"Oh, my God! My God!" exclaimed Spiller.

"What in the hell!" gasped Smith.

The first sergeant started yelling at the people, ordering them to get into the holding area. None could speak or understand English.

Spiller ran over to the first sergeant. "What in the hell are you doing? These people aren't VC or VC sympathizers. They're scared to death."

"Look, Corporal, we were sent on patrol, and according to intelligence, the village was supposed to be empty. If it's supposed to be empty, and these people are there, then they're suspicious."

"Did it ever dawn on you that the intelligence reports might be wrong?"

"Look, Corporal, you get your men over to that holding area and get these people corralled, or I will personally have you court-martialled."

Spiller joined Smith and Stilley.

"All right, men, let's see if we can get them inside the wire."

For the next 30 minutes the scouts attempted to corral the villagers. A few went inside the wire without any trouble, but most cried and shook their heads "no." Spiller attempted to get one pregnant woman inside the wire. Crying, she tried to hug Spiller. Spiller's eyes filled with tears as he tried in vain to explain that the scouts had no intention of hurting her or the other villagers. Finally, all the villagers were inside the wire. They hugged each other, afraid that the Marines might hurt them. The first sergeant walked up to Spiller.

"Well, we finally got them corralled."

Tears were streaming down Spiller's face. "You son-of-a-bitch!" he said to the stone-faced first sergeant.

"I'll have your ass!" yelled the first sergeant.

A Jeep pulled up. The lieutenant from intelligence got out and for a moment looked on in total disbelief at the number of villagers.

Turning to the indignant first sergeant, he asked, "What the hell is going on, First Sergeant?"

"Sir, intelligence reports indicated the village was supposed to be empty. We brought them in as VC sympathizers."

"Do you have your map, First Sergeant?"

"Yes, sir. Right here, sir."

"Show me the village."

He pointed to the map. "Right here, sir."

"That's what I thought. That's the wrong village! That's the wrong village! Get these people back on the choppers, and take them back to their village. Now!"

"Yes, sir!"

The lieutenant, Spiller, Smith, and Stilley watched quietly as the villagers were returned to the choppers. The choppers lifted off. The lieutenant turned to Spiller, "I want to see you in my office in one hour. I have a mission for you."

"Yes, sir."

Spiller walked into the intelligence office where Lieutenant Gruner and Sergeant Gray were waiting.

"Good morning, sir."

"Good morning, Corporal Spiller. Have a seat," ordered the lieutenant.

"Spiller, we're sending you on a mission into Nam Hoa village. The village is located here," said the lieutenant, pointing to a village on the map some 15 miles to the northwest of battalion headquarters. "We have reports that there's been a lot of VC activity in and out of that village. In the morning we're going to send you into the village. At this point, we haven't had anyone there. You'll leave in the morning at 0600. I want all the information possible when you return. Is that understood?"

"Yes, sir."

"I have to fly up to Da Nang in the morning. Sergeant Gray will take my place here while I'm gone. You'll report back to him."

"Yes, sir."

"Any questions?"

"No, sir."

"Very well then, Corporal. That will be all."

As Spiller was leaving the tent, Sergeant Gray smiled. "Hey, Spiller, good luck."

Spiller returned the sergeant's smile. "Thanks, Sarge. Thanks."

As the sun broke the horizon, the scouts passed through the battalion perimeter and headed northwest for the village. The temperature was well over 100 degrees. The Marines made their way across the rolling hills, elephant grass, and rice paddies, until they came within a half mile of Nam Hoa village. They found no sign of VC activity. The scouts halted. Spiller removed his binoculars from the case and scanned the area. Several Vietnamese were working in rice paddies at the outer

Villagers were busy with daily chores while Marines attempted to gather information about Vietcong activity.

edge of the village. Although some huts were visible, Spiller was unable to see the activity within the village because of trees and bushes surrounding it. Spiller noticed two paths, obviously used frequently by the villagers who worked in the rice paddies.

"All right, men, we're going in. Everything seems to be quiet in the village. Let's keep on our toes. There haven't been any Americans in this village before, so no telling what kind of response we'll get. Any questions? Okay, let's go."

The scouts moved cautiously toward the village. Smith, on point, knelt suddenly as he signaled for the others to get down. Spiller crawled to Smith's position, where he noticed a woven basket full of bananas lying on the ground in front of Smith.

"What's wrong?" asked Spiller.

"I just came nose to nose with a woman villager. She dropped her basket and ran like hell. She looked really scared."

"Where'd she go?"

"She ran up the path into the village. Do you think she's tipping off the VC or what?"

"I don't know. Intelligence said there have never been any Americans in the village before. Maybe they're just afraid of us. You know the stories the VC have spread about us."

"You mean about us killing babies and eating them?"

"Yeah, among others."

"How could they believe that, Harry?"

"Easy, Smitty. VC propaganda is very convincing, especially when the villagers haven't been around Americans before."

Spiller turned, facing the other scouts. "Okay, guys, they know we're coming, so let's be on our toes."

Once again, the scouts fell into a column and cautiously moved across the rice paddies on the open path, making their way to the village. The villagers were no longer in sight. The scouts moved through the foliage and finally stood at the outer edge of the village. Running through the middle of the village was a dirt lane about five feet wide. On both sides of the path were huts made from bamboo. The only thing moving in the village were a few chickens that clucked and pecked at the ground. The scouts observed the village for several minutes.

Spiller turned toward the scouts. "All right, men, we'll fall into a column and go straight through the village. Smile or wave if you see villagers. We don't want to scare them any more than they already are. Let's go. I'll take the point."

Spiller moved into the village slowly. The scouts fell into a column behind him. He passed the first hut and then the second. Looking through the openings of the huts, Spiller saw the shadows of the villagers. The scouts were close to the center of the village. Suddenly a villager, dressed in white pajama-like top and bottom, no shoes, a straw hat, and a fu-man-chu style beard stepped out of a hut. With a smiling face and hands together as if he were praying, he bowed as he approached Spiller.

"Good afternoon," Spiller said smiling.

The villager responded in Vietnamese.

"Do you speak English?"

Again, he answered in Vietnamese.

"Oh, boy! You don't have to be afraid of us. We're here to help you."

The villager once again spoke in Vietnamese.

"Quit bowing, old man. You don't have to be afraid. Are there any VC in the area? Have they been in your village?"

"VC, VC," the old man said and pointed to the hills behind the village.

"Have VC been here?"

Again, Spiller couldn't understand him.

"Does anyone in your village speak English? Quit bowing, damn it!"

Once more the old man rattled something in Vietnamese.

"All right, men, let's go."

The scouts proceeded to walk through the village. The old man walked back to his hut. Before entering the hut, he turned, and once again bowed. The scouts continued through the village, still seeing nothing but shadows of the villagers, who watched in silence.

"Let's head back to headquarters. The lieutenant will love this. Either we have to get someone that understands the Vietnamese language, or we're going to have to go to school for it. That is, if we're going to gather any intelligence."

"Did you catch when you said VC?" asked Smith.

"Yeah, that was the only part of the conversation that I caught onto."

"What do you think he meant?"

"I don't know. He might've been trying to tell us where they were located. I just don't know. We need to talk to the lieutenant."

The scouts arrived at headquarters just before dark. Spiller went directly to the intelligence tent, while the others returned to their squad tent. Spiller entered the tent and approached Sergeant Gray.

Gray smiled up at Spiller, "Well, how did it go?"

"Not so good, Sarge."

"What happened?"

"Well, we were spotted by one of the villagers about a quarter of a mile before we got to the village. By the time we got there, everyone was hidden. An old man came out, and as I questioned him, he just kept bowing. He was scared, Sarge. He was really scared. Nobody could speak English. Other than the old man pointing to the hills and saying 'VC, VC,' we didn't get any information and I'm not sure what he meant. He could have meant any number of things, Sarge. We need an ARVN or an interpreter to go with us."

"Did you see anything at all that might indicate VC activity?"

"Nothing, Sarge, except the old man pointing to the hills, saying 'VC, VC'."

"Okay, Spiller, you did your best. When the lieutenant gets back, I'll talk with him and see what he wants to do. Be back here in the morning at 0900."

At 0900 Spiller reported to the intelligence tent. As he entered, Gray and the lieutenant were discussing a map lying on the table.

"Spiller! I'm glad you're here. We've been planning your next patrol. Have a seat."

"Yes, sir."

"Okay, Harry, we have an interpreter reporting to us some time today. You'll take a patrol out tomorrow with the same game plan. I want you to make sure the interpreter talks to that old man. My hunch is that he's the village chief. Find out what he meant when he pointed to the hills and said 'VC, VC.' No doubt, they're in that area."

"Yes, sir. What about this interpreter? I mean, is he trustworthy?"

"I believe so. According to our information, he's been used by the recon unit without any problems. Do you have any other questions?"

"No, sir."

"Be ready to move out at 0600. I'll have the interpreter here at that time."

"Yes, sir."

"See you in the morning, Spiller."

At 0600 Spiller and the scout section met at the intelligence tent where they were introduced to the interpreter. They then proceeded on patrol. Four hours later the unit neared the village. Spiller scanned the village with his binoculars. As before, there were a few villagers working in the rice paddies. Things looked as they had a couple of days before.

"Okay, men, let's go! Stay on your toes. I'll take the point. Chin, you fall in behind me."

The scouts fell into a column and followed Spiller into the village. This time the villagers didn't quit working the rice paddies, but occasionally looked at the Marines. Before long the Marines stood at the edge of the village. Some children were playing, but once they spotted the Marines, they hurried into their huts. Many women did the same, while a few continued to work keeping one eye on the Marines.

As the Marines walked into the village, the old man came out of his hut, approached Spiller, and bowed again.

"Not again! Chin, would you talk to him? Tell him we're not here to hurt anyone. We just want information on the VC."

Chin walked up to the old gentleman and spoke to him in Vietnamese. They talked back and forth. Once in a while, the villager pointed to the hills.

"What did he say, Chin?"

"He said there have been some VC in those hills. He didn't know how many, but none had been in the village for many days."

"What else did he say?"

"Nothing! What do you mean, nothing? You've been talking to him for ten minutes."

"No, no. Nothing else."

"Bullshit! How many days? Three or four days, a week, what?"

Chin turned to the old man and started talking once again.

"He only knows many days, as you say, a long time."

"Why were they here?"

"He says to get rice."

"Are they giving it to them, or are the VC just taking it?"

Chin spoke with the old man again.

"He says the VC came and took the rice."

"When was the last time?"

"He says many days."

"Did he say anything else?"

"No, no. Nothing else."

"Do you think he's telling us everything?"

"Yes, yes. Everything."

"Okay, let's go."

Again, the patrol returned to headquarters. Spiller headed for the intelligence tent. The interpreter disappeared. The rest of the scouts headed for their squad tent. Spiller entered the tent and approached the lieutenant.

"How did it go, Spiller?"

"Better than the last time, sir. We did find out a little more. According to the village chief, the VC have been in the village to get rice. Also, they're supposed to be in the hills directly south of the village, but according to him, they haven't been there for many days."

"How many is many?"

"I don't know, sir. That's all he'd say."

"How many VC?"

"He didn't know, sir."

"Anything else?"

"Well, sir, to be quite frank, I think he was lying or the interpreter was. They would talk for ten minutes, then Chin would turn and say very little. When I asked him what else he said, Chin would say 'nothing'."

"What do you think, Spiller?"

"I think the VC are in the village all the time, sir. They probably take off when we hit the village. They know we're coming 30 minutes before we get there. Today some of the villagers stayed in the paddies, but they kept an eye on us. I think they're warning them, sir."

"Okay, Spiller, let me think about all of this. Be back here in the morning."

"Yes, sir."

The next morning, Spiller returned to the intelligence tent. The lieutenant had a plan to see if Spiller's hunch about the VC was correct.

"Spiller, we're going to play on your hunch. Tomorrow morning, the scout section, along with two snipers, are going by truck through Hue and down the river to a Vietnamese outpost located on Thu Bon River. That outpost is directly behind the hill ridge the old man was talking about. You will be here." The lieutenant pointed to the map. "Day after tomorrow, I want you to set up on the hill ridge behind the village. We'll send another patrol through the village and see if we can flush out the VC. Let's see if we can raise the casualty count for the other side."

"Yes, sir."

"The snipers will be reporting this afternoon. I want you to brief them."

"Yes, sir."

"That'll be all, Spiller."

"Yes, sir," said Spiller, heading for the exit.

"Oh, by the way, be careful and good luck."

The scouts were in the squad tent cleaning rifles and preparing for the next day's assignment. Two Marines entered the tent.

"Howdy, I'm Bob Thompson. This is Larry Schafer. We're snipers looking for the scout section and Corporal Spiller."

Spiller introduced himself and shook hands with Thompson and Schafer. "This is Smith and Stilley. Make yourselves at home, and we'll go over the game plan for tomorrow."

"We gonna get some VC?" asked Thompson.

"I hope so, if my hunch is right."

"What do you mean?"

"We've been on patrols in Nam Hoa village. The second time we took an interpreter. From what we found out, the VC have been in the village. I don't believe we were getting the whole truth. The village chief told us the VC had been in the village to get rice, but that was all. He said a lot more, we just never could get the interpreter to tell us what he said. I think he was lying. I believe the VC are staying in the village and heading out into the hills when we come in. They know well ahead when we're coming. Another thing, supposedly, we're the first Americans in the village."

"Sounds familiar. We were in the Da Nang area a couple of weeks ago. The units there are having the same problems. The villagers are either scared or sympathizers. Most of the time it's hard to tell which. The Third Marines have been finding weapons and ammo hidden in the villages. Your hunch is probably right."

"What type of rifles do you carry?" asked Spiller.

"Thirty-ought-six rifles with 10X scopes. We're good at a range of about 1,000 yards."

"Damn, 1,000 yards!"

"Yeah, 1,000 yards," grinned Thompson.

"Okay. We're leaving in the morning for a Vietnamese compound located here," Spiller said, pointing at the map. "There are 50 ARVN troops located at the compound and a Green Beret advisor. Day after tomorrow, we're to work our way to this hill ridge just behind the village. We have to be set by noon. A patrol is going into the village at approximately noon. Hopefully, they'll flush the VC out, if they're in the village."

"Hopefully, they'll fall right into our hands," said Thompson.

"Exactly."

The Marines spent the rest of the afternoon cleaning their equipment and preparing for the next day. The next morning they boarded trucks and headed for the ARVN compound. About an hour later, they arrived. Surrounded by consentina wire with a perimeter of foxholes some 20 yards inside of the wire, the compound was what remained of an old French fortress. A concrete building sat in the center of the perimeter. Several holes, hits by 106 recoilless rifles, were in the walls of the building. A Green Beret sergeant approached Spiller.

This picture was taken from the top of a concrete bunker emplacement, built by the French during the Indo-China war.

"I'm Sergeant Hill."

"I'm Corporal Spiller. Nice to meet you."

"Bring your men inside the headquarters building, Corporal. You can leave your equipment inside. When you get squared away, I'll show you the perimeter assignments."

"Okay, Sarge. Thanks."

The scouts laid their equipment on the floor and entered the building. Smith stuck his head through one of the large holes in the wall and looked around.

"I always wanted an air-conditioned room. Guess I got one, huh?"

Everyone laughed.

"Let's go find out where our perimeter assignments will be," said Spiller.

The Green Beret sergeant walked to the perimeter with the

Marines to show where each one should go in case of an attack. Four 3-caliber machine guns were mounted equally on the perimeter. A 155 howitzer was located at one side of the headquarters building. Behind the perimeter and at the back of the building were two 60-millimeter mortars.

"You have a good defense set up, Sarge," said Spiller. "How often do you get hit?"

"Up to a month ago, every night. Mostly harassment, nothing heavy, but it's been quiet lately."

For the remainder of the afternoon, Spiller went over the maps with the army advisor and briefed the scouts and snipers. Finally, they settled down for a good night's sleep before the next day's activities.

Kaboom! Tat-ta-tat! Kaboom! Kaboom!

"Let's get to the perimeter," yelled Spiller. "Incoming!"

Spiller and the Marines grabbed for cartridge belts and rifles as they quickly scrambled for the perimeter. Spiller dove through an open window, landing flat on his face. He stood up and ran for his foxhole. As he passed the location of the 60-millimeter mortar positions, he noticed the Vietnamese dropping shells down the tubes, as fast as they could. The entire perimeter of some 40 Vietnamese had opened fire. Grenades were thrown. The 155 howitzer crew fired rapidly. In the few short seconds it had taken Spiller to get to the perimeter, he couldn't help believing that the Chinese army must have attacked. Staying low, he hit the foxhole where he managed to get his cartridge belt around his waist. The Vietnamese soldiers continued firing rapidly until their clips emptied. Reloading, they opened fire again. Flares were fired for visibility. The perimeter continued to fire at a steady pace. Spiller rose slowly until he could see over the edge of the foxhole. He looked directly into the field in front of him, to the left, to the right, then back to the ARVN soldier on his left. Both fired rapidly. The flares went out. Then two more flares lit up in front of the perimeter. Again Spiller looked directly into the field, to the right, and then to the left. He saw nothing.

He shouted at the ARVN soldier on his right. "Hey, asshole! What the fuck are you shooting at?"

Ignoring Spiller, the ARVN soldier continued to fire.

Spiller turned to the ARVN soldier on his left. "Hey, what in the hell are you shooting at?"

Spiller heard someone screaming to cease fire. He turned to see the army advisor moving from foxhole to foxhole, shouting at the ARVN to stop firing. Ten minutes passed, and the perimeter was quiet. Spiller, staring into the darkness, wondered where the perimeter had been hit. Both the ARVN soldier to his right and to his left looked frightened. The ARVN lieutenant spoke over a portable loudspeaker. They only word Spiller understood was VC. He wondered what was going on. Suddenly, the ARVN lieutenant spoke in English.

"Surrender VC. Surrender VC, immediately. We have the United States Marines with us. If you do not surrender immediately, we will send the Marines after you."

"Like hell you will," yelled Spiller. "Sarge Hill, where in the fuck are you?"

Spiller leaped from his foxhole and walked around the perimeter. "Sarge Hill!"

"Here I am."

"What the fuck is going on? We have five of us and to boot, two with sniper rifles. We aren't going after anybody."

"Take it easy, Spiller. Take it easy. The lieutenant thinks this will scare the VC off. These troops are new and a little jumpy."

"Oh, I see. Where did we get hit, anyway?"

"We didn't, Spiller. A trip flare went off."

"What!"

"A trip flare went off."

"You mean to tell me that they fired all this ammo because of a trip flare."

"Yeah, like I said, they're fresh troops, a little jumpy."

Spiller shook his head and headed for the headquarters building. "I don't believe this."

He stopped and turned toward Sarge Hill. "Hey, Sarge! Just out of curiosity, do you have any ammo left, if we do get hit? I mean, they just fired enough to wipe out the entire North Vietnamese Army."

"Yeah, Spiller, we have plenty of ammo."

The night seemed short. The scouts prepared for the day's patrol.

"I hope today goes better than last night," said Smith.

"Boy, you can say that again," said Stilley.

"Everybody ready?" asked Spiller.

"Ready," replied Smith and Stilley.

"Us, too," answered Thompson.

"Let's go!"

The Marines fell into a column and walked for three hours through rice paddies, elephant grass, and across a number of hill ridges. Finally, they were on a hill ridge about 1,000 yards southwest of the village.

"What time is it?" asked Spiller.

"Ten-thirty," replied Thompson.

"Okay, we need to set in. The patrol should be moving into the village about noon. Stilley, take these binoculars and keep an eye on the village. We'll switch off every half hour."

Two hours passed.

"It's 12:30. Where the hell is that patrol?" snapped Spiller to himself.

"Hey! Hey! Take a look, Harry!" gasped Smith.

"There they are. I knew it. I knew it!" Spiller exclaimed.

Thompson grabbed the binoculars, "Four . . . five. There's five."

"Get 'em! Get 'em!"

Spiller took the binoculars back and watched the VC as they moved slowly in a column, rifles thrown casually over their shoulders.

"Bet the patrol hasn't got to the village yet. Bet they know they're coming!"

Bam! Bam!

"Damn, you got one, two. They're running. Hurry."

Bam! Bam!

"You hit another one."

"Where'd they go?" asked Thompson.

"They ran behind those bushes to the left. You got three."

The Marines watched for another hour, but the two remaining VC never came into sight.

"Let's go. The lieutenant will love this," shouted Spiller.

The Marines returned to the ARVN compound, and were quickly transported back to battalion headquarters.

They arrived just before dark. Spiller hurried to the intelligence tent to brief the lieutenant. As he entered the tent, the lieutenant was studying a map.

"Sir! We got three. We got three!"

The lieutenant looked up. "You're sure?"

"Yes, sir! I watched while the snipers fired, sir!"

"You are sure?"

"Yes, sir, I'm sure. Sir, is there a problem?"

"Wait here." The lieutenant left the tent for a few minutes, then returned with the battalion commander.

"Tell the major what you just told me."

"Sir, we got three VC. We set up on the ridge southwest of the village like planned. There were five of them. They came out in a column. I watched with binoculars while the snipers fired. The first two shots dropped two of them. They started to run, and the snipers fired again. They only got one when they fired the second time. We never could spot the other two after that. Sir, is there a problem?"

"The patrol came through the village. They didn't find any bodies," replied Lieutenant Gruner.

"Sir, I swear we got three. We watched for a good 45 minutes after the first shots, and all three bodies were in sight. I'm positive we got them."

"All right, we'll turn in the body count."

The major left the tent. Spiller smiled at the lieutenant.

"Good work, Spiller. Good work," said Lieutenant Gruner.

Spiller returned to the squad tent.

"What did the lieutenant have to say?" asked Smith.

"He said to pass on a job well done. I don't know what the major thought. The patrol didn't find any bodies, and I'm not sure he believes my story."

"Maybe they dragged them off or something," said Stilley.

"One thing for sure, they didn't walk off. They were nailed. I saw it with my own eyes. Oh, well, we got the body count, and the lieutenant was satisfied."

"This place is nuts. They'll be making us bring them in caskets next," snapped Smith.

Spiller laughed. "You're probably right. Hey, Smitty, why don't you go see if we got any mail."

Smith returned with the mail and a couple of *Stars and Stripes* newspapers. Spiller read a letter from home. Smith was reading the *Stars and Stripes*. Stilley was talking to Thompson about sniper training, and Schafer headed for the shower.

"Hey, hey! They got a letter off a dead VC up around Da Nang and printed it in the paper. Listen to this," said Smith.

"Marines will go anywhere in RVN. III MAF, Vietnam—The following document was found on the body of a VC killed in action May 5, 1965, in the area being protected by the First Battalion, Third Marines:

From: Chung Hoa Thuong
To: Mr. Tam

Following the common situation in the Hoa Thong Hamlet right now
is very hard. Last time the USMC have mop up and occupy all zones
such as Hoa Hon Phuoc Chan, Phuoc Gian, Dang Bich, Hoi Nuc. Their
manners were too bad, they did not scare anywhere. If they want, they
come. They came to the village, they search from outside to inside the
house, with the cruel faces. They told people to move down and they
stay. Don't stay here, the US will destroy all and they promise that
they will pacify the hamlets. Hoa Phu and Hoa Thuong, set up the
Hing-an-camp. The members in the council told people that all youths
16 years old have to go to district to make the pass no order to present
to the American why they come. As for population is very anxious.
They are afraid of these Americans only because they don't understand Vietnamese language so that they shoot sometimes. Population
is afraid of their cruel faces, because they do not scare anywhere, they
come anywhere they like. I am responsible to talk to the villagers but
it is not enough so that I report to you and have you any good opinions
in order to fight the United States Marines. They look like mad dogs.

Hao Thuong 10 April 1965
Chung'

"Teach them to mess with us, huh?" said Smith.

"Hey, I want one of them to send home," said Spiller.

"Me, too," said Stilley.

"Them gooks are really afraid of us, huh?" laughed Thompson.

Schafer popped through the door. "Hey, guys, I think I made the
battalion commander mad."

"How's that?" asked Spiller.

"He stopped me on the way down to the shower and asked me if
I was one of the snipers. When I told him I was, he wanted to know
if I was sure we killed the VC. I told him we were sure. He asked me
how I was so sure, and I told him the one I hit did a double flip and a
half gainer before he hit the ground."

Everyone burst out laughing.

"What did he say, Schafer?" asked Smith.

"He just stared for a minute, then told me to go take a damned
shower, and walked off."

The laughter continued.

7

Praying for War

Two days later Spiller walked into the intelligence tent to turn in the report on the patrol operation at the ARVN compound. A PFC administrator clerk was in the office.

"Jones, I'm going to leave this report on the lieutenant's desk. Make sure he gets it, okay?"

"Sure, Harry. Hey, want to play a quick game of darts?"

Spiller and Jones took turns throwing darts. All the while, Jones kept grinning as if he knew something Spiller didn't.

"How long you been here, Corporal?"

Spiller, startled by the voice, turned quickly. Sitting in the corner at the front of the tent was Sergeant Johnson.

"Sergeant Johnson! Where did you come from? I mean, when did you get here?"

"Yesterday."

"I knew that voice. I knew it!"

Spiller walked over to shake hands with Johnson.

"They assigned me to S-3 as Staff NCOIC. I'm afraid it's going to be more pencil pushing than anything. Maybe I'll get a chance to get some action," Johnson told Spiller.

"I'm sure you will, if you want. I sure am glad to see you, but I must admit you were the last person in the world I expected to see. When I heard that voice, I thought I was back in boot camp."

Johnson and Spiller both laughed.

"Well, I've got to get back over to the squad tent and clean up some gear. We have a meeting in the morning. We're going to have some kind of operation in a couple of days. Maybe you can get in on that."

The next morning Spiller went to the intelligence tent for the briefing of the upcoming operation. Two platoons were to escort a crack Vietnamese unit of 40 Black Panthers in Thu Bon River. The Marines were to provide cover for the Panthers as they crossed the river. When finished with that mission, the two platoons were to sweep five miles down the river in search of VC or signs of VC activities. They were then to return to battalion headquarters. The Marines were warned about booby traps, something the VC knew how to use very well. They were also reminded of the day the battalion had 26 casualties as a result of booby traps without spotting a single VC.

The two Marine platoons formed at sunup and met with the Black Panther unit. A civilian reporter traveled with the unit. As the troops formed for the move to the river, Spiller spotted Johnson. Smiling, he winked at Spiller. Spiller returned the gesture as the troops moved out.

The Marines and Black Panthers walked all day and half the night, arriving at a location one-half mile from the river's edge at 0300 hours. The foliage was thick. The troops looked forward to getting off their feet for a couple of hours before the Panthers started their move across the river at daybreak.

Spiller sat quietly watching in the night. It was so dark that the Marines could not see each other, even though they were but a few feet apart. Spiller sat for a few minutes then unbuttoned his shirt to get some air. He felt something on his chest. He reached inside. Land leeches! Three of them.

"Oh, shit," Spiller thought, "I can't even light a cigarette to get them off. I wonder what time it is. It should be daylight soon, then I'll get them off. They don't really hurt. Won't take much blood. I'll just sit here and try to rest."

Spiller sat for what seemed hours then rubbed his hand across his chest. The leeches had grown larger.

"It won't be long till daylight. Can't be. I'll just think about something else. Let's see. Only got three months and I'll be going home. Can't wait. It'll be great to get out of this god-forsaken place. Be good to see some of my old friends. Shit! I wish that damned sun would come up. These fucking leeches are driving me crazy. They're getting bigger."

Three hours later, daylight broke.

"Stilley, Stilley, you got a cigarette!"

"Yeah, Harry. Damn, you having a nicotine fit, or what?"

"Fuck, no! Get over here. Help me get these leeches off my chest. Hurry up!"

Stilley walked over as Spiller opened his shirt.

"My, they're pretty big, Harry," laughed Stilley.

"Hey, asshole, quit fucking around and light that cigarette."

"Okay, okay!"

Stilley held the cigarette to each leech until all were released.

"Damn, Harry, sure you can make it without a blood transfusion?"

"You're real cute, Stilley, real cute. Get your ass back over to your position. We'll be moving out soon."

The two platoons spread out along the riverbank as the Black Panther unit started across the river.

Rat-ta-tat! Rat-ta-tat!

"We're getting fire from across the river."

The Marines fired in the direction of the far bank.

Kaboom! Kaboom!

A Marine screamed. "Rifle grenades! They have rifle grenades!"

The two platoons continued firing for another five minutes, then stopped. The VC played their usual hit-and-run, cat-and-mouse game. For a moment everything was quiet.

"We need help down here. We have casualties!"

With Smith holding his position, Spiller and Stilley rushed in the direction of the call for help.

Two Marines had been hit by shrapnel from the rifle grenades. One was hit in his right arm, the other had a graze to the head. A corpsman was attending to them.

"Where do you need help?" yelled Spiller.

"Over here!" a Marine called out.

Two Marines and a corpsman were kneeling. Spiller and Stilley ran up. Spiller couldn't believe his eyes as he looked down at the Marine lying on the ground.

"Oh, my God! It's Staff Sergeant Johnson. Man, he's only been here five fucking days!"

"He must've been standing right on top of that rifle grenade," said the corpsman. "We've looked all over, and there isn't a bit of his leg left. I mean nothing!"

"We have a chopper coming into a clearing about three-quarters of a mile from here to pick up the casualties. We need a few men to help carry him back," said Spiller.

The Marines covered Johnson with a poncho. Aside from the leg missing from his hip, there wasn't a scratch on Johnson's body. The Marines placed Johnson's body on a portable stretcher and headed for the clearing where the other two casualties lay. Spiller couldn't help thinking back to boot camp days, remembering the first morning he met Johnson at the receiving barracks and the respect he had for him. Johnson's death was difficult for Spiller to accept. He felt ill all over. The choppers landed and the casualties were loaded. As the choppers pulled away, Spiller spoke up.

"I wonder if Gunnery Sergeant Anderson would still want us to pray for war if he were here right now?"

"What?" replied Stilley. "Who? What are you talking about? Who is Gunnery Sergeant Anderson?"

"Nothing. Nothing. Just forget it. Let's get back to the unit."

When Spiller and Stilley returned, the Black Panthers had crossed to the far side of the river, and the two platoons were preparing to make their sweep down river. Spiller and Stilley fell into formation. Mile after mile, the Marines struggled through the thick foliage, crossing streams, fighting mosquitoes, watching for snakes, and always keeping an eye open for booby traps and VC. Suddenly the platoons stopped. Word was passed back from the point that an outpost had been spotted. The Marines moved slowly into the area. The outpost consisted of five huts in a clearing. Behind the huts was a group of fruit trees and an area used for gardening. Tunnels were located all over the place. The VC outpost was empty, and from all signs, had been for some time. Orders were given to destroy the huts and tunnels. Half-pound blocks of TNT were placed on the heavier structures of the huts and also thrown on the tunnels to cave them in. The Marines, using cigarette lighters, set fire to the grass roofs of the huts, meanwhile, the news reporter took pictures of the activities. A couple of hours later ashes were all that remained of the outpost.

For the next three weeks the scouts rotated from perimeter watch to ambush patrols within a three-mile area of the base perimeter. Other than a few sniper rounds fired into the battalion area, there'd been no contact with the VC.

During a night off, Spiller slept while Smith and Stilley read.

"Hey, Stilley. Does it bother you to read with these kerosene lamps?" asked Smith.

"Hell, no, Smitty. Nothing bothers me anymore."

Crack! Zing! Zing!

"Them fucking snipers again," snapped Smith as he blew his lamp out.

Stilley just layed there as if nothing happened and continued reading.

"Hey, Stilley, didn't you hear that? Put your light out!"

"Fuck it!"

Spiller, awakened by the fire, rolled from his bunk onto the floor along with Smith.

Crack! Zing! Zing!

"Stilley, blow that fucking light out. There's sniper fire," yelled Spiller.

"Fuck 'em! Fuck 'em! I've been trying to read this goddamned book for three months, and I'm reading it. Fuck the snipers!"

"You crazy bastard," yelled Spiller as he quickly crawled to the lamp and blew it out. "Now get on the deck before you get your ass shot off."

Stilley grunted, then reluctantly rolled to the floor.

"Fucking VC, can't even read for the gook sons-of-bitches."

The next morning a Marine from First Platoon, which had been in the operation with the Black Panthers, stormed into the scouts' tent.

"Look at this, guys. Look at this!"

The scouts scrambled to look at the magazine the Marine was holding. In it were pictures of the VC outpost being burned.

"We're on both pages."

"Hey, man, that's the VC outpost we destroyed," said Smith.

"Yeah, but look what it says."

The headline read: "Marines Destroy Vietnamese Village." The pictures showed Marines using their lights to set fire to the huts.

"Hey, it doesn't really say it, but this looks like it. It makes us look like we're running around burning villages. Why didn't they tell it all? Man, that was a VC outpost, and an abandoned one at that," snapped Spiller.

"One of our guys saved that bastard's ass when we got hit down at the river. He didn't have enough sense to get down, and one of my guys pulled him down and fell on top of him so he wouldn't get hit by rifle grenades," said Schafer.

"With shit like this, no wonder people are starting to demonstrate against us at home," yelled Spiller. "They probably think we killed women and children in the village."

"Why would they do this to us?" asked Stilley.

"I don't know. I just don't know," said a disgusted Spiller.

8
Operation O.P.

For seven months the Marines endured temperatures of 110 and 120 degrees, leeches, mosquitoes, snakes, and booby traps. Monsoon season was now upon them, bringing rains that lasted for days without stopping. The monsoon winds were so fierce that the rain fell sideways. At the snap of a finger the rain could start or stop, leaving the four-foot trenches flooded. Staying dry was difficult, if not impossible. In a futile attempt to keep their feet dry, the men changed socks constantly. Most of the time, it was a matter of changing from wet socks to damp socks, which caused many to get jungle rot.

The scouts had just returned from patrol. They were in their tent changing into dry clothes. Suddenly the wind started to blow intensely. As the rain poured down, the tent stakes worked their way upward from the ground, and the trenches around the tent overflowed.

"This fucking weather," complained Smith.

"Quit yelling and grab the tent poles," Spiller shouted. "The tent's going to blow over."

The scouts split up into pairs and grabbed the two poles that held the roof of the squad tent. By now, the rest of the stakes came completely out of the ground. For 30 minutes the scouts held tenaciously to the poles, preventing the tent from collapsing. Suddenly, the rain stopped and the wind calmed. The tent walls and part of the roof draped over the soaking wet scouts.

"Much more of this and I may never take another bath," remarked Stilley. "I've seen all the water I want for a lifetime."

"Let's try to get this fucking tent back up," snapped Spiller.

The men grumbled as they reassembled the tent. Two hours passed.

Spiller turned in his patrol report only to receive another assignment. When Spiller returned to the tent, he informed the other scouts of the mission. This time their destination was Hill 110, ten miles from base camp. There they were to set up an observation post. The VC were much more active in the monsoon season, and there were reports that they'd been moving in the area near Hill 110. The scouts were to remain on Hill 110 for three days or until their position was given away by calling in a fire mission.

"That's just fucking great," said Smith. "We can go lie in the rain for three days."

"Doesn't matter," said Stilley.

"What do you mean, it doesn't matter?"

"It doesn't matter. We're wet all the time anyway. Look at my cot! Look at yours! Everything's wet! It doesn't fucking matter."

Spiller sat on his cot, scratching at the sore on the ball of his right foot.

"I wish they'd get those boots in that we've been promised for the last three months. Maybe, just maybe, I could get this sore cleared up," he said.

Stilley laughed, "Hey, Harry, let's see that hole in your boot."

Spiller held his boot up, stuck his finger through the hole and wiggled it at Stilley.

"Shit, man, look at this. Yours is only the size of a quarter. Mine is twice that size." Stilley showed Spiller his boot. "We're both lucky though."

Puzzled, Spiller looked at Stilley. "What's that supposed to mean?"

Stilley laughed, "The VC don't have any boots at all, man."

"Funny, Stilley, very funny."

Smith had just finished tying a rope lengthwise from the two tent poles. "Okay, men, Smitty's dry cleaning is now open. Bring your shorts, socks, and shirts! We have a special on today. We guarantee dry service against Ho Chi Minh Monsoon."

Spiller and Stilley both grinned at Smith.

"This place getting to you?" asked Spiller.

"No. No, not really."

The scouts squeezed out their socks and other clothing, and hung them on the homemade clothesline.

Smith looked at Stilley, then at Spiller.

"Hey, guys, ever wonder why we're here? I mean, what the fuck is this mess all about? Why are we here? We put up with this weather, leeches, mosquitoes, bad food, people we don't understand, and now from everything we're hearing, everybody is mad at us back home. What's the point?"

"Somebody has to do it," replied Spiller. "I don't know all the answers, but somebody has to do it. Let's get our rifles cleaned and oiled for the patrol tomorrow."

"The way it rains, we need a barrel of oil for these rifles to keep the rust off of them," said Stilley.

"Do you think it'll ever stop?" asked Smith.

Everyone just looked at each other, then silently began to clean their rifles.

The night passed too quickly for the scouts. They left their squad tent in the early morning hours and headed for Hill 110. The clouds and the mist in the air reminded Spiller of a dreary mid-winter day back home. Only a short distance from the battalion's perimeter, even though the rain had stopped, Spiller could feel the dampness of the ground through the hole in his boot.

"Hey, Stilley! Your feet wet?" asked Spiller.

"No, shit! It won't be long 'til I'll be barefoot. Think they'll issue us some black shorts then?"

"Probably, and a bowl of rice to go with 'em."

"Let's hold up and eat chow," said Smith.

The Marines spread their ponchos on the ground, sat down and fumbled through their backpacks for C-rations. Spiller removed a can opener from his pocket, and opened a can of ham and lima beans and a small can of cheese. He dumped the cheese into the greasy beans and ham and stirred. Then he crumbled some crackers into the mixture and stirred once more. Smith and Stilley both watched Spiller consume his strange concoction.

"Harry," said Smith, "You've been here too long."

"Why?" asked Spiller.

"Why! You act like you like that garbage," replied Smith.

"I do. It's great. Want a bite?"

"Hell, no!"

"You don't know what you're missing, guys."

Smith and Stilley shook their heads as they opened their C-rations and began to chow down.

"You know, you're right," admitted Spiller, "I have been here too long. But if I make it just two more months, I can get out of this place."

"I've got three months," said Stilley.

"I'm leaving with you," Smith said to Harry. "I can hardly wait. What's the first thing you're gonna do when you get out of here, Harry?"

"I'm gonna find a grocery store and drink all the milk I can hold. How about you?"

"I'm going to the store with you, but I think the nice thing is going to be able to just walk down the street without looking over my shoulder all the time."

"Yeah, man, that'll be nice. How about you, Stilley?"

"I don't care what I do. I just want to get out of this god-forsaken place."

"We'd better get going. We're another two hours from 110," said Spiller.

The scouts folded ponchos, put their backpacks back on, and headed for the hill. Once again, the rain fell and Spiller felt the moisture from the ground penetrate his boot.

Three hours later the scouts reached the finger of Hill 110. At the top of the hill, the Marines spread out and sat down for a break. The hilltop was only some 20 yards wide. To either side was a straight 300-foot drop-off. The hill was a good observation post, providing a view for miles in any direction. Intelligence reports indicated the main concern was the area directly to the north where the jungle started. Taking advantage of the low visibility from the monsoon, the VC had been conducting a lot of movement from the jungle area.

Wrapped in ponchos, the Marines tried in vain to stay dry.

"Okay, men! We need to put a trip grenade along that finger," said Spiller.

"I'll do it," offered Stilley. "Maybe we'll get one of those sneaky, little, gook bastards."

"I'll help him," replied Smith.

"Okay, I'll get this scope set up," said Spiller.

Spiller fumbled in his pack, pulled out the ten-power scope and tripod, screwed the tripod on the bottom of the scope, and placed the scope in position. As he scanned the area with the scope, Stilley and Smith busily secured a hand grenade to a small tree that stood about three feet above the ground. Using comm-wire left behind by fellow

Marines, Smith and Stilley secured the body of the grenade to the tree trunk, leaving the spoon of the grenade free. Stilley straightened the carter pin on the grenade and pulled it out so that it barely held the spoon. Smith then tied a piece of comm-wire to the ring of the carter pin, stretched the wire across the path, and tied it to a bush directly across from the tree.

"Man, the slightest tug of that wire, and the pin will pull," said Smith.

"No, shit! Let's get out of here. If we hit that wire, we don't have any place to go but 300 feet straight down."

Smith and Stilley walked lightly back up the finger of Hill 110 to Spiller's location.

"See any gooks?" Smith asked.

"No, but that jungle sure is thick. I'm not sure if we can spot any unless they come right out in the open. Did you get the grenade set up?"

"Sure did," said Stilley. "Don't even need to trip it. Just breathe on it, and it's gook heaven."

"I checked along the front slope of the hill while you were rigging the grenade. There are two places where it looks like there's been some movement up and down the slope. We'd better rig something up to give us a little warning tonight in case we get company."

"We got some comm-wire. Are there any cans around?" asked Smith.

"Don't know. Let's see if we can find some," Spiller replied.

The scouts rounded up several cans, punched holes in the sides, ran comm-wire through them, then stretched them across the anticipated paths, and placed rocks in each can. Spiller shook the wire on each can. The cans clanged as the rocks hit the sides.

"That should do it, huh, guys?"

"We'll know they're coming," said Stilley.

The scouts went back to the top of the hill and spread out some ten yards apart. Spiller took the first watch. He laid on the wet ground and stared into the darkness. The rain had stopped, but the wind continued to blow.

"It really doesn't matter who's on watch," Spiller thought, "since no one can sleep in this weather anyway."

As the chill went through Spiller's body, he thought back to junior high school. A full eclipse of the moon was to occur at 2:00 A.M. one January morning. Even with a foot-and-a-half of snow on the ground, nothing was going to stop him and his friend, Larry Bratton, from pitching their pup tent, setting up their telescopes, and watching the eclipse. They sat all night just to watch that eclipse, and the freezing cold didn't even bother them.

"Guess nothing bothers kids," Spiller thought.

The cold sure bothered him now. Spiller wrapped the poncho even more tightly around his body to keep the wind out and stared for what seemed days. Finally, he crawled to Smith and shook him.

"It's your watch, Smitty."

"Okay, Harry," whispered Smith. "I wasn't asleep anyway."

Spiller crawled back to his position and snuggled up in his poncho.

"Just two more months of this. If I can just hang on two more months."

Daylight came and the Marines gathered to eat breakfast.

"I believe that's the longest night I've ever spent in my life," gasped Smith.

"Me, too," snapped Stilley. "I didn't sleep a wink."

"Me, either," snarled Spiller. "Maybe we can get a fire mission today and get out of here."

"I'll volunteer to run them out of the jungle by myself if we can just get out of here."

"I know now why we aren't getting any boots," said Stilley.

"Why?" asked Spiller.

"It doesn't matter. If we have holes in our boots, we'd still have wet feet. Besides my feet are the last thing I'm worried about. I mean, I'd be glad if just my feet were wet right now."

"You eating them damned lima beans again?" growled Smith at Spiller.

"Yeah, want a bite?" smiled Spiller.

"No. Fuck, no!"

"They sure are good."

"Sure, Harry, sure. Told you this place was getting to you."

"I'm gonna use the scope first. Try to get us a fire mission," said Spiller. "You two check the comm-wire. Make sure nothing's been tampered with."

Spiller scanned back and forth across the jungle line watching for movement. Smith and Stilley checked the trip grenade and the two areas where they'd placed the tin cans. When they returned they took a prone position on each side of Spiller.

"See anything, Harry?" asked Stilley.

"Nothing yet. Everything okay?"

"Fine," replied Smith.

"Hey, hey. Looky here. One, two, three, damn!"

"What! What is it?"

"Get on the radio, Smitty. Call in for a fire mission. Stilley get our coordinates. Hurry!"

Stilley scrambled for the map. Smith called battalion for the fire mission.

"How many are there?" asked Smith excitedly.

"I lost count, at least 30, a platoon."

"Stilley, got our coordinates?"

"Sure do, Harry."

"Okay, go to the ridge in front of us and figure the coordinates."

"Got it, Harry. Coordinates are grid 40 northeast by 49 southwest."

"Smith, call in. See if artillery is ready."

"Yank, this is Yank One. Over."

"Yank One, this is Yank. Over."

"Yank, are you ready for the fire mission? Over."

"Yank One, this is Yank. Go ahead with your coordinates."

"They're ready, Harry."

"Okay, give us a round at 40 northeast, 49 southwest."

"Yank, this is Yank One. One round at 40 northeast and 49 southwest."

"Damn!" yelled Spiller. "They're out of sight. They went behind that ridge."

"Here it comes!" yelled Stilley.

The round made a whistle-like sound and passed over the Marines. It exploded on top of the ridge that hid the VC.

"Okay, Smitty, tell them to add 100 and fire for effect."

"Yank, this is Yank One. Over."

"Yank One, go ahead. Over."

"Yank, add 100 and fire for effect."

"Here they come!" yelled Stilley.

Eight to ten rounds whistled over the scouts and exploded on the far side of the ridge. When the explosion stopped another eight to ten rounds whistled over. Spiller watched through the scope. Stilley was on his feet yelling and laughing.

"We got them bastards. We got 'em."

"How many did we get?" asked Smith.

"I don't know. They were out of sight behind the ridge, but we must have got 'em. That artillery was right on top of 'em. Get battalion. Tell them to fire one more volley."

"Yank, this is Yank One. Over. Yank, this is Yank One. Over. Damn." Smith banged the radio. "Yank, this is Yank One. Over. Our radio's out."

"Great, just great. Keep trying."

"Yank, this is Yank One. Over. Yank, this is Yank One. Over."

"Hey! Hey!" yelled Stilley. "They're coming over the ridge. We didn't get 'em."

"Let's get the hell out of here! screamed Spiller. "They know our position."

The scouts grabbed their equipment and took off in a dead run down the finger of the hill. They hurried across about a mile from the finger and then stopped. Spiller grabbed the scope and scanned Hill 110.

"Damn, we got out of there just in time. There are VC all over the top of that hill. Let's keep moving."

The Marines moved briskly covering another three miles before stopping. Spiller, once again, scanned the area with the scope.

"They aren't following us now," reported Spiller. "Damn!"

"How the fuck did they know we were there?" asked Smith.

"Every damned unit in the battalion has used that hill. We never change. We're predictable. They knew what hill, and they knew damned well that there weren't very many of us. Smitty, see if the radio's working."

"Yank, this is Yank One. Over. Yank, this is Yank One. Over. Nothing Harry. It's dead as a door nail."

"Okay, we'd better keep moving. We have several miles to go before we get to headquarters."

The Marines moved swiftly. The rain had stopped but the wind continued to blow. The muddy ground slushed under the quick feet of the Marines.

"Hey, Stilley, feel that water in your boots?" asked Spiller.

"No!"

"Me either."

"Who's worried about the weather?" snapped Smith.

"Not me," said Spiller.

"Me either," said Stilley. "Weather's fine, just fine."

The cold Marines continued to walk briskly back to headquarters.

9
Who's Who

The monsoon season had ended. Smith and Spiller, both short-timers, had only a month to go before leaving Vietnam. A month was a long time. The scouts had a new assignment. Phu Bai had been getting hit constantly by VC. The scouts were to assist the Marines and ARVN, already in the village, in ambushes on the outskirts of the village.

The scouts reported in Phu Bai to Sergeant Swift, who introduced them to several of the Marines stationed in the village.

"We'll meet at 1600 hours for a briefing on tonight's ambush. In the meantime, take a look around at the village. Leave your packs in the headquarters building. These kids'll steal you blind."

"Okay," said Spiller as the three scouts walked to the headquarters building.

Phu Bai was criss-crossed by Route 1 and a small stream. There were bamboo huts everywhere. Vegetable stands, on both sides of the road, attracted Vietnamese shoppers. The villagers carried honey buckets or baskets full of fresh vegetables. They seemed friendly, some nodding, while others smiled at the Marines. Who would think there was a war going on? The children, wanting C-rations and candy, clung to the Marines. A small girl offered Spiller a bite of rice and raw intestines from a water buffalo. Spiller politely refused with a kiss to her cheek. Bus after bus passed through Phu Bai. Some stopped to load and unload Vietnamese. The busses reminded Spiller of those he'd seen in the United States loaded with migrant workers.

"We'd better get back to headquarters, guys. It's almost time for the briefing," said Spiller.

The Marines and ARVN soldiers gathered in a small room in the

Marines were often confronted by Vietnamese children begging for C-rations and cigarettes.

headquarters building. Spiller leaned against the wall, Stilley stuffed his large hand in his shirt pocket fumbling for a cigarette, and Smith shifted his blue-green eyes from one ARVN soldier to another. All three 19-year-old Marines listened carefully. There'd been contact with the VC almost every night. In the past two weeks, 23 VC and 2 Marines had been killed; 5 Marines wounded. The scouts were going to set up an ambush a mile down from the small stream. A route, near a small footbridge, was believed to have been used frequently by the VC to cross the river. The Marines and ARVN were to leave at dark.

Spiller grabbed carbon paper and mosquito repellent from his backpack. He handed some to Stilley and Smith. Spiller squirted the carbon with repellent and smeared it on his face and hands. Smith and Stilley did the same.

"How do I look?" asked Spiller.

Smith laughed, "Like Al Jolson!"

"Very funny, Smith. Very funny."

"The mosquitoes will be able to chow down tonight," said Stilley. "This repellent is just like calling chow."

The scouts checked their rifles and grenades, then walked outside the headquarters building to meet with the rest of the patrol. Swift was standing in front of headquarters, studying the map that lay before him.

Swift looked up and grinned, "Ready to get some gooks?"

"Sure," Spiller replied anxiously.

Swift looked in both directions, then walked up close to the three scouts.

"Have you been on patrols with the ARVN before?"

"No," said Spiller. "We've been in an ARVN compound with 'em. They sure are trigger happy."

"Well, I couldn't say anything earlier, too many ears. I'll give you a little tip. Watch the ARVN. Watch them close."

"What do you mean?" Spiller inquired.

"You may think I'm crazy, but you can tell when we're going to get hit, or at least, when VC are in the area. Watch the way the ARVN act. If they're clowning around when we start the patrol, or act like they're on a Sunday stroll, we won't get hit. If they look scared to death and they're very quiet, look out."

"They know when the VC are there?" asked Spiller.

"You got it."

"How do they know?"

"I wish I knew, but remember what I told you."

Spiller looked at Stilley and Smith. "Crazy, fucking war, isn't it? Just fucking crazy."

The rest of the Marines and ARVN gathered for patrol. The ARVN, talking Vietnamese, laughed back and forth as the patrol lined into a column. Swift led the patrol. Every other man was an ARVN soldier. As the patrol moved, Spiller watched closely, wondering if the ARVN's laughter really meant there'd be no contact. Carrying his rifle in one hand and looking mostly at the ground, the ARVN in front of Spiller didn't seem to be too concerned. Just another surprise in this wonderful war. With an ARVN soldier in front and one behind, Spiller felt insecure. How could they know when or where the VC were, unless they were in contact with the VC, or maybe, they were VC themselves? What a thought in the middle of the night on an ambush mission.

"They couldn't be," thought Spiller as they arrived at the ambush site and took the prone position.

For the rest of the night Spiller watched silently cursing the mosquitoes and wondering about the ARVN. Shortly before daylight, not having made any contact, the patrol moved out of its ambush position and returned to the village.

The scouts had been on patrol ambushes for five nights, and in those five nights, there'd been no contact. The Marines gathered once again for the same mission, but with a new ambush location.

In column, the Marines and ARVN walked into the darkness. The ARVN in front of Spiller was not as relaxed as he'd been before. One hand on the trigger guard of his rifle, the other holding tightly to the forearm of his M-1 rifle, the ARVN watched cautiously as the patrol unit moved toward its ambush position. Spiller glanced back at the ARVN behind him. His behavior was the same. Spiller turned back and peered both left and right, recalling what Swift had told him about the ARVN soldiers.

"If Swift was right," Spiller thought, "we're going to be hit."

Kaboom! Bam! Bam! Tat-ta-tat!

The Marines and ARVN ran for cover behind a dike at one end of a rice paddy. The VC were at the other end behind the opposite dike. Fire was exchanged.

Spiller looked over at Swift, who was lying on his stomach, adjusting the sights of his M-79 grenade launcher. Spiller reloaded his rifle with another clip of ammo as shot after shot whizzed over his head.

Crack!

A Marine yelled as he grabbed his shoulder and rolled onto his back. Spiller crawled toward the wounded Marine while Swift fired his grenade launcher. Spiller reached the wounded Marine.

"Take it easy, man. Take it easy. Where are you hit?"

"Shoulder, my shoulder," mumbled the wounded Marine.

Spiller grabbed a pressure bandage and unbuttoned the Marine's shirt. The bullet had shattered the Marine's collar bone, which partially protruded through the skin. In his effort to tie the bankage, Spiller failed to notice the shooting had stopped.

"How many wounded?" yelled Smith.

"One over here!" yelled Spiller. "I need the corpsman."

As the corpsman crawled toward Spiller and the wounded Marine, Swift and half of the patrol worked their way to the dike at the opposite end of the rice paddy. The M-79 had made a definite impact. The mangled bodies of eight VC lay scattered behind the dike.

"Sergeant Swift, Sergeant Swift!" yelled the corpsman. "This man's bleeding internally. We gotta get him back to the village quickly, or he's gonna bleed to death."

"All right, men, we're gonna leave these VC. Let's go back," ordered Swift.

The Marines hurried back across the rice paddy.

"Let's go!" yelled Swift.

Spiller held his hands under the Marine's head. Four others grabbed his arms and legs, and the Marines hurried toward the village. Swift, watching for VC, took the lead of the column. Spiller and the others walked awkwardly, but quickly, through the jungle. The ARVN, obviously frightened, looked cautiously in all directions.

"Oh, shit! My leg," complained Stilley.

"What's the matter?" asked Spiller.

"I got a charlie horse in my leg."

"Shut up. Damn! A man's bleeding to death and you're worried about a charlie horse."

"Man, this is the worst charlie horse I've ever had, though."

"Get one of those ARVN to take your leg and try to get rid of it."

Stilley motioned for an ARVN to take the leg. Stilley hobbled along and fell back into the ARVN's position.

"Man, it hurts."

"We only have a half mile or so to go," said Spiller.

In a short time, the Marines entered the village. Two corpsmen waited with a stretcher to help with the wounded. Spiller and the others quickly placed the Marine on the stretcher. The corpsmen, grasping each end of it, hurried into the aid station. Spiller and the other Marines sat. They wiped sweat from their brows as they tried to catch their breath. Stilley was walking in a circle, still complaining about his leg. Spiller and the other Marines stared silently at Stilley as if he'd lost his mind. The ARVN soldiers disappeared. The corpsman came out of the aid station and walked slowly toward the Marines.

"He's dead. Bled to death."

"Damn!" snapped Spiller.

"The bullet glanced off the bone and down through his chest."

"My leg. Oh, shit."

"Let the corpsman look at it, Stilley," Spiller said angrily.

"What's the matter?"

"I've got a charlie horse, worst I've ever had."

"Let's get in the aid station where I can see."

Spiller, the corpsman, and Stilley entered the aid station. Stilley got on the cot, stomach first, and the corpsman lifted his pant leg.

"Hell, man, you haven't got a charlie horse. You've got a piece of shrapnel in the calf of your leg."

"Oh, no. Oh, shit!" yelled Stilley as he grabbed his leg. "I'm gonna die. I'm gonna die."

"No, you're not," Spiller insisted as the corpsman snickered.

Stilley fell to the floor rolling back and forth, "I'm dying. I'm dying."

Spiller and the corpsman looked at Stilley with disbelief.

"Stilley!" yelled Spiller. "Stilley, quit rolling around."

"What?"

"You just walked five miles, four of them carrying another Marine. Your leg's quit bleeding. You're gonna be fine."

"Am I, Doc? Am I?"

"Sure. I'd have had that piece of shrapnel out of your leg if you hadn't been carrying on so much. Get back up on the cot. We'll fix you up."

"Harry, you stay with me till they get it out. Okay?"

"Sure. Just take it easy. You just got a band-aid wound."

"Okay, okay, but stay here!"

"I'm gonna stay. I'm gonna stay."

Spiller sat on the edge of the cot thinking about the night's events as the corpsman attended to Stilley's leg.

"If we could've been just a little quicker, maybe we could've saved him. What luck. A man gets hit in the shoulder and bleeds to death. Stilley was lucky though. Who knows for how long. We're short-timers, and tonight was close. We've got less than a month. We gotta make it. Just got to."

"Okay, Stilley, your leg is good as new. Come back tomorrow and I'll change the bandage for you. He handed Stilley two penicillin pills. Take these tonight. They'll help keep your leg from getting infected," the corpsman instructed.

"Okay, Doc. Okay."

"Hey, Doc, how long before that guy was to go home?" Spiller asked.

"He was short. Maybe a month or so."

Spiller looked at Stilley then back to the corpsman. "This fucking war stinks, you know it? It really stinks."

For the next four days Stilley rested in the village. Spiller was assigned to a bunker on the south end of the village, which faced Route 1. Each night Spiller stood watch, and each night a patrol was sent out on an ambush mission. They were lucky. There'd been no contact. On the fifth night, Spiller with Stilley, who was back on his feet, once again prepared for an ambush mission near the same location where they had been ambushed. Stilley and Spiller smeared mosquito repellent and carbon on their faces.

"Hey, Harry, are you a little jumpy?"

"Yeah, I am!"

"Me, too. I keep thinking about how short we are, and well, I wish we didn't have to go on this patrol."

"Me either, me either. We just have to be careful. We'll make it," said Spiller.

"Yeah, we gotta be careful."

The two Marines grabbed rifles and met with the rest of the patrol in front of the headquarters building. The Marines and ARVN lined into a column and headed for the ambush position. Spiller looked to his right, left, then at the ARVN soldier in front of him. He thought about his conversation with Stilley. "Man, we're short, real short. We have to be careful. How the hell are we supposed to be careful? We can't see ten feet in front of us. Them gookfuckers could open up any time. We just gotta be lucky. Not like the guy we carried in the other night. Talk about bad luck. A fucking shoulder wound and he dies. I wish I could just ask this ARVN gook soldier in front of me if we're gonna get hit. That little, gookfucker knows. This is crazy. I wonder if all wars are as crazy and useless as this one. You don't know if the VC are ARVN or if the ARVN are VC, and the people in the village act like there isn't even a war going on."

The Marines arrived at the ambush position and took the prone position.

Spiller was keeping watch in the night. He thought more about his talk with Stilley. "We get killed here tonight, and what's been accomplished? Gooks get a couple of rice paddies, so what? These ARVN and the rest of the villagers could care less. Gotta be careful so we can get out of here. Somebody needs to know about this place. This fucking war. This useless, fucking war."

Just before daylight the patrol gathered in a column and moved silently toward the village. Daylight had broken the horizon, as Spiller,

Stilley, and Smith sat on the ground in front of the headquarters building preparing their breakfast of C-rations. Spiller prepared his usual ham and limas with crackers and cheese. Smith and Stilley watched Spiller then looked at each other, shaking their heads.

"He's been here too long," said Smith.

"I know," laughed Stilley.

Spiller looked up and grinned, then began eating again.

A Jeep pulled up in front of the village headquarters. The PFC administrator from battalion intelligence perched on the passenger side. He smiled at the scouts.

"Smith! Spiller! Your orders are here."

"Yea ha! Yea ha!" Spiller yelled as he threw his ham and limas into the air.

Smith yelled. Both of them were laughing and dancing.

"When are we leaving? When?" Spiller asked excitedly.

"Tomorrow."

"Great, great!" yelled Smith.

"Let's go get our gear!" said Spiller.

"Better wait for a minute, Harry. Headquarters says you can stay till the morning. It's up to Sergeant Swift."

"Let's go talk to him. This is crazy. I'll be damned if I'm gonna get killed the night before catching a plane out of this hell hole."

"Me either," snapped Smith.

The three hurried inside the village headquarters to Swift's office.

"Hey, Sarge, battalion says we can leave today if you say it's okay, otherwise we're leaving tomorrow."

Swift sat in his chair silently for a moment and rubbed his hand under his chin.

"Spiller, I'm short of men, you know that."

"Yeah, Sarge, I know, but we're leaving in the morning. I'm afraid we might not make it if we go on another ambush. I mean one night left in Vietnam and to have to go on ambush."

"I want everybody to make it out of this place in one piece, Spiller! I'm short of men. There's a war to be fought. I need you. You're staying!"

"But, Sarge!"

"That's all, Spiller. Get out of here, now!"

Spiller, Smith, and the administrator turned and walked out of the headquarters. Spiller paced back and forth, eyes to the ground.

"I wish you hadn't told us. Why the fuck didn't you just wait 'til tomorrow and come and get us?"

"Hey, man!" said Smith. "We got one more night. One more and we're out of this place! We can handle it."

"Yeah, you're right, Smitty. It's just that I've been about to jump out of my skin for two weeks. We're so close yet so far from being out of this place."

"I've got to get back to battalion but I'll be back in the morning to pick you guys up."

"Yeah, I hope it's alive," said Spiller.

"It will be. It will be," said the administrator. He got into his Jeep and smiled. "See you in the morning."

"Okay, in the morning," said Smith.

Smith and Spiller, both wishing that tomorrow was today, watched as the Jeep pulled out and headed down Route 1 toward battalion headquarters.

"We'd better get ready for tonight, Smitty. I want to be prepared. We're going to be on that Jeep in the morning . . . grinning."

Smith smiled at Spiller. "Damn right we are!"

For the rest of the day Smith, Spiller, and Stilley cleaned their weapons. Spiller and Smith packed everything they weren't taking on patrol with them, so they'd be ready when the Jeep arrived in the morning. While packing, Spiller was informed that he was assigned the M-79 grenade launcher for the night's ambush.

"Hey, Smitty! We'll make it out of here. I'll blow the fuck out of anything that moves."

Smith laughed, "Sounds good to me. We might as well let them bastards know we've been here."

"That's right. We will. We will."

The patrol gathered in front of the village headquarters at dusk. As the patrol prepared to leave, Spiller, with the M-79 grenade launcher and two bandoleers of M-79 shells criss-crossed over his chest, and Smith, with his M-14, both watched the ARVN soldiers. They weren't joking around. As a matter of fact, they were very quiet.

Spiller looked at Smith, "That's what I thought. Of all nights. Let's watch it."

Smith nodded at Spiller as the patrol moved toward the ambush sight. The ARVN were cautious, looking to their right, then to their left. Spiller and Smith were both jumpy, too. At the ambush location, the Marines took prone positions parallel to the path along the river. It was hot and muggy. The mosquitoes chowed down. Spiller's thoughts were on one thing, daylight. At daylight this war was over for him and Smith. Just a few more hours. Spiller imagined what it would be like to be back home with his friends and family and how safe it would be not looking over his shoulder every minute. The ARVN soldier to Spiller's right reached over and shoved Spiller on the shoulder.

"What's wrong?" Spiller whispered. "See something?"

"No, no. You no sleep."

"I wasn't asleep."

Spiller looked back to his front.

"That stupid, little bastard thought I was asleep. Silly, little fucker thinks I'd go to sleep on my last ambush."

Spiller wondered how much longer before daylight. Time had passed slowly since they'd arrived at the ambush position. The ARVN soldier to his right shoved Spiller's shoulder again.

"You no sleep. You no sleep."

Spiller crawled a few inches, then grabbed the ARVN soldier by the shirt and stuck the M-79 to his chin.

"You little chicken-shit fucker, I wasn't asleep. How would you like for me to pull the trigger on this and disconnect your fucking, little gook head?"

"No, no, no!"

"Then keep your fucking hands off of me. Understand?"

"Quiet down there! Quiet!" ordered Swift.

Tat-ta-tat! Boom! Tat-ta-tat! Bam! Bam!

Silence.

"They're about 30 yards in front of us," whispered Smith.

"I'll get 'em," yelled Spiller as he raised and fired six shots rapidly from his left front to his right front.

Kaboom! Kaboom!

The Marines and ARVN began firing. Spiller reloaded the M-79 and fired repeatedly. Six more rounds exploded, then silence.

"Fucking gooks aren't getting me my last night in Nam. Just move, fire one shot," Spiller thought to himself as he stared into the darkness.

Everything became silent as the Marines listened for movement. Spiller, breathing rapidly, looked back and forth. Everything seemed to return to normal.

"It's gonna be daylight soon," thought Spiller. "It's got to be."

"Grenade!" yelled a voice across the river.

Kaboom! Rat-ta-tat! Bam! Bam!

"Oh, shit! They've been hit across river, right behind us!" The firing went on for ten minutes, then stopped.

"Watch it, men. They'll probably run the VC right into us."

Spiller could see the silhouette of the footbridge from the glare of the water and watched closely for movement.

The ARVN soldier hit Spiller's shoulder and pointed. "VC, VC!"

Spiller aimed at the point where the bridge and path met on their side of the river and started firing, moving down the bridge each time he fired.

Kaboom! Kaboom! Kaboom!

The patrol once again opened fire. After about five minutes silence crept over the area. A slow fog covered the moist ground. Sweat poured from Spiller's brow. He wondered if the night would ever end. A flare popped overhead and the area lit up as if it were midday.

Kaboom! Kaboom!

The ground shook beneath the Marines.

"Who in the fuck called in artillery?" Swift screamed over the radio.

The flare went out and the Marines grabbed for the ground as the earth shook beneath them. Once again, silence. Spiller lay hugging the ground wondering what was next. Finally, the order came that Spiller and Smith were waiting for, time to move out. The patrol quietly and slowly moved back to the village. Spiller looked at the headquarters building in the village and gave a sigh of relief. Smith and Spiller looked intently at one another for a moment, then embraced.

"We made it! We made it!" gasped Spiller.

"Yeah, man, we sure did."

The Jeep from battalion headquarters rolled into the village at daylight. The PFC administrator smiled at Spiller and Smith who were standing in front of headquarters with rifles in one hand and backpacks in the other.

"See. Told ya you'd make it."

Spiller looked at Smith. Both turned back to the PFC.

"Yeah, man, we did. Didn't we?" said Spiller.

"Let's get the fuck out of here."

Spiller, Smith, and Stilley climbed aboard the Jeep. As they drove out Spiller watched the Vietnamese busily working and walking around the village.

"They have no idea what we went through last night," thought Spiller, "but even worse, they don't care. I'm just not sure why we're even here. Not sure at all."

The Jeep arrived at headquarters, and as the Marines jumped out, a gunnery sergeant walked out of the battalion intelligence tent.

"Smith, Spiller, take your rifles to the armory and turn them in, then get all your gear, and report back to me."

"Okay, Gunny!" yelled the two Marines.

Spiller and Smith hurried to the armory. Each handed his rifle to the armory sergeant. The sergeant looked each rifle over and then looked down the barrel.

"These rifles are filthy, Marines. You should be court-martialled."

"But, Sarge, we just got off ambush last night."

"Yeah, sure. Likely story. They let you youngsters get by with too much nowadays. Not enough discipline today. You should've been in Korea."

"Yeah, Sarge, that was the tough war, I'm sure. Can we go?"

Spiller and Smith left the armory and ran for the tent. Both crammed what loose gear they had into the sea bags.

"Let's get back up to the intelligence tent before they change their minds about us leaving," said Spiller.

The two hurried to the intelligence tent. The gunnery sergeant came out of the tent.

"All right, men, dump your sea bags."

"What!" said Spiller in a startled voice.

"Dump your sea bags! Want to make sure you don't take off with anything you're not supposed to take."

Spiller and Smith looked at each other then grabbed their sea bags and dumped them. The gunnery sergeant searched through the clothing. He grabbed a VC helmet Spiller planned to keep for a souvenir and threw it to the side. He opened a pair of socks and dumped several punji stakes that Smith had hoped to take home.

"Okay, men, you can put your gear back, but you don't need these items," he said, pointing to the helmet and punji stakes. "When you get finished, report to the supply tent and get back here. Your plane will be leaving in about an hour."

Spiller and Smith stuffed their clothes back into the sea bags and headed for the supply tent.

"I wanted that helmet," snapped Spiller.

"Yeah, I wanted them punji stakes, too. What's the big deal?"

"I don't know. I'm just glad we're getting out of this place."

The Marines entered the supply tent and walked up to a counter. A lance corporal stood behind the counter, his elbows resting on the countertop.

"Can I help you?" asked the lance corporal.

"Yeah, the gunny from intelligence told us to report down here. We're leaving today."

"Okay, what size boots you wear?"

Spiller looked at the lance corporal startled. "Size eleven. Why?"

"How about you?" he asked, pointing to Smith.

"Size ten."

The Marine turned and walked to a shelf at the back of the tent and very shortly returned with two pairs of boots for both Spiller and Smith. Spiller looked at the boots, then at Smith.

"Must be a mistake," snapped Spiller.

"No mistake. Everyone going stateside gets two pairs of new boots. It's orders," explained the lance corporal.

"Fucking orders. We've been walking around with holes in our boots for two months. Now we're leaving, and we get new boots. You kinda got it turned around, don't you?"

"It's orders, Corporal. I just follow orders."

Spiller and Smith reported back to the intelligence tent and stuffed the boots in their sea bags. The PFC clerk pulled up in a Jeep.

"Ready to go?"

"Ready!" said Spiller and Smith simultaneously.

"Let's go! The plane's gonna pull out in about 30 minutes."

Spiller and Smith arrived at the Phu Bai Airport. Both jumped from the Jeep, shook hands with the Jeep driver, and walked up the ramp at the rear of the plane. Not long after they'd taken off, they landed again in Da Nang. The Marines departed and met a liaison officer who instructed them to wait inside a hangar at the side of the runway. Spiller and Smith walked into the building, where approximately 100 other Marines stood waiting for that final flight out of Vietnam.

"I feel almost naked without my rifle," said Spiller.

"Me, too. Kinda funny. I never thought I'd miss that rifle."

"All right, listen up!" yelled the liaison officer. "We have a 707 flight leaving in 30 minutes. When I read your name from the roster, speak up, then get aboard the plane and stay there. Understand?"

Everyone was silent.

The liaison officer called names, and one by one the Marines boarded the plane. Spiller leaned back as the plane took off. His mind wondered back through the time he had spent in Vietnam. The death of the little girl. Going for almost a month without a bath. How grateful he'd become for simple things like cold water and showers, things most people take for granted. Then there was Wilson. In Hawaii he and Spiller talked about winning all those medals and how glamorous war would be. Now Wilson was dead, and aside from his family and close friends, no one seemed to care. What a waste.

The no-smoking and fasten-your-seat belts sign came on. Spiller pulled his seat belt tight. He looked at Smith and grinned. The pilot spoke over the loud speaker.

"Gentlemen, please fasten your seat belts. We'll be landing in Okinawa in about ten minutes."

Smith reached over to Spiller and slapped him on the arm.

"We made it, man. We made it!"

10
Homeward Bound

The Marines got off the plane and boarded busses that took them to Camp Butler. The busses pulled up in front of the mess hall, and the Marines got off the bus and lined up for breakfast. Spiller and Smith approached two cooks who were fixing eggs, bacon, and sausage.

"Man, I never thought anything would look as good as that food," said Smith.

"Or smell as good," added Spiller. "I'm gonna drink at least a gallon of milk."

"Me, too."

Spiller and Smith finally reached the cook. He turned grinning. "Bacon, sausage, or both?"

"Both," replied Spiller and Smith hungrily.

Each received four eggs, three sausage patties, five pieces of bacon, and three slices of toast. Spiller and Smith joined several other Marines at a table and began devouring the food.

"This is good," said Smith with a mouthful.

"Yeah, good," mumbled Spiller. "Let's get some milk."

They jumped up and walked to the machine. Spiller took one spout and Smith the other.

"Hey, man, chocolate milk," said Spiller, still chewing.

"White over here," said Smith.

Both stood in front of the machine and downed the milk, then switched spouts and repeated. Both returned to the table with a cup of milk and continued eating. The sound of chewing and slurping echoed through the mess hall.

Spiller got up and walked to the mess line.

"Could I have a couple more eggs and some bacon?"

"Sure can," smiled the cook.

As Spiller waited for the eggs, he noticed a warrant officer in tropical uniform standing near the milk machine. The warrant officer stood erect, his arms folded across his chest. Tears rolled down his cheeks as he watched the Marines eat.

"Wonder what's the matter with him?" thought Spiller.

The cook slapped bacon and two more eggs on his tray.

"Thank you," said Spiller. He walked back to the table.

Smith was looking down, still stuffing his face.

"I think we've eaten the mess hall out of business. We've got that warrant officer in tears," remarked Spiller.

Smith laughed and half choked, "You're crazy, you know that. Just crazy."

After half-a-dozen eggs, twelve pieces of bacon, five sausage patties, five slices of toast, and eight cups of milk, Spiller leaned back in his chair and smoked a cigarette.

"I'm full, but I could eat some more," he said.

"Me, too. I never knew how good real food could be."

"Beats spam and peanut butter and jelly, doesn't it?"

"Then damned C-rations, too."

"All right, let me have your attention!" yelled the liaison officer, standing at the far end of the mess hall.

"Directly across the road is a group of Quonset huts where you'll bunk during your stay at Camp Butler. We have not assigned bunks, so when you leave, grab a bunk. Be in formation tomorrow morning at 0700 for roll call."

Spiller and Smith left the mess hall and walked across the street to the Quonset huts. As they entered the hut and chose bunks, Spiller was reminded of his old boot camp days.

"These mattresses sure are gonna feel good. It's been a year since we've slept on one."

"This is like heaven," said Smith as he plopped down on the mattress.

"You really never know how lucky you are 'til you do without for a while," said Spiller as he too laid down.

Other Marines came in one at a time until all the bunks were taken. The signs and moans of comfort fell into a long silence.

Spiller stared at the overhead, thinking of the night before. "This time last night, we were in the middle of an ambush, not knowing whether we'd make it out of that hellhole alive. And now we're here, safe, bellies full, and not a care in the world. Life sure can change fast in this old world."

"Hey, Harry. You asleep?"

"No. Believe it or not, I can't go to sleep. This mattress is too soft."

"Me either. I've got the same problem."

"You think they'd take us to a mental ward if we slept on the floor?"

"No, not really," Spiller chuckled as he grabbed his pillow and crawled to the floor.

"This is much better," said Smith who'd done the same.

At 0600 the lights came on in the barracks. Spiller and Smith both rose quickly.

"What was that?" snapped Spiller.

"The lights, the lights," said Smith.

"The lights, oh yeah. Wait a minute. We're in Okinawa, not Nam."

Spiller and Smith looked around the room. Thirty bunks in the hut, and two-thirds of the Marines were on the floor, all sitting up. After a few seconds, the Marines started moving around, some chuckling and snickering.

"I forgot about electricity," Smith said.

"Me, too. It's been a whole year since we were woke up like that."

"Where is the formation held?" asked Smith.

"Don't know. We'd better ask."

The two Marines walked out into the fresh morning air. A lance corporal, smoking a cigarette, stood near the roadway.

"Hey, Lance!" yelled Spiller. "Know anything about these formations? We supposed to eat first or stand for roll call?"

"Stand for roll call. It won't take long."

"Thanks."

Spiller fumbled in his shirt pocket for his cigarettes and matches.

"Want a cigarette?" asked Smith.

"No, thanks. I got some," replied Spiller.

The two Marines puffed on cigarettes as they walked slowly toward the headquarters building.

"You know, I was a little jumpy when those lights came on, but once I realized we weren't in Vietnam, it sure was a good feeling," Spiller said.

"It sure is. We're safe, but I keep trying to grab for my rifle."

"Yeah, me too, Smitty. Me too."

The Marines went into formation. A staff sergeant stood at the front of the formation with a clipboard and blurted out names. After roll call the staff sergeant gave instructions.

"All right, men, we'll have another formation at 1500, liberty at 1600. You have cinderella liberty only. You can pick your liberty cards up at the window." He pointed to a side window in the headquarters building. "Make sure you have all your gear gathered in one place in case you're called for a flight out. Your time is yours until 1500. Any questions?"

A voice from the formation called, "Hey, Sarge, can you get us any pussy?"

Everyone in the formation chuckled.

The staff sergeant tried to hold back the chuckles. He cleared his throat, "Be back at 1500. Dismissed!"

Spiller and Smith walked around the base, stopped at the PX, turned in dirty clothes at the base laundry, and ate every time they could get their hands on food. As they walked back to the barracks, they passed fresh troops lined in the road standing inspection.

"Hey, Marine!" The platoon sergeant yelled at Spiller.

Spiller turned, "Me?"

"Yes, you, Corporal. Here, call the roll call for this platoon," he ordered and handed the clipboard to Spiller.

"Uh, Sarge?"

"Oh, hell, Corporal, read that list."

"Yes, sir," grinned Spiller.

Smith stood to the side snickering at Spiller.

"Don't call me sir. I'm a staff sergeant."

"Yes, sir, I mean, Staff Sergeant."

Spiller looked down at the list, as the staff sergeant turned to talk to another staff sergeant on the sidewalk near the platoon.

"Anderson!"

"Here, sir!"

"Atwood!"

"Here, sir!"

Spiller turned his head to the right and grinned at Smith. Smith was still snickering at Spiller.

"Jones!"

"Here, sir!"

"Oh, hell, you're all here. Platoon dismissed!"

Smith laughed loudly as the platoon of new troops mingled around not really knowing what to do. Spiller handed the clipboard to the staff sergeant.

"They're all here, Sarge."

"What the hell do you think you're doing? I'll have your ass. Just look at you, no starch in those dungarees, and those boots. You got on jungle boots. You just back from Nam?"

"Sure am, Sarge, sure am. If you'll excuse me, Sarge, we have to be in formation, so we can go on liberty."

Spiller walked off with Smith, who held his hand over his mouth, still snickering.

"You smart ass! I ought to...."

The staff sergeant looked at his confused platoon.

"Get in formation. Get in formation."

Spiller and Smith stood side by side waiting for roll call.

"You crazy fucker," said Smith. "I wish you could've seen the look on that staff sergeant's face when you dismissed his platoon," said Smith as he burst out laughing again.

Spiller, chuckled a little. "What the fuck. I'm not in boot camp. And another thing, it's his platoon. Let him call roll call." Spiller reached up and scratched his chin. "Besides, what's he going to do, send us to Nam?" he said as he burst out laughing.

At 1500 the staff sergeant yelled, "Roll call." Spiller, Smith, and the other Marines answered as their names were read from the list.

"All right, men! No plane today. You have liberty call at 1600. Be here in the morning at 0700. Dismissed!"

"Yea ha!" yelled Smith. "Yea ha! Let's get ready for liberty, man. Let's get ready."

Spiller and Smith headed for the Quonset hut. Both put on the civilian clothes they'd purchased at the PX and headed for the headquarters building for liberty cards. They signed a roster list beside a list of numbers, then took the liberty card with the corresponding number beside their names.

"Where do you want to go first?" asked Smith.

"Let's hit the base club, first. See who's there."

"Okay, then let's go to town."

"Sounds good to me," said Spiller.

The two Marines entered the enlisted men's club and sat at a round table large enough to seat eight people. A Japanese waitress came to the table.

"May I help you, gentlemen?"

"Yes, ma'am. Could we have a pitcher of beer, please, and two glasses?" said Smith.

"Sure can."

Spiller lit a cigarette and looked around. The center of the room was filled with tables. A few Marines, sipping on beer, were scattered at different tables. The waitress returned with a pitcher of beer, setting it between them. Spiller reached into his pocket and handed her a dollar.

"Keep the change, ma'am."

"Thank you, sir."

The door opened and three Marines entered.

"Hey, Fred! Over here!" yelled Smith.

The three Marines came over, pulled out chairs, and sat down. Everyone knew Fred McCluskey, that is everyone connected with the Third Battalion. Fred was a lifer. Had 18 years in the Marine Corps. A veteran of Korea, he received the Bronze Star for bravery while he was a platoon sergeant. He was one of the best combat Marines in Vietnam. Now he was a private. Fred went AWOL a couple of times, and he had problems with rank, but he was a great guy.

"Hell, my old lady's mad at me," Fred said.

"Why's that?" asked Smith.

"Got a buddy in communications, and he let me call home. Well, I told her we were going to have to stay for another year in Nam, the Red Chinese had invaded. Fuck, I was just teasing. She started crying, and it took me ten minutes to get her to stop. When I told her I was only teasing, and I'd be home in a few days, she got mad and hung up. Fucking woman, just doesn't have a sense of humor." Everyone burst out laughing.

Fred ordered two pitchers of beer. After consuming several pitchers between them, the five Marines decided to hit the town. Fred supposedly knew this great bar in town, and the Marines decided to try it.

The five men stood on the curb across from the main gate. A small cab pulled up and the driver, a Japanese man wearing a red ball cap, held up four fingers.

"What's the problem, man? There are five of us," said Fred.

"No, no. Four only. MPs stop me."

"Aw, shit, man, I'm an MP myself. No problem," said Fred as the Marines stuffed their way into the cab. "Go, go. Shit, I'll take care of those MPs," chuckled Fred.

The cab looked like a sardine can with windows and wheels. The driver headed down the curved road. Spiller, Smith, and the other Marines were quiet as they watched the road in front of them. The driver, afraid the MPs might see him with five passengers, drove 75 miles per hour, taking one sharp curve after the other. Fred started laughing and the rest of the Marines laughed, too. All at once Fred reached over, grabbed the bill of the driver's cap, and pulled it down over his eyes.

The driver quickly grabbed the hat and pulled it up.

"No, no, you crazy, fucking Marine!"

Fred laughed and grabbed at the bill of the cap again. The driver hit Fred's arm.

"No, no. You crazy! You crazy Marine!"

"We're all crazy," yelled Fred as everyone laughed.

The driver pulled into town.

"Let us out at that bar," yelled Fred.

As the driver pulled up in front of the bar, the Marines piled out and all handed Fred a dollar.

"Here, Pappa San. Thanks for the ride."

The driver grabbed the money. "You crazy, fucking Marines. You crazy."

For a couple of hours the Marines drank in the bar that Fred recommended, then bar hopped the rest of the night.

"Hey, Smitty," Spiller said, "we'd better see if we can catch a cab and get back to the base. It's getting late."

"Okay, man. I'm drunk."

"Me, too."

"Hey, Fred, let's go," said Smith.

"Naw, I'm gonna stay for a while. You go ahead."

"Okay, see you tomorrow," said both Spiller and Smith as they staggered out of the bar.

The cab pulled up in front of the base's main gate. Smith and Spiller fumbled in their pockets and paid the driver. Smith opened the door and fell into the street. Spiller got out, grabbed Smith by the arm, and helped him up.

"You okay?" laughed Spiller.

"Fuck, yes! I'm all right. Shit, man, that ground got there fast," laughed Smith.

They started through the front gate. The officer of the day, a second lieutenant, was checking post. A private first class stood at attention while the lieutenant questioned him. Smith, with both hands in his pockets, began to whistle. The lieutenant turned to Spiller and Smith.

"Marine, come here," yelled the lieutenant.

Smith looked at the lieutenant and stopped whistling.

"You mean me?"

"Yes, you. Get over here."

Smith staggered over to the lieutenant.

"What do you want, Lieutenant?"

"Your hands cold, Marine?"

"Nope, got 'em in my pockets."

The guard, standing behind the lieutenant, attempted to keep a straight face.

"Get your hands out of your pockets and stand at attention."

"Oh, shit, if it'll make you feel any better," mumbled Smith. He took his hands out of his pockets and stood at attention.

"What unit you with, Marine?"

"None, just got back from 'Nam. Going home."

"You know what time it is?"

"No."

"No, what!"

"No, God damn it. I don't know what time it is."

The guard snickered, and Spiller turned his back to Smith and chuckled.

"It's 'yes, sir' and 'no, sir.' You understand?"

"Yes, sir."

"You, too, Marine," he said, speaking to Spiller.

"Yes, sir," replied Spiller.

"All right, both of you report to headquarters building at 0900 in the morning."

"Yes, sir!"

The Marines walked back to the hut with their arms slung over each others shoulders.

"Fuck, man, we may not get out of here, yet. That little, fucking prick," said Spiller.

"We haven't been out of that country but one day, go on liberty for the first time in almost a year, and we're AWOL. I don't believe it," Smith said.

"Believe it, man, believe it. We're still in the corps."

At 0700 Spiller and Smith stood for roll call.

"My head is throbbing," complained Smith.

"Mine, too, and my stomach."

"Roll call," yelled the staff sergeant.

"He doesn't have to yell. Shit!" Smith said.

"You all look real good this morning, men. How do your heads feel?" snickered the staff sergeant.

Everyone stood silently. One by one, their names were called, until the end of the list was finished.

"All right, men, I have some good news for you. The people on the roster whose names I just called will be leaving tomorrow night. You'll have liberty tonight, but make sure you're here for tomorrow morning's roll call. Understand?"

The hangovers were forgotten when the news of leaving came. The Marines cheered.

"All right, listen up. I want Smith and Spiller to report to me after you're dismissed. Dismissed!"

"Oh, shit, man! We aren't even going to make it out of here tomorrow," scoffed Smith.

"Fuck!" said Spiller.

They walked with the staff sergeant into headquarters building.

"Wait here," snapped the staff sergeant.

"Yes, sir," replied Spiller and Smith as the staff sergeant walked into the office and shut the door.

Painted on the door were the words, 'Battalion Commander.'

"We're fucked, man. We're fucked," gasped Smith.

Spiller stood just shaking his head.

The staff sergeant opened the door. "You can go in now."

Spiller and Smith entered the office. Sitting behind the desk with his hands folded in front of him was a stocky major. The second lieutenant stood in front of the major's desk. Spiller and Smith stopped about a foot in front of the major's desk and snapped to attention.

"Sir, Corporal Spiller reporting as ordered, sir."

"Sir, Corporal Smith reporting as ordered, sir."

"At ease, Corporals," barked the major. "Had a little problem last night, didn't you, gentlemen?"

"Yes, sir."

"Let's see, 30 minutes late, which makes you AWOL, and disrespectful to an officer. Is that right?"

"Yes, sir."

"You've been here since night before last. That was your first liberty in how long, men?"

"A year, sir."

"A year, huh? How old are you, Spiller?"

"Twenty, sir."

"Smith?"

"Twenty, sir."

"Smith, Spiller, go sit down on the couch."

"Sir?" replied Spiller and Smith with startled voices.

"Go sit on the couch."

"Yes, sir."

They walked to the couch, caps in their hands, and sat as the major ordered.

"Lieutenant, how old are you?"

"Twenty-one."

"Twenty-one what?" growled the major.

"Twenty-one, sir!"

"Ever been in combat?"

"No, sir."

"Lieutenant, these men have been in country fighting in the rice paddies for a year, with no liberty, no nothing. They get back here, and you write them up for being AWOL after being 30 minutes late, when you know my orders were to let them be, if they were late."

"Yes, sir!"

"They need time to adjust, Lieutenant. Time to adjust."

"Yes, sir."

"And you want to play boot camp."

"Yes, sir. I mean, no sir."

The major, arms extended as he leaned over his desk on his fists, was face to face with the lieutenant.

"You say as much as one word, Lieutenant, one word to another vet coming through transit, and I'll have your fucking bars! You understand?"

"Yes, sir!"

"Get out of here!"

Spiller and Smith sat dumbfounded on the couch as they watched the lieutenant scurry from the office. The major sat in his chair.

"Here are your ID cards back, men."

They walked to the major's desk and took the cards.

"Thank you, sir."

"Have a good trip home, men."

"Yes, sir," they replied as they left the office.

Spiller and Smith walked back to the Quonset hut.

"I'm going to wake up after a while, and we're still going to be in Nam," said Spiller.

"No shit! I think I'm dreaming, too. I've never seen anything like that."

"Me, either."

"Did you see the look on that lieutenant's face when the major was yelling at him?"

"Looked scared to death, didn't he," laughed Spiller.

"Things sure are happening fast," said Smith. I mean, one night we're in the middle of an ambush, and the next night we're on liberty. Today we're watching a major chew out a lieutenant, tomorrow, the United States! Things are just happening real fast."

Spiller began stuffing the clothes he wouldn't need the next day into his sea bag.

"Know something, Smitty? Just night before last we were on an ambush. For a while, we didn't know if we were going to make it out of there or not. Now we're here. Everything's happening fast, but not so fast that I can forget that deep feeling in my gut. That feeling of safety. I mean, knowing I don't have to look over my shoulder every minute. I mean, it's not just the safety. I didn't realize how much I was looking over my shoulder, or how cautious I really was, until now. Now that we don't have to be looking every minute."

"How come we keep looking over our shoulders then? And how come we keep looking for rifles?" asked Smith.

"Habit, maybe. Habit."

"Let's go get our laundry," interrupted Smith.

The two Marines left the Quonset hut.

Spiller continued, "Habit, man. I mean, when we were in the country, we ate, slept, and fought with our rifles. We were always looking over our shoulder, but we were just reacting to the point that it was everyday life. Maybe we just adapted to the dangers of war."

Spiller went on. "Remember the time we were sitting in the squad tent and all the new troops were in temporary pup tents because there wasn't enough room. Artillery called in a fire mission, and when all the rounds went over, they were running for cover."

"Yeah, I remember."

"What did we do?"

Smith laughed. "We started clapping and cheering."

"That's right. Those guys were scared to death, and we just cheered and laughed."

"Fuck, man, it was funny."

"And look at the time we had the night off and the sniper fire started. Stilley refused to blow out the lanterns. We adapted to the dangers of war, man. Things that are normally dangerous, we were laughing at. I never really thought about it or realized it 'til now – now that we don't have to worry about being killed."

"Fuck, man, there wasn't a day that went by that I didn't think about being killed. I always wondered if I was going to make it out of there in one piece."

"Me, too, Smitty, everyday. But we still laughed at the dangers."

"Yeah, you're right. We did. I'll tell you, man, I'm just glad to be out of that hole."

"Me, too, Smitty. Me, too."

Smith and Spiller stuffed their clean laundry into the sea bags and headed for the PX.

"We'd better get some cigarettes. They're a lot cheaper here than in the States," said Spiller.

"Everything's cheaper here than in the States."

"I'm going to buy my ribbons, too."

Spiller stood in front of the glass counter looking at what must have been a thousand ribbons. There were ribbons for World War II, Korea, and, of course, the individual ribbons for the Purple Heart, Bronze Star, Silver Star, or any other metal for bravery in battle.

"May I help you, sir?" asked the cashier.

"Yes, sir," Spiller said as he turned looking for Smith. "Hey, Smitty, come over here."

Smith walked over to the counter and stood by Spiller. "What?"

"Let's get our ribbons." Spiller turned back to the cashier. "Sir, we need the National Defense, Vietnamese Service with two stars, Vietnamese campaign, good conduct, and Presidential Unit Citation."

"One of each, sir?"

"How much are they a piece?"

"Each ribbon is ten cents, the star clusters are a penny each."

"Let me have two of everything," Spiller said.

"Me, too," said Smith.

The clerk placed the order of ribbons in two separate paper bags and handed a bag to each.

"That will be $1.04 each, gentlemen."

Both paid the clerk and headed back to the Quonset hut.

Spiller sat on the side of his bunk and stared at the wall. Smith was looking through the bag of items he'd purchased at the PX. He looked up at Spiller.

"What's the matter?"

"I was just thinking, Smitty. When I joined the Marine Corps, I'll never forget how impressed I was when I saw that recruiter walk up in those dress blues. Man, he had three-and-a-half rows of ribbons. Then I watched every war movie I could. Thought it was just great. Then when we were in Hawaii and thought we were going to be shipped over here, what did we do? We went to see *The Sands of Iwo Jima* and almost tore the theater down. Me and Wilson were always arguing over who was going to win the most medals. Hell, the night we were at the New Year's party, his New Year's resolution was to get more medals than I did. Then we came to Nam, Wilson's dead, and who cares? Only us and his family. All the killing and destruction, the leeches and mosquitoes sucking blood out of us, jungle rot from walking around in those rice paddies full of human shit, seeing our friends killed, and Smitty, you know where the glamor and heroics is? Do you know? It's in this little paper bag, Smitty. A $1.04 fucking cents worth of glory, and $1.04 fucking cents worth of glamor."

"You're right, Harry," Smith mumbled as both men silently stared off into space.

"Let's go take a shower and get a beer," Smith suggested a few minutes later.

Spiller and Smith stopped at the enlisted men's club, and then hit the town. They were more cautious this time, however, returning to base at 2300 hours. Neither wanted to miss the flight home.

The group of Marines stood in front of the headquarters building, anxiously awaiting roll call and the word to move out. The streets were lined with busses, and the Marines knew they must be for them. The staff sergeant came in front of the formation and called the names on the roster. After the last name was called, the staff sergeant paused for a moment, then spoke up. "All right, men, go back to your Quonset hut and get your gear. Make sure you've left nothing behind, then get on the busses. Make sure you're on the busses, or you'll be left. Understand? Dismissed!"

Spiller and Smith went to the Quonset hut, picked up their gear and headed directly for the bus. It came as no surprise that all of the others whose names were on the roster were ready too. The busses were loaded within 30 minutes. The line of busses made their way across Okinawa to Clark Air Base. It was 1000 hours when the busses pulled up to a stop in front of a building just inside the main gate. The liaison officer got off the bus and had a short conversation with an Air Force captain who walked from the building to meet him. The liaison officer returned to the busses.

"All right, men, there's been a delay. The plane will leave at 1400, not at 1200 hours."

Moans and groans burst from the bus windows as the word was passed.

"Fucking hurry up and wait!" snapped Spiller.

"Yeah, we can blame it on the Air Force this time instead of the Marine Corps," Smith snarled back.

The liaison officer went back to the Air Force captain. He spoke to him for a short time, then returned to the lead bus. The busses began to move.

"Where the fuck are we going now?" asked Smith.

"I don't know. I just wanna go home. Why can't they get their shit in one bag, man?"

The busses stopped in front of a mess hall, and once again the liaison officer got off the bus. He was met at the front door by an Air Force mess sergeant. With the windows lowered on the busses, the Marines listened to the conversation.

"Sergeant, we have a delay on the flight out. Captain Swinford from the liaison office sent us over so we can get noon chow."

"We can't feed them. God damn it! That's an extra hundred men. We just can't do it. Chow is already being prepared!"

A voice came screaming from the first bus. "You feed us or we'll take the fucking mess hall over!"

The busses exploded with yells and banging on the sides of the busses. The liaison officer ran to the first bus, then the second, and on down the line, quieting the Marines. When he departed the last bus, he approached the mess sergeant once again.

"Sarge, these men have been out of country four days. They've been shuffled around, and all they want is to get home. Now one more delay. Can't you get hold of an officer?"

The sergeant interrupted, "They act like a bunch of animals. I said no chow."

"Let's take it," a voice screamed out.

The Marines began to yell and scrambled off the busses.

"Jesus Christ!" yelled the mess sergeant as he ran inside the mess hall, locking the doors behind him. "Call the MPs. Call the MPs."

The Marines beat on the door with their fists. Others lined up in front of the windows.

"Let us in, motherfucker!"

"We want chow!"

"Teach you to call us animals, you fucking air poge!"

Five Jeeps full of MPs pulled up in front of the mess hall. Some of the MPs ran for the main door, the rest tried to back the Marines away from the mess hall windows. In ten minutes the MPs had quieted the Marines. An MP sergeant walked up to the liaison officer who was trying to catch his breath.

"Let's go inside. I wanna know what's going on here."

The mess sergeant opened the door to let the MP and the liaison officer in. He quickly shut the door and locked it. The mess cooks and mess men stood back from the windows as they watched the Marines, some of whom made hideous faces at them. The MP sergeant, the liaison officer, and the mess sergeant huddled for about five minutes, then the three came outside.

"All right. They're going to feed us," yelled the liaison officer.

Everyone started yelling and waving their caps. The MPs looked back and forth in disbelief. The Marines jumped and cheered.

"I don't want any more trouble, you understand," screamed the MP sergeant. "Any more trouble and you won't be on that plane today."

The Marines settled down and lined up for chow as the MPs quickly boarded the Jeeps and left the area. The Marines passed through the chow line, ate, and one by one, boarded the busses, as the mess sergeant watched cautiously. Once again the busses moved to the airfield, where an Air Force 707 sat.

"That must be ours," gasped Spiller.

"I hope so. Man, I hope so," replied Smith.

The busses came to a stop in front of the plane, and the Marines were instructed to leave the busses. Five baggage carts sat near the back of the plane. The Marines placed their sea bags on the carts and boarded. Spiller and Smith sat side by side and fastened their seat belts.

"If this thing doesn't crash on us, we've just about made it," said Smith.

Spiller grinned. "You're right, but let's not talk about crashing, not after what we've been through."

The plane was in the air and the captain's voice came over the loud speaker.

"Welcome aboard, gentlemen. This is Captain Glasgow. I'm sure you're all looking forward to getting back to the States. The flight time will be eight-and-one-half hours. We have a steward who will be showing you some emergency procedures. Enjoy your flight."

A man, dressed in a flight suit, walked to the front of the compartment.

"Gentlemen, may I have your attention, please? I'm your steward. My name is Bill. I would like to show you some emergency procedures."

"Hey, Tootsie, come on back here, I've got a hell of an emergency," said a Marine in the back of the plane.

Everyone burst out laughing as the steward's face turned red.

"Come back here, sweetheart, and sit on my lap," said Smith.

"I'm in love! Oh God, I love her," came another voice.

"Gentlemen! I need to show you these emergency procedures. They're important."

"Let's see some leg, honey," yelled another Marine.

"Bend over, baby," shouted Spiller.

Everyone laughed. The frustrated steward threw the oxygen mask down and plopped into a seat at the front of the plane. "Just let 'em die, crazy bastards. They'll be sorry, if we have an emergency."

The laughing fell into silence and the sound of snoring. The plane came closer and closer to the United States. A bell rang and the seat belt sign came on. The captain's voice came over the loud speaker.

"Gentlemen, we'll be landing in 30 minutes. Please fasten your seat belts."

Spiller and Smith grinned at each other as they fiddled with their seat belts. Then both leaned back against the seat. The engines roared and the tires squealed as the plane landed and slowly rolled to a stop. The Marines quickly unfastened their seat belts and crowded the aisle, as the side door of the plane came open. Just as the Marines started for the door, a sergeant stepped inside the plane.

"All right, gentlemen, wait up just a minute. Wait up. First of all, I want to welcome all of you back to the United States. Now, when you get off the plane, we have a corporal that will take you to your barracks and will then give you further instructions. Also...."

"Also, hell! Let us off this plane, damn it," came a voice from the rear compartment.

Everyone moved forward as the sergeant moved to the side. Spiller and Smith walked down the ladder, gaping at the scenery.

"This is the most beautiful airfield I've ever seen," yelled Smith.

"Me, too, Smitty. Me, too."

Spiller stepped off the ladder onto the runway. He fell to his hands and knees and kissed the ground.

"Hello, United States of America. You're beautiful."

Several Marines, hooping and hollering, threw their hats into the air. The sea bags were brought out on baggage carts and the Marines fumbled through the pile. Once all the men had their belongings, they followed the corporal across the base to a barracks, where once again, the men were told to grab a bunk.

"You all have liberty call until Monday morning. You can pick up your liberty cards in the duty office," he said, pointing to the far end of the barracks. "Welcome home," the corporal said with a big grin.

"Let's get a quick shower and go on liberty," suggested Spiller.

Both the Marines quickly opened their sea bags and grabbed towels and soap. In record time, they'd taken showers and dressed.

"I think everybody in this barracks has set an all time record for quick showers," remarked Spiller.

Smith laughed, "I can believe that. What time is it?"

Spiller looked at his watch. "It's 2200, why?"

"I wanted to call my brother after I talk to Mom and Dad, and I just wondered if he'd be home. He's kind of a night owl."

"With the two-hour time difference, it'll be midnight at home."

They hurried to the duty office, grabbed a liberty card, and headed for the main gate. Just inside the gate was a bus stop and a line of phone booths.

"Let's call. There are some phone booths," said Spiller.

Smith ran for a booth with Spiller right behind him. First Spiller tried to call his mother, but there was no answer. He picked up the receiver and dialed the operator.

"Operator."

"Yes, ma'am. I'd like to make a collect call to area code 618-993-8609."

"Your name, sir?"

"Harry Spiller."

"Thank you. Just a moment."

"Hello."

"Yes, ma'am, you have a collect call from Harry Spiller, will you accept the charges?"

"Yes! Yes, I will!"

"Hello? Hello, Sis? It's Harry. We're back."

"Hi there. Welcome home. When did you get back?"

"We just flew in about an hour ago. They let us have liberty until Monday morning. Boy, Sis, it sure is good to be home. Sis? Sis?"

"I'm, here! How come you haven't written? We thought they'd kept you over there. We heard there was a big build-up of Chinese on the border and were afraid that you had to stay longer."

"No, I was on patrol in Phu Bai for the last month. Couldn't write then. When we did get our orders, it was a day in Da Nang, and three days in Okinawa, and now here, so I just didn't get a chance to write."

"Well, when will you be home?"

"I don't know yet. We're waiting for our orders to come in. They'll probably tell us Monday. I'll call again as soon as I find out for sure. I'm sure it'll be some time next week. Boy, it sure is good to be home. Me and Smitty are going to walk around all night in this good old USA. Sis? Sis? What's the matter? You falling asleep on me?"

"No, no. I was just listening."

"Listen, I'm gonna get off here. There are a lot of guys waiting to call home. I'll call you the first of the week as soon as I know something for sure. Okay?"

"Okay. You be careful tonight."

"I will," chuckled Spiller. "Bye now."

Spiller stepped out of the phone booth and lit a cigarette while he waited for Smith to finish his phone call.

Spiller chuckled as he thought of what his sister had said. "'Be careful.' A year in Vietnam, and 'be careful' on liberty. Damn."

Smith opened the door and stepped out of the phone booth. He reached into his pocket for a cigarette.

"They glad to hear from you?" asked Spiller.

"Yeah, except I couldn't get Mom to quit crying. Hell, I'm okay now. No need to cry."

"I had a little bit of the same problem, not quite that bad though. Sis tried to hide hers. I expected it though. She's always been like a mother to me. Hey, let's hit the town."

The two Marines walked out the main gate and down the street about two blocks where they found a local night club.

"Let's get a beer," suggested Spiller.

"All right, man, all right. Let's see what that good old American beer tastes like," chuckled Smith.

The two walked into the bar and sat in a booth. They watched two couples on the dance floor. A waitress was going from table to table taking orders.

"Look at that waitress, Smitty. Look at those beautiful eyes."

"Round eyes. Man, it's great to see those round eyes."

The waitress walked to the booth where they sat and rested the small round tray on the table.

"May I help you, gentlemen?"

"Ma'am, you're the most beautiful thing I've seen in a year," gasped Smith.

The waitress rolled her eyes slightly.

"What are you having, gentlemen?"

"I'm having a draft beer," Spiller said.

"Me, too," replied Smith.

"I need some IDs."

"Well, ma'am, we just got back from Vietnam."

"You just got back from Vietnam, right? Well it doesn't matter, where you came from, the drinking age is twenty-one. IDs, gentlemen."

They handed the waitress their IDs.

"That's what I thought – under age. The bar policy here is that no one under age can hang around. I'm going to have to ask you to leave."

"But, ma'am."

"But, nothing. Leave, or I'll call the manager."

"Yes, ma'am," said Spiller in a low voice.

Smith grunted slightly as they walked out the door.

"Great homecoming, huh, Smitty? First place we go and we're thrown out?"

"Hell, I understand not being served, but getting thrown out!"

"Yeah, she didn't have to be so nasty."

"Oh, well, maybe she just had a bad night."

"Yeah, maybe. What time is it?"

"2330."

"Let's get a cup of coffee."

"Sounds good, Smitty."

They walked into an all-night restaurant located in the middle of town. A counter with several stools was on the left, square tables filled the rest of the room. Just inside the door, three tables were filled with several people who had obviously had too much to drink. They were drinking coffee. Spiller and Smith walked to the center of the room and sat at an empty table. A waitress walked toward them.

"Don't do it, Smitty, not this time."

"Don't do what?"

"Don't tell her she's beautiful. We'll be in trouble."

Smith chuckled as the waitress approached the table.

"What do you need?"

Smith looked at Spiller, then back to the waitress.

"Coffee, please."

"Me, too," said Spiller.

The waitress wrote their order on a pad, then turned and walked away without saying a word.

"Do we smell or something, Harry? I mean, maybe we took a shower too quick or something."

"I don't know, man."

The waitress walked back to the table with a cup of coffee in each hand.

"You motherfucker," a voice screamed at the front of the restaurant.

Spiller and Smith turned quickly as two men grabbed each other and fell across the table. The waitress tossed the two cups on the table. Coffee splashed everywhere. She ran to the phone and called the police.

No sooner had she hung up the receiver than in walked a six foot three, 220-pound cop wearing a helmet. He grabbed each man by the shoulder and dragged them out the door without saying a word.

Spiller turned back, reached for a napkin, and wiped the coffee off his shirt while Smith wiped coffee from the table.

"What the hell else is going to happen?"

"I don't know, Smitty. Why don't we go walk for a while."

"Yeah, let's get out of here."

The two paid for their coffee and left the restaurant.

Pow!

Smith and Spiller quickly turned and knelt.

"Fuck, man, must have been a back fire," snapped Spiller.

"Must have. Let's go back to the barracks. I've had enough for one night."

"Me, too. I'm starting to wonder if we should've come home."

"No shit. Let's go."

On Monday the Marines formed outside the barracks. A sergeant walked to the front of the formation.

"Men, your orders will be in within the next two days. We'll have a formation at 1500 hours and 0700 hours each day. Liberty will be sounded at 1600 hours. We're going to have a field day today and get these barracks cleaned up. Is that clear?"

The entire formation burst into laughter.

"What's so funny? If these barracks don't pass inspection by 1600 hours, there will be no liberty."

"Sure, Sarge, probably send us to Nam, too, huh?" came a voice from the formation.

"Who said that?" snapped the sergeant.

"I did," replied a Marine.

"No, sir, I did," snapped another.

"I did it," said another and another, until everyone in the formation had confessed.

"There will be no formation at 1500. Understand? Dismissed."

The sergeant walked away briskly. The Marines clapped, laughed, and whistled.

"Hey, Smitty, I'm gonna call home."

"I'll go with you."

The two Marines headed for the phone booths.

"A collect call from Harry Spiller, will you accept the charges?"

"Yes, I will."

"Hi, Sis! Wanted to call and let you know that I'll be home in a couple of days."

"Good. Will you be here by Thursday?"

"I hope so. Maybe if there isn't any delay in orders."

"You need to be home by Thursday if you can."

"Sis, I've been gone for a year and a half. What's a couple of days?"

"Well, you're supposed to be on TV Thursday."

"What! TV? For what!"

"You were in *Life* magazine!"

"Oh, bull, Sis."

"You were. I have two copies right here. Remember Bruce Travelstead, the insurance man that sold you your life insurance while you were in high school?"

"Yeah, I remember."

"He brought the magazine out the other day. He saw the picture and thought it was you, and it was. A two-page photo."

"I don't believe it."

"Yeah, you're a celebrity around here. They had your life history on WSIU at Carbondale last week with all your baby pictures."

"Sis, I don't remember. There were a lot of newsmen around. My baby pictures? Oh, no, on TV!"

"Yes, sure was."

"Well, I'll be home by then, I guess. That's what they're telling us."

"You're supposed to be on by 10:00 A.M."

"Okay, see you in a couple of days."

"All right. Bye."

Spiller stepped out of the phone booth with a puzzled look on his face. This time Smith was waiting for Spiller.

"What's the matter. You look flabbergasted."

"Damnedest thing I ever heard of."

"What?"

"Smitty, do you remember anybody from *Life* magazine being with us in Nam?"

"No. *Newsweek* once, but there were newsmen all over. Why?"

"My sister just said I'm a celebrity back home. I've had my life history on TV. It's been in the papers. Smitty, she says that I'm in a two-page photo in *Life* magazine."

"No shit!"

"Yeah, I have a TV interview at 10:00 A.M. Thursday."

"Well, you're a hero, man," Smith chuckled.

"Oh, bullshit! I don't remember any pictures being taken of me by *Life* magazine. And besides, even if they did a picture, that's all it is, a picture. What's the big deal?"

"They took a lot of pictures over there, maybe you didn't know about it, hero."

"Fuck you, Smitty," Spiller said.

They both began to laugh.

Wednesday morning, December 15, the Marines received their orders. After a 30-day leave, Spiller was to report to Marine Corps Recruit Depot, San Diego. Smith was assigned to Camp Pendleton. Both dressed in Marine Corps greens and caught a cab to the airport. They walked to the counter at TWA.

"May I help you?" asked the clerk.

"Yes, sir. I'd like a flight to Oklahoma City."

"We have a flight leaving in five minutes. If you hurry, you can catch that one."

"Okay," said Smith as he grabbed quickly for his billfold. "How much?" he asked.

"Sixty-five dollars."

Smith quickly counted out the money and asked, "What gate?"

"Twenty-nine."

"Thank you." He turned and quickly shook Spiller's hand. "See you, man. Take care."

"You, too, Smitty. Have a good leave."

Spiller watched with a grin as Smith turned and ran down the hall.

"May I help you, sir?" asked the clerk.

"Yes, sir. I need a ticket for St. Louis."

11
Hero's Welcome

The engines roared loudly as the wheels of the twin-engine plane touched down on the runway and slowly approached a small terminal. Spiller peered out the small window of the plane. It was a cold December day in 1965, snow flurries fell softly. Spiller scanned the crowd.

There she was, his sister, Natalie, almost hidden by the crowd. In an effort to catch sight of her brother, she swayed back and forth looking over the shoulders of those surrounding her. The plane came to a halt. Spiller quickly unfastened his seat belt and walked to the back of the plane. The stewardess fumbled with the door and, with a push, opened it. Spiller proceeded down the ladder. Natalie, waving, made her way through the crowd.

"Hi, there," said Natalie as she embraced her younger brother.

"Hi, Sis. I sure am glad to be home," Spiller said happily.

Arm-in-arm, he and his sister walked to the parking lot. They got into her car.

"Ouch!" Spiller gasped. "I'm not used to this weather. That cold goes right through me."

"I'll turn the heater on."

"Where's this picture you were talking about?" asked Spiller.

"Right here," she said as she picked up a magazine and fumbled through the pages.

In the middle of the magazine was a two-page, color photo of several Vietnamese villagers. Standing behind them was a Marine with a rifle slung over his shoulder and two bandoleers of ammunition across his chest. Spiller closely examined the face of the Marine whose resemblance to himself was uncanny.

"This isn't me, Sis. This isn't me."

"Well, yes it is. You just tell them at the TV station that it's you. It looks like you. It is you."

"I know it looks like me, but it isn't."

"They had your life history on TV last week, and they're expecting us in 30 minutes to interview you."

"I'm not telling them I'm the person in this picture when I'm not!"

Both were silent as they stopped at the traffic light. When the light turned green, Natalie turned left and pulled into a parking lot some two blocks down the street from the university campus. Hippies with long hair, beards, and clothes that looked as if they hadn't been washed for months were walking in a circle. They carried signs that read "No More Draft" and "Stop the War."

"Come on. We're late," said Spiller's sister.

"Look at that. Look at them fuck heads."

"Watch your language, and come on," Natalie insisted as she tugged at his arm.

Just as Spiller turned, a hippie looked in the direction of the parking lot and pointed toward Spiller.

"Murderer!" yelled the hippie.

"Warmonger!" yelled another.

Spiller responded angrily. "Fuck you, hippie!"

His sister continued to pull him by the arm.

"Come on, come on. Don't pay attention to them."

Spiller turned angrily and entered the building.

A receptionist greeted them from behind a desk. "May I help you, sir?"

It was Natalie who responded. "Yes, my brother is here for an interview. He just got home from Vietnam."

Spiller looked around the room while the receptionist called the studio. She hung up the phone and said, "Okay, you can go on back."

"Thank you," replied Spiller and Natalie. They proceeded down the hallway and into the studio.

The host of "Personality of the Week," Bill Jackson, and the guest, a female college student, sat in chairs angled, but facing one another. A cameraman was focussing in on the two.

"Oh, hi, Natalie," said the host. "We didn't think you were going to make it. We were just getting ready to tape with our fill in."

Looking at Harry, he said, "You must be Harry Spiller."

"Yes, sir."

"Natalie, why don't you take a seat over there," said the host, pointing to a closed circuit TV, "where you can watch the program and see what it will look like on TV."

"Harry, come on over here and sit down so we can get you hooked up with a microphone. We're a little behind schedule. This program is aired at one o'clock."

Spiller walked to the chair. The college student moved across the room and took a seat behind the camera. The cameraman attached a small microphone to the front of Spiller's uniform then took his place behind the camera.

"Ready to roll," said the cameraman. "You're on."

Facing the camera, the host said, "Good afternoon, and welcome to 'Personality of the Week.' Last week we had the history of a young man from Southern Illinois, Harry Spiller, who was born and raised in Marion. Harry, now a corporal in the United States Marine Corps, has just recently been photographed in a two-page, color photo in *Life* magazine. We mentioned this week that we hoped to have Harry with us. Arriving about an hour ago at the Williamson County Airport, Harry has just returned from Vietnam and is with us today." Looking directly at Spiller, he continued, "Harry, thanks for being with us, and welcome home."

"Thank you."

"Harry, after a year in Vietnam, how does it feel to be home?"

"It feels great. I've been looking forward to this day for a long time."

"Harry, can you tell us a little bit about your background in the Marine Corps?"

"Well, sir, I enlisted in 1963. I went through boot camp in San Diego, and then I was assigned to the Third Battalion, Fourth Marines, First Marine Brigade in Hawaii. I was there from December 1963 until we were shipped to Nam in March 1965. I was assigned to Battalion Intelligence in Phu Bai, where I was stationed until now. When my leave is up, I'll be stationed at Marine Corps Recruit Depot, San Diego."

"What can you tell us about the weather and the terrain in Vietnam?"

"The weather was very hot most of the time. The temperature ranged from 110 to 120 degrees, except during monsoon season. The temperature was the least of our worries. We were more concerned with staying dry. It rained for days at a time, sometimes the wind would blow so hard it rained sideways."

"That must have been difficult for fighting conditions."

"Miserable is a better word. We were wet all the time. Difficult in the sense that the VC moved a lot during that time because of low visibility, and we had a hard time detecting them. As for the terrain, our battalion headquarters was set up beside the Phu Bai Airfield. Most of the terrain around us was flat and sandy. Further out from the headquarters area, there were a lot of hills, most of them not too heavily vegetated, then the jungle which you could get lost in real easy. It was so thick in there, a person four or five feet in front of you could be completely out of sight. There were also a lot of rice paddies. They seemed to be everywhere."

"I heard that there were tigers over there and that there had been a couple of incidents where Marines were attacked by them."

"That may be true, but as far as I know, there were never any tigers seen in the area where I was. We had a lot of snakes, land leeches, and mosquitoes, but no tigers."

"What about food?"

"We had C-rations most of the time, B-rations when we were in headquarters."

"What's the difference between the two?"

"B-rations are cooked in the mess hall. C-rations come in small boxes, and that's what we'd take into the field with us."

"Can you tell us some of the types of food that are in the B- and C-rations?"

"Both B- and C-rations have mainly the same kinds of food. Let's see. There is ham and lima beans with cheese and crackers. That was my favorite. And, chicken and noodles, beef chunks, and chopped ham and eggs."

"How did you prepare the food?"

"We had sterno tablets that we'd light and that would warm the can. If we didn't take the tablets with us, we just ate the food cold."

"I bet you're looking forward to some home cooking."

"I sure am, sir."

"I'm sure you've heard of the war demonstrations on a lot of the college campuses around the country. How do you feel about that?"

"Well, it certainly doesn't help morale any. But I don't think it's college students that are doing it. Just a bunch of cowards that are worthless to the human race. I saw three hippies outside as I came into the studio. Looked like they came out of a cave. We should take those fucking bastards and kill them."

Jackson's eyes grew large and his face turned red.

"Hold it. Hold it. Cut! We'll have to cut that out. Harry, I'm sorry I asked the question. I didn't realize it was such a sore spot with you."

"I'm sorry too, sir. I kind of lost it."

The host's face returned to its normal color. Both he and Spiller settled down for a moment.

The cameraman zoomed in. "You're on."

"Harry, I'd like to thank you for being with us today, and I hope you enjoy your leave at home."

"Thank you, sir. I've enjoyed being here."

Facing the camera again, the host spoke. "That's our program for this week. I hope you've enjoyed the show. We'll see you next week on. 'Personality of the Week.' Have a good day."

The cameraman and the college student walked out of the studio. Spiller, his sister, and Jackson walked to the back of the building and entered a small room, where he and his sister sat at a square table in the center of the room. Jackson poured three cups of coffee.

"Cream or sugar?" asked Jackson.

"I take mine black," said Spiller.

"A little sugar for me, please," said Natalie.

The three sat at the table. "Harry, I want to apologize to you again for asking about the demonstrators. I really didn't mean to upset you," said Jackson.

"That's okay. It's a sore spot with me, but I guess I shouldn't have spouted off like that. I just couldn't help myself."

"I was trying to be careful about what I asked. I mean, I know some people suggested I ask you how many VC you killed."

Spiller, setting his coffee cup down, looked silently at Jackson, then at Natalie.

"Sis, you about ready to go? I wanna go home."

"Sure, when you're ready."

"Let's go," said Spiller. He stood up.

Jackson and Natalie both stood, and Jackson reached out to shake Spiller's hand.

"Thanks for being on the show."

"You're welcome, sir."

"Have a good leave, Harry."

"Thank you, sir."

Spiller walked out of the building with his sister. He looked across the street where the hippies had been standing earlier. The sidewalk was now empty.

On the way home Spiller thought of the conversation he had with Jackson. "He didn't believe me when I told him that the photo wasn't of me. Sis doesn't want them to believe it, either. What are they trying to prove? All I want to do is get my car, go see my friends, and have a good time. I just want to forget Nam."

"Sis, where do you think I can find a convertible?"

"Oh, I forgot to tell you! I located one for you, and they're checking it over. We can look at it this afternoon. If you like it, they'll have it ready for you late this afternoon."

"That's great. What kind is it?"

"It's a '63 Chevy Impala. White with black interior. It's got low mileage, and the interior looks good."

"That's great! Just great! It sounds like what I wanted. Have you heard from Jeff or anyone?"

"Yes. Jeff called yesterday and wanted to know if you were home yet. I told him you'd be home today. He's looking forward to seeing you."

Spiller was finally home. He grabbed his suitcase from the back of the car while Natalie unlocked the front door. Spiller hurried in and looked around for a moment.

"It sure is good to be home. I'm gonna take a shower. Can we go look at the car when I get finished?"

"Sure can."

Spiller grinned, then hurried to the bedroom where he grabbed a change of clothes and headed for the shower. As he walked back to the living room, he laughed.

"I think I just set another record for shower taking."

"That was quick."

"Can we go now?"

"Let's watch the TV show. It's coming on in ten minutes, then we can go."

"I don't want to watch that show. I'm not interested."

"Well, I want to see it before we go. Oh, the Marion paper called while you were in the shower. They want you to call them."

"Why?"

"They want to interview you about *Life* magazine. You can call while I'm watching the program."

Natalie turned on the TV. Harry walked into the other room to the phone. He thumbed through the phone book for a moment then laid the book back in place. He lifted the receiver and dialed.

"Hello."

"Jeff!"

"Sure is!"

"This is Harry."

"Hey, man, how's it going?"

"Great, man, just great, now that I'm home."

"Guess what I'm doing?" snickered Jeff.

"What's that?"

"Watching you on TV. You're getting to be a celebrity. How does it feel?"

Spiller paused for a moment.

"Jeff, I'm gonna look for a car in a little while. If everything can be worked out, I may have it by late this afternoon. You gonna be home, Jeff?"

"Yeah, man. I'm sorry. I was listening to you on TV. What did you say?"

"I said, I may have my new car this afternoon. You gonna be home?"

"Sure! Come on over."

"Okay. I will. See you tonight."

"All right, Harry. Bye."

Spiller hung the phone up and paced through the family room, where his sister was watching the program.

"Don't you wanna watch this? You're doing good."

"No! I wanna go look at the car."

Spiller returned to the bedroom and proceeded to unpack his clothes. A few minutes later, Natalie was ready to go. Spiller grabbed his jacket and the two headed for town.

"I don't know why you didn't want to see the show," said Natalie.

"I'm not interested in the show, Sis. I've been waiting a year for this car. I've dreamed of it. I wanna forget Vietnam."

"Well, we're just proud of you."

"Proud of what! Being on TV for a picture? And besides, a picture in a magazine that isn't me. You act like you're trying to make a hero out of me!"

They drove in silence. They pulled into a car lot off Main Street. Angled toward the street were several cars parked side by side. Above them was a banner that read: "Used Cars."

"The car's inside. They're changing the oil. That's it over there," Natalie said pointing to a far corner of the building.

Spiller hurried over to the car. The hood was up and both doors were open. Spiller examined the white exterior carefully, checking for scratches and dents. He crawled inside and rubbed the black vinyl seats and dashboard. He emerged from the car smiling.

"Man, this car doesn't have a scratch on it. The top's in good shape, too. How's the engine?" Spiller asked the mechanic, who stood beside the car.

"Young man, I can't find a thing wrong with it. It looks to be in excellent shape."

"Do you like it?" asked Natalie.

"I sure do."

"Okay, we want to take it today, so he can drive it. Also, I have a friend who's going to look it over. If there's no problem, we'll sign the papers in the morning."

"That'll be fine," smiled the mechanic. "I'll pull the car out front for you." He closed the passenger door then walked to the front of the car.

Spiller beamed at Natalie as they both walked back to the front of the building.

"I'll meet you back at the house and we can call Jack Franklin. He's a friend of Jim's. He's been a mechanic for 20 years. We'll take the car over to him so he can give it a good going over."

"Okay. See you in a few minutes."

The mechanic pulled up in the car and got out leaving the driver's side open.

"There you are, young man," he said to Spiller.

"Thank you, sir."

The mechanic grinned at Spiller.

"Oh, by the way. I saw your picture in *Life*."

Spiller grunted. He jumped into the car, shut the door, and hit the accelerator.

Pulling up to a four-way stop, Spiller almost threw himself through the windshield.

"Damn! 'This baby sure does have the brakes,' that bastard could've told me instead of 'I seen you in *Life*.'"

Spiller continued down Main Street and out of town to Natalie's place. He thought of the past year in Nam. "Man, every two weeks I sent a money order home to buy this car. I've dreamed of it, and now here I am. It's sure hard to believe. I sure hope I don't wake up in a foxhole."

Spiller pulled into the driveway and came to a not-so-sudden stop this time. He jumped from the car and ran inside.

"Boy, Sis, it sure does drive good! I really like it. Damned good brakes, too!"

"Watch your language!"

Spiller paused for a moment then asked, "Did you get in touch with the guy that's going to look at the car?"

"Yes, he'll be home at five. We can go then. Let's go pick up Susie. She'll be out of school shortly. I kinda think she's looking forward to seeing that uncle of hers."

"She is, huh?" Spiller asked with a grin.

Just before 3:00 P.M., Harry and Natalie arrived at the school to pick up 12-year-old Susie. She greeted her Uncle Harry shyly.

When they returned Bob Wilson from the newspaper called. He wanted to interview Harry. They set up a meeting for the following morning. Harry hung up the phone. He felt depressed. Rather than give into his feelings, he joined Susie who was playing records. Listening to the Beatles, Turtles, and the Animals helped ease the feelings that no one seemed to understand.

Before long Natalie had supper ready. Susie and Harry pulled their chairs close to the table. Natalie placed a dish in the center of the table.

"What are we having?" Spiller inquired.

"Rice and chicken stew," said Natalie.

With a frown on his face, Spiller plopped back into his chair.

"What's the matter?" asked Natalie.

Spiller paused for a moment, then looked up.

"I hate rice. All I've done for a year is wade in rice paddies and look at rice. Now you want me to come home and eat this shit!"

"Well, you used to like. . . ."

Spiller interrupted, "I may used to have liked it, but I don't anymore. I hate it. Understand?"

Spiller stood up and walked out of the room. Natalie was at his heels.

"Harry, you want me to fix you something else to eat?"

"No, I'm not hungry anyway."

"Let Susie finish eating, and we'll take your car over and get it checked out."

"Okay."

After dinner the three drove to the mechanic's house. Mr. Franklin was friendly, but Harry winced when he said, half chuckling, "You look a little different without that machine ammo that you were carrying in that picture."

Natalie and Susie went into the Franklin home. Harry looked on as Franklin proceeded to check the car over.

After having driven the car five miles, Franklin said, "Well, Harry, as far as I can tell, the car seems to be okay. I think you're making yourself a good buy."

"Thank you, sir."

"Would you like to come in for a few minutes?"

"Well, thank you, sir, but I was supposed to be at a friend's house an hour ago. Maybe some other time."

On the way home, Natalie scolded, "You don't have any manners at all. Why didn't you come in? His family wanted to meet you."

"Sis, I told him some other time. I want to go see Jeff."

"Well, Jack's family wanted to meet you. They bought a *Life Magazine* and cut your picture out. You just don't have any manners."

Spiller was silent for a moment. "I wonder, if they would've wanted to meet me if I hadn't been in *Life*."

"What! What do you mean? Those are good people."

"You just don't understand, do you, Sis? You just don't understand."

Everyone was quiet as Spiller pulled into the driveway.

"Aren't you coming in before you go over to Jeff's?"

"No, I'm . . ."

Spiller paused as lights flashed in his eyes from the rear view mirror, "Well, shit!"

"Watch your mouth."

Spiller got out of the car and watched as the silhouette of a man walked toward him.

"Hi, Harry. Bob Travelstead."

"Oh, hi, Bob."

"I was the one that noticed the picture of you in *Life*. Natalie didn't know it, until I brought the magazine out."

Spiller shook hands with Travelstead. "I appreciate it. Could you pull back just a little? I'm really in a hurry."

"He doesn't have any manners at all, Bob."

"Oh, that's okay. I realize he just got home."

Travelstead walked back to his car and backed his car out of Harry's way.

Spiller headed toward Jeff's house. He parked his car in front of the house and hurried for the front door. Just as he raised his arm to knock, the door swung open.

"Hi, Harry!" Jeff yelled.

"Hi, Jeff!" said Spiller as he shook hands and stepped inside.

"You look good, Harry."

"Thank you."

"Hey, what do you think about rounding up some of the old gang and maybe tomorrow night, we can have a little party," grinned Jeff.

"Sounds great to me. Your mom working?"

"Yeah, she works every night but Sunday."

"Hey, man, want to go get a cup of coffee? I'd like to see Mrs. Thompson. Do you remember her? I grew up with her boys, Dick and Ralph."

"Yeah, I know who you mean."

"I promised to come and see her when I got home. Besides I want you to go for a ride in my new car."

"Let's go, man."

When they got out to the car, Jeff walked around it slowly examining the exterior. He opened the passenger door and slid in shutting the door behind him.

"This is sharp. It's in damned good condition."

Spiller started the car and they drove toward town. "It rides good, too," said Jeff.

"I sure am proud of it, and you know something else?"

"What's that?"

"It sure is good to be home."

"I know it must be. I bet Vietnam was really horrible."

"It's hard to put into words, Jeff. I just want to put it behind me."

"I don't blame you, man. I don't blame you."

Spiller pulled into a parking stall and the two headed for the restaurant. Jeff sat down at a table in the middle of the room.

"Jeff, I'll be back in a minute. I wanna see if Mrs. Thompson is working."

"Okay. I'll order some coffee."

Spiller walked up to a lady standing behind the cash register. "Ma'am, I just came home on leave, and I was wondering if Mrs. Thompson is working."

"She sure is. She's in the back. Why don't you go on back?"

"Thank you," said Spiller. He walked through a swinging door into the kitchen where Mrs. Thompson was busy preparing a dinner plate.

"Hi there," Spiller said.

Mrs. Thompson looked up, dropped the plate, and ran to Spiller. As she hugged him, she began to cry.

"I sure am glad to see you made it home all right. I've been worried about you."

"I'm fine."

"When did you get home?"

"Today. I told you when I left the last time, I'd be back to see you the day I got home."

"I remember."

"Listen, I'll be over to see you. I'm going to be home for 30 days, and I know you need to get back to work."

"Okay. Now you come over."

"I will. I will," laughed Spiller.

He walked back to the table and sat down across from Jeff.

"I bet she was glad to see you, wasn't she?"

"Sure was," said Spiller.

Two teenage boys walked up to the table as Spiller and Jeff sipped their coffee.

"Hey, aren't you Harry Spiller?" asked one teenager.

"Yes, I am."

"We saw your picture in *Life* magazine. How many did you kill while you were over there?" the boy grinned.

"I didn't. . . . You shouldn't ask questions like that."

The other teenager spoke up. "My dad said you didn't kill anybody or do anything while you were over there. He was in the Army in World War II, and he said the Marines were always trying to take credit for everything. Besides that, he said you weren't fighting a real war anyway."

"Come on, man, did you kill anybody over there?" the other prodded.

"Let's go, Jeff."

The two boys followed Spiller to the door.

"Yeah. A real hero you are. You think you're too good to talk to us."

Spiller and Jeff got into the car. Spiller sat quietly for a moment, then started the car and drove off.

"You okay, Harry?"

"Yeah, I'm okay. They were just a couple of crazy kids. People just don't understand. I mean when I was their age, I was the same way. You watch all these movies about war and how glamorous it is. I remember when I enlisted. When I first saw that recruiter in those dress blues, I was ready to leave right then. And you know why?"

"No. Why?"

"Because I saw myself in that uniform with all those medals, and how great I thought it would be. I didn't really know what war would be like. It was nothing but death and destruction, Jeff. That's all. You wanna know something else?"

"What's that, Harry?"

"Everything you do, you do to survive. You're like a drowning rat just trying to hold on to the side of a barrel. I bought all my heroism in Okinawa. It cost $1.04. That's all there is, Jeff."

Spiller pulled up in front of Jeff's house and parked.

"I wasn't in *Life Magazine*, Jeff. It wasn't me."

"What? It looks like you. I saw it."

"It isn't me."

"But you were in the newspaper, on TV, and well. . . ."

"It isn't me. Jeff, let me ask you something. Let's suppose it was me. What I mean is, what is a picture?"

"Well, it's a picture."

"That's all. A picture, Jeff."

"Hell, man, everybody thinks it's you."

"I know. I told the host at the TV station it wasn't me, and he just laughed."

Jeff sat just shaking his head.

"Let's forget this, man. I just want to put it behind me. We going to have a party tomorrow night?"

"Sure are!"

As Spiller drove home he thought about everything that had happened that day. "I wonder how everyone would have reacted if they hadn't thought I was in *Life* magazine? I wonder, if they would even care that I was home. I know one thing for sure, if there were any heroes I sure wouldn't want to be one. My God, when I was in high school, I thought that there would be so much glory in war and so much glamor in being a hero. Boy, when you're young, you really have a distorted view of life."

Spiller shut the car door and locked it. He walked into the house. Natalie sat quietly on the couch watching TV.

"You're back early. Something the matter?"

"No, I was up all night last night, and it's been a long day. Thought I'd get a good night's sleep."

"Jim will be home tomorrow," grinned Natalie.

"Oh, really? It'll be good to see him."

"You sure you're all right? You look depressed."

"I'm fine, Sis. I always look depressed when I get tired."

"Did you eat anything?"

"No, I'm not hungry."

"You're going to have to start eating. You've lost a lot of weight."

"You're right about that. I weighed myself when I took a shower today, and I only weighed 139 pounds. I'm going to bed. See you in the morning, okay?"

"Okay, goodnight."

In the morning Harry's eyes opened to focus on the swirled plaster on the ceiling. Startled, he sat up quickly.

Okay, I'm home, he thought as he lay in bed taking a deep breath.

He lay for a moment thinking how good it was to be home. Before long he got up and got dressed. After shaving, Spiller went into the kitchen where Natalie sat sipping coffee.

"Good morning," said Natalie.

"Good morning."

"Want something to eat?"

"Yes. I'm starved to death."

"What do you want?"

Spiller laughed, "Half dozen eggs, a pound of bacon, and a loaf of bread."

"You are hungry, huh?"

"Yeah, but maybe you'd better just fix me a couple of eggs and not quite so much bacon."

Spiller finished breakfast.

"What time is it, Sis?"

"Eight-thirty."

"I'd better get going. I'm supposed to be at the newspaper office at nine."

"Are you excited?"

"Excited? Hell, no! I just want to get it over with. I'll see you later," said Spiller as he started for the door.

"Don't forget, Jim will be home today."

"Okay. I'll be back after a while."

Spiller walked into the newspaper office. Stretching from wall to wall was a counter piled waist high with newspapers. A small, gray-headed woman was typing at the desk behind the counter.

"Excuse me, ma'am. I'm looking for Bob Wilson," Spiller said.

The lady smiled.

"He's the first door on the right as you go down the hall."

Spiller stepped up to the door and knocked.

"Come in."

Spiller opened the door and entered the office. Sitting behind a small desk covered with papers was a medium-sized man, wearing a white shirt and dark rimmed glasses.

"Hi, I'm Harry Spiller."

"Yes, Harry, I recognized you from your picture. Have a seat."

Spiller sat down and reached for a cigarette.

"Harry, I wanted to ask you a few questions about Vietnam if you don't mind."

"Sure," said Spiller.

"What do you think of the demonstrators?"

"Demonstrators against U.S. policy in Vietnam are a bunch of mama babies too scared to fight for the freedom they enjoy. If they're really unhappy about the United States policy, let them go join the Vietcong. I'm sure we'll accommodate them with all the fighting they want."

"What about the morale of the troops from the demonstrations?"

"Well, at first our morale was hit pretty hard, until we realized it's but a small group doing it."

"What was the fighting like?"

"Most of it was patrols and ambushes, mostly at night. It's jungle warfare, and there aren't any lines like in conventional warfare. The biggest problem was knowing the VC from the Vietnamese. You just couldn't tell who was who. They use a lot of booby traps over there. We had a lot of casualties from the traps."

"What about the future?"

"Well, right now, I want to catch up on some home cooking, and I'm trying to look up my old friends."

"You have about a year-and-a-half left on your enlistment. What then?"

"Well, I'm not going to make a career out of the military. When I finish my hitch, I plan to go to college."

"Is there anything else you'd like to say or add?"

"No, sir. That's about it."

"Okay then, Harry, I appreciate your coming by, and we'll try to have this in tonight's paper."

"Thank you, sir," he said as he stood and walked out of the office. As Harry drove home, he thought of the interview with the reporter. "I wonder why he didn't ask me how many VC I killed. The host of the TV station didn't come right out and ask, but he wanted to know. People have such a distorted view of war. If you're at war, it's okay to kill each other. It's heroic to kill another human being. What a waste."

Spiller turned onto Boswell Road. At the far end of the gravel, dead-end street was a yellow, Peterbilt semi-truck. Jim was home.

Spiller walked into the living room and was met by his sister. Moments later, they were joined by Jim, who welcomed Harry home heartily. Eventually, the conversation got around to the Vietnam War, and Harry quickly changed the subject. When the Vietnam War came up again, Spiller excused himself. He decided to visit his brother, Frank, and his wife.

Spiller drove across town and pulled into the driveway at 117 Clark Drive. He walked to the front door of the house and knocked. The door opened and Spiller was greeted by Frank's wife, Janice, a short, gray-headed woman.

"Well, hi there," said Janice with a smile.

"Hi," replied Spiller as he stepped in the door and hugged Janice. "Where's Frank?"

"He went hunting. He won't be back till late this afternoon."

"Oh, I see."

"Well, have a seat and stay a while."

"Okay," said Spiller as he plopped down on the couch.

"How long did you tell us you have been home?"

"I got home yesterday morning at about nine."

"I bet you're glad to be back, aren't you?"

"I sure am, but I haven't had time to see many people. Between getting my car and the interviews."

"Speaking of the interviews. You know I've been disappointed in you."

"What do you mean?"

"Both the news article and the TV program said Corporal Spiller is spending his leave at 208 Boswell Drive with his sister. You do have a brother, you know."

"Well, yeah, I know, but that article and TV program were released, and I didn't have anything to do with it."

"Well, you were on TV yesterday, weren't you?"

"Yes."

"You didn't say a word about your family."

Spiller sat silently for a moment thinking. "Boy, I'm beginning to wonder if I wouldn't have been better off if I hadn't come home. They're more worried about my being in the paper than seeing me."

"Want to go look at my new car?" he asked Janice.

"It's too cold out there. I'll look at it from here," she said as she pulled the curtain back and looked from the window.

"It's pretty. You really deserve having a new car."

"Thank you. I like it really well."

Janice walked back and sat in the chair. A blank expression spread across her face.

"Well, I need to get going. I have a party to go to tonight."

"Okay, I'll tell Frank you stopped by."

"Tell him I'll be back tomorrow or the next day. I'll be home till the middle of January so I have plenty of time to visit."

"I'll tell him."

Spiller drove back to his sister's home. He parked behind a blue Chevrolet station wagon. He walked into the living room and found Natalie carefully examining a paper. Beside her was an opened brief case and a short, chubby man, filling out a form.

"Oh, hi, Harry. This is Mr. Jones with State Farm Insurance. The bank called while you were gone and okayed the loan for your car. Mr. Jones is going to insure your car for you."

"How much is the policy going to cost?"

"Full coverage insurance for a year will be $147," said Jones as he continued to write.

"Not bad," Spiller said. He got up and went into the kitchen to get an ashtray.

"Harry, this is the coverage you'll have on your car and personal injury," said Jones, handing Spiller the form.

Harry sat back, lit a cigarette, and began to read the insurance contract. Natalie walked over to him and grabbed his cigarette.

"What the hell are you doing?"

"You're smoking too much. Little boys shouldn't smoke anyway."

Spiller, turning red in the face, looked at Jones then back down at the contract.

"Little boy," Spiller thought, "you'd have thought I never left home."

"This looks all right to me," he said.

"Okay. If you'll sign on the bottom line, where I marked the X."

Spiller signed the paper and handed it back. Jones smiled and handed Spiller a newspaper asking, "Have you seen tonight's paper?"

"No, sir," said Spiller, taking the paper.

In big letters the title read, "Marion Marine Who Fought in Vietnam Says Demonstrators Are Too Afraid to Fight." Beside the caption was the picture from *Life* magazine. Spiller read the article then placed the paper on the table.

"I'm beginning to understand what is meant by freedom of the press."

"What do you mean?" asked Natalie.

"You don't know, do you, Sis?" Spiller snapped as he left the room.

After taking a shower and dressing, Harry came back into the living room. By then, Mr. Jones had left, but Natalie was still sitting on the couch looking at the paper.

"Didn't you like the article?"

"No, Sis, I didn't."

"Why?"

"Well, first of all, the picture wasn't of me. Then look how he phrases the sentence. 'His closeness to death' and all that bullshit. It's all bullshit. I'm leaving!"

"Where are you going?" Natalie asked.

"To a party. Want to call the paper for that, too!"

Spiller stormed out of the house, slamming the door behind him.

Spiller, Natalie, and Susie entered the church and walked down the aisle to the second pew from the front. Several people smiled at Spiller as he looked around at those attending.

The church services began with a prayer from the minister and then a few songs. The minister walked to the podium.

"We thought it would be appropriate for the next song that everyone had a candle. We'll hand out the candles, and when everyone has one, we'll turn out the lights and all join in to sing 'Silent Night.'"

The church choir stood behind the podium. Each member, in a white robe, held a large candle. Everyone else held a small birthday candle with a small piece of aluminum foil wrapped around the bottom. With the lights out, everyone sang "Silent Night." When the song ended, and the candles were all blown out, the lights were turned on. The minister stepped to the podium to begin his sermon.

Spiller sat for a moment holding the candle then reached forward and stuck it in the collar of a coat laid across the pew in front of him. Susie giggled.

Spiller leaned toward her and whispered, "I'll get it when the services are over. I got tired of holding it."

Natalie elbowed Susie.

The three sat listening to the minister. A short time later, Susie, pointing at the coat, elbowed Spiller.

"Oh, shit!" Spiller whispered as he quickly grabbed the coat, pulled the candle out of the collar, and slapped at the smoky area. Natalie bowed her head, putting her hands over her face. Susie giggled. The minister looked with disbelief, and then continued. Spiller laid the coat back across the pew. A woman in her mid-fifties, wearing a flowered hat, turned slightly and stared at him with a hard look.

"Um, ma'am, I'm sorry. I just laid the candle there till the services were over. I thought the candle was out," Spiller whispered.

"Well, I never," said the woman in a low voice.

"Lady, I wouldn't doubt that a bit," Spiller whispered.

In the morning Spiller heard a yell then felt someone grab his ankle. He jerked his leg and quickly rolled off the bed.

"My rifle, my rifle, where the fuck is my rifle?" he thought as he heard laughter in the background.

"Wait a minute, I'm home. What the hell?"

He felt his heart pounding in his chest. He looked up from the floor. There stood Susie, Natalie, and Jim at the end of the bed, all laughing.

"What's the matter, Harry? Think we were VC?" Jim chuckled.

"We just wanted to scare you a little," Natalie said.

Spiller, sitting in his shorts, grabbed a blanket and took a deep breath.

"My God! You scared me!"

The three were still laughing.

"It isn't funny, damn it. I thought I was in Vietnam again. Grabbing me like that might get you hurt."

"We were only teasing, Harry," said Natalie.

"Yeah, just having a little fun," said Jim.

"Hell of a way to have fun. Why don't you all get out of here so I can get my clothes on."

After they all left the room, Spiller sat silently, looking at the wall.

"Nobody understands," he thought. "You'd think I just came home from summer camp."

Spiller dressed and shaved. He joined Jim and Natalie, who were sipping coffee in the kitchen.

"You've lost your sense of humor, you know that?" said Natalie.

When Harry's leave was up, he drove to San Diego, California, to the Marine Corps Recruit Depot. A year passed. The war was escalating and there was a big push for re-enlistment. A promotion to sergeant, a choice of duty, and a large re-enlistment bonus of $3,200 looked inviting. Spiller re-enlisted for six years. He reported to recruiters school at Paris Island, South Carolina, on January 4, 1967. After five weeks of recruiters school he was stationed at Cape Girardeau, Missouri.

12

The Death Angel

Twenty-one year old Sergeant Spiller was dressed in typical military athletic attire: Marine Corps green shorts and a camouflage t-shirt. A slogan across the back of his shirt read: "If you can read this, you're too damned close." It was a slogan learned and well-respected by any combat veteran of Vietnam. It was 5:00 A.M., April 30, 1967. Spiller thought the night had passed too quickly. He had returned home late from enlisting four seniors at a high school career day.

Spiller stepped out of his apartment into the fresh morning air and began his daily two-mile jog. Halfway through the run, he became more alert, and got his second wind. As Spiller continued to run, he wondered what Gunnery Sergeant Pierce would say when he found out the May quota was filled. The thought of Pierce reminded Spiller of the first day he reported for recruiting duty.

As Spiller stepped out of the car at 439 Broadway, Cape Girardeau, Missouri, he noticed two large display windows at the front of the recruiting office. One window displayed a variety of Navy posters and plastic model ships. The other contained a dress blue Marine Corps cover, white gloves, and a sword all backgrounded by red velvet material. When Spiller opened the door, the Navy recruiter rose quickly and headed for the back room. At the desk, sitting erect with his arms folded in front of him at the desk, was Marine Gunnery Sergeant Jack Pierce. Spiller knew by the stern look on his face that he was already in trouble. Yet he couldn't help thinking that with Pierce's jet black hair, dark complexion, and prominent nose, if he only had a band, a feather, and a tomahawk, he'd have been perfectly cast as an Indian in a western movie.

"Sergeant Spiller," Pierce growled, "I want to tell you something right now. This job is tough. It's tougher than any combat mission you could ever be assigned to. I've been in this man's Marine Corps for 24 years, served in World War II and Korea. I've seen some crazy things, but I never thought I'd see the day the Corps would assign a kid to this job. I don't know what this man's Marine Corps is coming to. Listen, just one screw-up, just one, and you're gone. Do you understand?"

Back from his morning jog, Sergeant Spiller entered the apartment. He turned on the TV and listened to the top story. As usual it was about the television war: Ellsworth Bunker had arrived in Saigon to replace Lodge as Ambassador. The daily casualty count was 23 dead, 115 wounded. The news story continued with a speech by President Johnson indicating the escalation of the war by committing more troops, and finally, some photos of troops huddling behind a tank in a search-and-destroy operation.

Spiller turned off the TV, left the apartment, and headed to the recruiting office. As he drove to the office he fiddled with the tape deck.

"This thing never has worked right," he grumbled while trying to insert a tape by the Supremes. "You can't buy anything that works these days. Probably made by Orientals. I guess I'll have to take it back to the car dealer. The warranty's still good." He parked the car.

Spiller entered the office and smiled. "Hi, Gunny. How are you this morning?"

"Fine, Spiller. How was your career day?"

"It went well, Gunny. We filled our May quota. It's your turn today."

The gunny, fumbling with his literature and enlistment applications, looked up.

"That makes 19 applicants in the four months you've been here Spiller. That's a pretty impressive record, but it'll get tougher when you have to go out and get your own applicants. You've been riding on the past work of your predecessor, so don't get too cocky. Understand?"

Pierce looked back down and continued to fumble with the papers. Spiller noticed a slight smile on Pierce's face as he picked up his briefcase and headed for the door.

"See you tonight," said Gunny. "I'll see if I can fill the June quota today."

Spiller grinned, "See you tonight."

Thirty minutes later, while Spiller was working on the applications for the enlistees recruited the night before, the phone rang.

"Marine Corps Recruiting Station, Cape Girardeau, Sergeant Spiller."

"Sergeant Spiller, this is Captain Baker, Casualty Section, Headquarters Marine Corps."

"Yes, sir."

"I have a KIA for you."

"Yes, sir. Can you hold just a moment while I get a casualty card?"

"Certainly, Sergeant."

Spiller grabbed nervously for a card then said, "Go ahead, sir. I'm ready."

"Private First Class John W. Williams, age 19, Third Battalion, Fourth Marines, First Marine Regiment. Killed in action April 27, 1967, Da Nang area, hit by a mortar round. Next of kin: Mr. and Mrs. Ralph Williams, 209 Mary Ann Drive, Chaffee, Missouri. Religion: Protestant. You have until noon to contact the next of kin. If you're unable to contact them, call the casualty section so we can hold up the telegram. Do you have all the information, Sergeant?"

"Yes, sir."

"Very well, Sergeant. Good luck and have a good day."

"Yes, sir," Spiller said, hanging up the phone. His eyes widened. Spiller looked across the room at Chief Petty Officer Johnson.

"Chief, I have my first KIA."

"So I heard."

"I'd better call the courthouse in Farmington and get Gunny Pierce so I can use the car."

"You don't have time, Spiller. Pierce has only been gone 30 minutes. It'll take him another hour to get there, and by the time he gets back your telegram will be sent."

"What should I do?"

"Take your own car and keep the mileage. Uncle Sam will reimburse you for gas," said the chief.

As Spiller stood, he hit his coffee cup.

"Damn!" he exclaimed. "Where are the paper towels, Chief? I've made a hell of a mess."

The chief reached in his desk drawer and handed Spiller some towels. After cleaning the desk, Spiller grabbed the coffee-stained casualty card and headed for the door. The chief looked over the top of his newspaper at Spiller.

"Good luck, son."

As Sergeant Spiller drove the 20-mile stretch to Chaffee, he thought to himself, "I've got to find a minister. Shouldn't be that hard to find one. Chaffee isn't that big a town. Boy, Gunny Pierce sure has timing. He was going to break me in on three or four of these before I went by myself. Man, they didn't even mention casualty calls in recruiters school. This damned tape deck! Can't buy anything that works anymore. Probably gook made. I should've kept my old Chevy. I guess the minister will know where the address is. The family will know as soon as they see us what's happened. I wonder how they'll react. Let's see, I'll step out of the car, snap to attention, and just say it. I'll think about something else when I tell them. That's what I'll do. I'll just block it out. Damned Gunny. Of all times to be gone."

Sergeant Spiller took a deep breath as he read the sign: Chaffee – Population 2100. A few blocks into town Spiller spotted a church.

"There's one. I lucked out."

Quickly, he got out of the car and entered the church. At the far end of the room he saw a priest dressed in black. As he approached the back of the room, the priest turned and smiled.

"Good morning, Sergeant."

"Good morning, sir. I have a casualty notification to make and I was wondering if you would accompany me, sir."

"Oh, my. Who is it?" he queried with sad surprise.

"John Williams, sir," Spiller replied.

"Has he been wounded, Sergeant?"

"No, sir. He's been killed in action."

The priest paused for a moment. "Sergeant Spiller, I'd be glad to accompany you, but I believe the Williams family is Protestant."

"That's right, sir. They are Protestant. Well, could you direct me to a Protestant church in town?"

"I can, Sergeant, but the pastor is out of town today."

"Are there any other churches in town?"

"The closest church is about six miles from here."

"What time is it, sir?"

"It's 11:30, Sergeant."

"Could you give me directions to the home?"

Spiller thanked the priest, then left. As he passed through the churchyard, he noticed that the sign on top of the bulletin board was still lighted. It read: "Catholic Church."

Spiller perspired as he read the house numbers, 109, 206 . . . there it is, 209 Mary Ann Drive. He parked the car on the street directly in front of the house. Reaching for the casualty card, he opened the car door and slowly got out.

With his back to the house, he heard a voice. "Johnny! Johnny, you're home!"

Sergeant Spiller turned quickly. Looking up at him was a slightly heavy-set woman with silver-gray streaks in her hair.

"I thought you were Johnny. You're not John."

The expression on her face changed to sadness. Her eyes narrowed and filled with tears.

"Oh, my God! What's wrong? What's wrong?"

Spiller's lip quivered. "Are you Mrs. Ralph Williams?"

"Yes. What's wrong?"

Spiller snapped his six-foot frame to attention.

"Mrs. Williams, as a Representative of the President of the United States and the Commandant of the Marine Corps, it is my duty to inform you that your son, John Williams, was killed in action on April 27, 1967, in the Republic of South Vietnam in the defense of the United States of America."

Sobbing uncontrollably, Mrs. Williams fell into his arms. Spiller stood rigid with both arms around her staring straight ahead. He tried to control his emotions as she spoke. "I thought you were my son. He was due home any time."

"Ma'am, ma'am, let's go up to the house."

"Okay," she replied softly, and he walked with her to the front porch. As they sat in the porch swing, Mrs. Williams questioned him.

"When will they bring him home?"

"It'll be 10 to 14 days, ma'am."

"Where will they send him?"

"Whichever funeral home you request, ma'am. Headquarters Marine Corps will be sending you a telegram this afternoon to confirm your son's death. I'll have to send a telegram requesting a military escort and the funeral home you choose. We'll give a full military funeral, if you request it."

"He was coming home any time," Mrs. Williams cried while she rocked back and forth, both hands clasped in her lap. Spiller gazed across the yard trying to think of something to say that would help. His thoughts were interrupted when a young boy about ten years old came running up the sidewalk. Spotting Spiller, the boy smiled.

"Hi there," called out Spiller as the boy came toward him.

The boy stopped at the top step of the porch abruptly. "What's the matter, Grandma?" he looked at Spiller then back to his grandmother.

The smile disappeared from the boy's face.

Mrs. Williams whispered, "We need to find Grandpa, Billy. Do you remember how to get to the construction site."

"I think so."

"Go with this Sergeant, and find Grandpa."

Innocently the boy followed Spiller to his car.

They drove out of Chaffee into the countryside where they came upon an open field that had recently been cleared. At the far end of it, two men worked busily on a caterpillar tractor.

Spiller picked up the casualty card as he emerged from the car.

"Billy, you stay here."

As he made his way across the field, Spiller was unsteady with each step slipping and sliding in the mud. His patent leather shoes and uniform trousers became blotted with brown spots from the knees down. At the same time golden sparkles surrounded him from the reflection of the sun against his belt buckle, buttons, and Marine Corps emblems on his dress blue uniform. When Spiller was within 20 feet of the tractor, an older man looked up and acknowledged his presence.

"May I help you?" he asked.

"Yes, sir. I'm looking for John Williams."

"That's him right there," he said nodding at Williams who was up to his elbows in grease and continued to work as though he'd heard nothing.

"Mr. Williams?"

"My son's dead, isn't he?" he inquired with tear-filled eyes as both arms dropped like lead weights from the caterpillar engine.

Spiller snapped to attention and the mud splat in all directions from under his feet.

"Sir, as a Representative of the President of the United States and the Commandant of the Marine Corps, it is my duty to inform you that your son, John Williams, was killed in action in the Republic of South Vietnam in the defense of the United States of America."

Mr. Williams sat back and hung his head as if all life had been drained from his body.

As Spiller drove back to the office, he couldn't get the Williamses out of his mind. That morning, when he pulled up to the front of the their house, Mrs. Williams's son was still alive. For a moment, just for a moment, as Spiller walked across the field that beautiful spring morning, Spiller felt like a death angel. Until he reached Mr. Williams, young John Williams was doing fine and would be home soon. But the moment Mr. Williams acknowledged Spiller's presence, the closer Spiller came to him, the closer Williams's son came to death, and when Spiller finally said it, there was nothing else to say.

Spiller walked into the office and plopped into the chair.

"How did it go?" asked Chief Johnson.

Spiller sat quietly for a moment then spoke almost inaudibly. "She thought I was her son."

"My God!"

"And the look on his dad's face. It was like everything was drained from his body. My God, he looked like he'd worked his ass off all his life, and then this had to happen. I feel like I've ruined their lives."

"You can't feel that way, Spiller. You were just delivering the message," Johnson tried to reassure him.

"Yeah, Chief, I suppose you're right. I thought of that, but it doesn't make me feel any better."

"Hell, go on home, take a hot shower, and have a couple of beers. You'll be all right in the morning."

"I think I'll do just that. See you in the morning."

"Okay. Have one for me."

"No, Chief, I think I'll have two," replied Spiller. He slammed the door shut behind him.

The next morning Spiller returned to the office and found Pierce at the desk seated with his arms folded across his lap.

"I hear you had a tough one."

"Yeah, you can say that again."

"You need to find out from the family if they want a military funeral so we can send the telegram today."

"Yes, sir. I was going to leave about 0900 so I won't be getting there too early, if that's okay," Spiller replied sullenly.

"Snap out of it," yelled Pierce. "You're always kicking yourself in the ass. You were just delivering a message. It's your job. We take care of our own. Think of it that way. If you start blaming yourself or letting these calls get you down, you'll be crazy in six months. Understand?"

"Okay, Gunny! Okay."

"All right then, get out there, and take care of that family, then get back here. We have a quota to fill."

As Spiller drove he thought about what Pierce said. "We have to take care of our own." They had nine counties in Missouri and two counties in Illinois. In addition, they assisted in funeral details with the Poplar Bluff and Benton recruiting stations. Poplar Bluff had 18 counties southwest of their area. Benton had 14 counties on the east in Illinois. Spiller wondered just how many of "our own" they'd have to take care of.

Spiller pulled up in front of the Williamses' residence in a government car. This time nobody ran out to meet him. He knocked on the door.

"Good morning, Sergeant," Williams said solemnly, and he opened the door.

"Good morning, sir."

Williams led Spiller into the living room and sat on the couch by his wife. Spiller sat in a chair across from them. The Williamses sat silently. Their eyes were red and swollen.

"Mr. Williams, we'd like to know what funeral home you'd like your son to be sent to."

Mrs. Williams whimpered as her husband spoke. "Jackson Funeral Home."

"Is that located in Chaffee?"

"Yes."

"We'll request a military escort to accompany your son. Do you want a military funeral?"

"Yes, sir. I think he'd like that."

"We provide the casket and vault and a military headstone if you request."

"That'll be fine, Sergeant."

"I'll send the telegram today. It'll be about ten days before your son will be returned. If you need any assistance whatsoever, please feel free to contact us." He walked over to shake both their hands then left.

Two weeks later Spiller and Pierce sat sipping coffee and discussing quotas with four other recruiters in the recruiting office. Two recruiters were from Popular Bluff, Missouri, and two others were from Benton, Illinois. Gunnery Sergeant Maze was the non-commissioned officer in charge of Poplar Bluff. A 16-year veteran, and a cook in the Marines, Maze was always cracking jokes. His partner, Staff Sergeant Roberts, was a 12-year veteran artillery-man and a much more sober person. First Sergeant Ledue was the non-commissioned officer in charge of the Benton recruiting station. He was a 22-year veteran infantryman and appeared to be a strictly-by-the-book Marine. His partner, Sergeant Beck, had 10 years in the Corps and was also infantry.

"We have our May and June quotas filled," said Ledue. "Only need two for the July quota. How about you, Maze?"

"We got May's filled. We need two for June and two for July. We've got three career days left, so we'll make it. Damn, my nuts itch."

Pierce snickered then spoke up. "We'd better get going. It's a 45-minute drive to Chaffee."

They grabbed their caps and gloves as they stood, then everyone headed for the cars.

"We'll follow you," yelled Maze.

"Okay," replied Pierce as he and Spiller got into another car.

An hour later, the three government cars pulled in front of Jackson Funeral Home in Chaffee. The recruiters squared their caps and put on their gloves as they emerged from the car.

"All right, let's go into the lobby and line up in a column. We'll file in a column and sit in the front row. The funeral director said the services aren't going to be long," said Pierce.

The Marines lined in a column. Spiller stood behind Pierce and in front of Maze. "Amazing Grace" played softly throughout the funeral home and the scent of fresh flowers filled the air. All eyes were on the Marines as the music stopped. The Marines snapped to attention, marched down the center aisle, and stood at attention in the front row.

"Ready, seats," snapped Pierce in a low voice.

The Marines sat at attention. The pastor spoke. "No greater man than the man who lays down his life for a friend."

Spiller just tried to black out everything. This was the first funeral he had attended since his father died. That was when Spiller was eight years old. His father was the first dead person he had ever seen and Spiller was scared to death when he saw him. Since that time Spiller hadn't gone into a funeral home. But this time, when he entered the funeral home, Williams's mother saw him, and again it was as if he'd taken her son's place. It was probably all in his head, but that was the way Spiller felt. Like Pierce said, maybe he was too young for the job.

The funeral home emptied as the Marines took their places on each side of the casket.

"Ready, men? Let's go," said Pierce.

The Marines lifted the casket and walked out the door, down the steps, and into the crowd. Slowly they made their way to the open door of the hearse. They placed the casket inside and returned to their cars. Maze and Roberts jumped in the back seat. Pierce drove and Spiller sat on the passenger side.

Maze spoke as the motorcade pulled out. "Well, we'll plant this one, and see if we can recruit one to replace him. The name of the game is to stay ahead. We got to recruit more than we plant. My nuts itch, I think I got the crabs."

Pierce snickered.

Spiller just shook his head. Roberts spoke up. "Stay away from me if you have the crabs."

"They don't bite much," Maze laughed.

Ten minutes went by and the motorcade stopped on a narrow gravel road in the cemetery. The Marines quickly got out of the car and lined up three on each side of the hearse door. The funeral director opened the hearse, and the Marines carefully pulled the casket out. Slowly they marched to the burial site. Family and friends followed close behind. Placing the casket on the stand, Pierce and Maze took positions at each end of the casket. Spiller and the other Marines hurried for the car. Each grabbed a rifle and took a position some 200 feet from the gravesite. The minister prayed, then Pierce nodded.

"Half right, hau!" snapped Ledue.

"Port arms."

"Ready! Aim! Fire!"

The shots ran out and echoed across the cemetary.

"Ready! Aim! Fire!"

"Ready! Aim! Fire!"

A high school student had volunteered to play taps. As he played those in attendance, some sobbing loudly, bowed their heads.

When the taps ended, Pierce and Maze folded the flag. Maze handed the flag to Pierce and saluted. Pierce walked to the family and stood at attention.

"We present this flag to you in recognition of your son who gave his life in the defense of the United States of America."

Pierce bent over and placed the flag in Mrs. Williams's lap. He stood erect, saluted, then turned and walked away.

13
Plant One, Enlist One

For the next two weeks the recruiters were busy with paperwork. Spring and summer quotas were easy to fill because a number of high school graduates enlisted at that time. Spiller and Pierce had filled May, June, and July quotas and were working hard on August and September. Spiller was gathering literature and preparing for the last high school career day of the year. Pierce was typing out enlistment forms for the applicants he had recruited. He'd peck out three or four words on the typewriter, then cuss for five minutes. Meanwhile, Spiller left the office and drove to Fredericktown High School.

When Spiller arrived he grabbed the briefcase full of literature and made his way down the hallway to the gymnasium. The stage was located at one end of the gym where five folding chairs were placed in a semicircle. The podium and microphone sat directly in front. In the center of the gym floor, 60 folding chairs were lined in rows. Close to the walls on each side were tables with cardboard signs taped to them. Each sign designated the name of the branch of service.

Spiller walked to the table with the sign that read, "Marine Corps." There he neatly placed books and pamphlets.

"Hello there," said a tall thin man with slightly grey hair. "I'm Jack Palmer, the guidance counselor."

"Hi, Mr. Palmer. I'm Sergeant Spiller."

"We have a few minutes before we begin, but what we planned to do was give each recruiter five minutes to make a presentation then let the students come to the tables of their interest."

"That'll be fine, sir. If I could, I'd like to speak last."

"That's fine, Sergeant. I'll be introducing each of you. I don't believe anyone can complain about you going last."

The rest of the recruiters arrived. They each arranged literature on their tables, and took a seat on the stage. As the students filed into the gymnasium, Spiller sat erect in his full dress blues. The Army recruiter went first. Nervously, he thumbed through a booklet and explained the many guaranteed programs the Army offered. The Navy recruiter stood and spoke about the nuclear and electronic programs. He was followed by the Air Force recruiter, who explained the pilot programs. Spiller went next.

Spiller stood and walked to the podium. He looked out over the student body, scanning from left to right. While some students watched, others whispered, and still others giggled among themselves.

Spiller paused for a moment. "The first thing I want each and every one of you to understand is that we don't guarantee or promise anything."

He looked over the crowd. The students became very quiet.

"We are the greatest fighting force on the face of the earth. We are the only fighting force that serves on land, at sea, and in the air. Now we have every occupational field that any other branch of the service has, but we don't promise you an occupation. You have to earn it. We have a 120-day delay program with a two-, three-, or four-year enlistment. If you want to be a part of our team, I'll be at my table over in the corner. If you want promises, go to some other table."

Spiller walked back to his chair. He sat proud and erect.

The counselor walked to the podium and said, "We're going to dismiss in a couple of minutes. If you're interested in talking with any of the recruiters, do so at that time. If not, return to your classroom."

The recruiters walked to their respective tables. The students were dismissed and those interested gathered around the tables. Several grabbed at the literature placed on Spiller's table. Four baby-faced, flat-topped boys, wearing the usual, blue jeans, tennis shoes and sweatshirts approached the side of the table.

"Sergeant, we want to join the Marines."

As the boys filled out forms, Spiller recalled a day in October 1962 when a young Harry Spiller had just mailed a letter at the post office. As he came out of the building and started down the steps, there were two Marines in full dress blues. Harry looked them up and down, and as he did, he thought, "Man, it would be neat to come back home and parade down the street looking like that. Wow, look at the medals."

Spiller was completely mesmerized by the glamor of the uniform, and when he found out the Marine Corps offered a 120-day delay program, he decided to join their ranks instead of the Navy's. Since he wasn't 18, he needed his mother's permission to go. Spiller blasted into the house. "Mom! Mom! I'm joining the Marines!"

Spiller's mother, a small woman weighing 100 pounds, set a pot of potatoes on the stove as she fixed her eyes on Spiller. "What?"

"I'm joining the Marines! But you have to sign a parent's consent since I'm not 18 yet! Mom, you ought to see the uniform. Wow!"

"Son, you were going into the Navy. You don't want to go into the Marines. They have to do all that fighting. What if we have a war? Why don't you think about it?"

"I'm a man, Mom! I want to fight for my country if I have to. They're tough. I'm tough. Besides there isn't going to be any war. I want to make something of myself. I want you to be proud of me, Mom. Please. After that, Spiller counted the days until finally, it was time to report to boot camp.

Spiller entered the office all smiles.

"We made August quota, Gunny. I got four today."

Pierce sat at his desk frowning.

"What's the matter?" asked Spiller.

Pierce paused for a moment. "We have another KIA."

"Damn! Damn! Where at this time?"

"St. Genevieve. We only have a couple of hours to get up there before headquarters releases the telegram. Put your gear up. We're going to have to step on it."

Spiller and Pierce made their way up Route 61. Both smoked one cigarette after another. Finally, they arrived in downtown St. Genevieve, and Pierce pulled up in front of the post office.

"I'll be back in a minute."

Spiller grunted. It was minutes before he saw Pierce coming back toward him.

"They live on Route D. The third house on the right." He seated himself behind the wheel, and they drove away.

"You want me to tell them?" asked Spiller.

"No, I'll tell them," Pierce said.

"I'll do it, Gunny, if you want."

"I said I'd do it. It isn't going to bother me half as much to tell them he's dead as it will be to tell them how he was killed."

"How was he killed?"

"Read the card."

Spiller picked up the casualty card and began reading. "L/Corporal Jack Simmons, killed in action May 5, 1967, Quang Tri. Killed in an ambush by his own troops."

"Oh, shit!"

Pierce turned onto Route D. They passed the first house, then the second, and finally pulled into the driveway of the Simmons's family. To the left was a two-story farmhouse. To the right was a large barn with farm equipment on each side of the barn door. Spiller and Pierce got out of the car, squared their caps, and walked toward the house.

"Can I help you?" a voice echoed from behind them.

They turned. A tall man wearing bib overalls, a flannel shirt, and a farm hat, stood in the doorway of the barn. Spiller and Pierce stood for a moment then walked toward him. The farmer chewed on a wad of tobacco a couple of times and than spat toward the ground.

"Can I help you?" he asked again.

"Are you Mr. Simmons?" Pierce inquired.

"Sure am," he replied.

"Mr. Simmons, as a Representative of the President of the United States and the Commandant of the Marine Corps, it is my duty to inform you that your son, Lance Corporal Jack Simmons, was killed in action on May 5, 1967, in the defense of the United States of America."

Simmons eyes narrowed as he quickly chewed his tobacco then spit. After a moment he spoke up. "You must be mistaken. My boy just got there."

"I'm sorry, Mr. Simmons. There's no mistake."

The farmer reached for his hat, removed it from his head, then wiped his brow. Placing the hat back on his head, he mumbled, "We'd better go in the house and tell the wife."

The three walked across the yard to the back door and into the house. A heavy-set woman stood in the middle of the room wiping her hands on a dish towel. She glanced at her husband's disturbed face.

"What's the matter?" she asked.

Mr. Simmons looked up with tear-filled eyes. "It's Jack, Mom. It's Jack."

"He isn't dead, is he? Oh God, no!"

Mr. Simmons grabbed her. They embraced each other as Mrs. Simmons cried, "Oh, God, no! Not my baby!"

Suddenly the kitchen door opened and a teenage girl entered the room.

"Dad? Mom?" Seeing the strangers, she asked, "What's going on here?"

"It's Jack, honey. He's been killed in action." The young girl stood horrified. "No, not Jack, not Jack!" Her screams filled the room as she turned and ran out of the room. Mrs. Simmons followed closely behind.

Simmons took a handkerchief from this back pocket and wiped his eyes. "Gentlemen, come on into the living room." The room was modestly furnished.

Spiller stared at a picture hanging on the wall of Jack Simmons in his dress blues. To the left was a picture taken during World War II of Jack's father in his military uniform. To the right of the pictures was a picture of the American flag. From where they stood the men could hear loud angry voices, filled with pain and anguish. Spiller could see Simmons was fighting to keep back the tears. "How did it happen?" he whispered.

It was minutes before Spiller could speak. Finally he managed to say, "Your son was killed in an ambush."

"He was ambushed by his own troops," interrupted Pierce. "We don't have all the details."

"Oh my God!" yelled Simmons as he bowed his head and sobbed into his hands. In a moment he looked up with a confused, angry look on his face.

"I thought the Marines were good fighters. Supposed to know what's going on. Killed by his own goddamned men." Silence filled the room.

"Now, Mr. Simmons, take it easy. We don't have all the details, but things like this can happen in a war. Your son's commanding officer will contact you personally to give you all the details."

At this point Mrs. Simmons entered the room and sat beside her husband on the couch.

"Honey, don't get mad at them," she managed to say between halting sobs. "They're only doing their jobs."

"He was killed by his own men. His own damned men!"

"I know," Mrs. Simmons began to cry again. "God has taken him. It's His will," she said mournfully.

"When will they send him home?" he asked.

"It'll be 10 to 14 days, sir," replied Pierce.

"We'll have your son sent to whatever funeral home you request. If you'd like, we'll give your son a full military funeral."

"He'd like that," Mr. Simmons said in a low voice. "Have him sent to the Mitchell Funeral Home. We want a full military funeral."

"We also provide a military escort, if you like."

"Yes, yes, we want the escort."

"We'll send the telegram today, sir. Shortly, you'll be receiving a telegram confirming your son's death from Marine Corps headquarters. Now, if you have no further questions, we'll be leaving."

Spiller handed Mr. Simmons a business card. "If you need us for anything, just call."

"Thank you, Sergeant. Thank you both for being so kind."

Neither man spoke on the way back to the office. Spiller thought about his two casualty notifications: the mother that thought he was her son and the Marine that was killed by his own men. He remembered his own words earlier that morning. He'd told those high school seniors the Marines were the best fighting force in the world. Now three hours later, he and Pierce were telling a family their son had been killed by his own men. Maze had said it was a game – plant one, enlist one. Spiller wondered just how long this game would go on, and just how long he could continue to play that game.

For the next couple of weeks Spiller and Pierce traded off days on the road, going from town to town in the eleven-county area. The four seniors who'd applied at career day in Fredericktown, passed their physicals in St. Louis. The recruiters had locked in the August quota. Spiller had taken one application from a walk-in, and Pierce had picked up two while on the road.

It was Friday, May 16, 1967. It was Spiller's turn on the road. He checked his briefcase to make sure he had plenty of enlistment forms. He closed the case and sat back to finish a cup of coffee.

"Harry, when you get to St. Genevieve, stop by the funeral home and make sure everything's going all right. If you have any problems, give me a call," said Pierce.

Spiller took a last swallow of coffee and placed his cup on the desk. "Okay. Will do."

Two hours later Spiller pulled up to the funeral home in St. Genevieve. As Spiller approached the front door, he was greeted by a doorman.

"Good morning, Sergeant."

"Good morning, sir. Is the funeral director in?"

"Yes, sir. He is."

A tall, well-dressed man walked up to Spiller and extended his hand. "Sergeant, I'm Ralph Mitchell."

"Yes, sir, I'm Sergeant Spiller. I came up to make sure everything was okay."

"Come with me, please."

Spiller followed the director into the east room of the funeral home. The gray military casket lay centered at the far end of the room, close to the back wall. The American flag draped the casket, and on it sat a portrait of Jack Simmons in his dress blue uniform. On each side of the casket were baskets of flowers.

"Where's the escort, sir?"

"He's in the back room."

"I'd like to talk to him, sir."

"Follow me."

The director led Spiller to the back office. There sat an unshaven Marine sipping a cup of coffee.

"Hi, Sarge."

"Hi, hell! Why aren't you dressed and at your post?"

"Well, Sarge, nobody's here so I figured I'd take it easy as long as I could."

"Corporal, you get your ass cleaned up and dressed and get in there by that casket. If I find out you've left your post for one second before that family leaves, I'll have your ass. Now hurry up! The family will be here any minute."

"Yes, sir."

"Is there anything I can do for you before the funeral?" Spiller asked the funeral director.

"I think we can take care of everything, Sergeant," replied Mr. Mitchell.

"Very well, sir."

Spiller left the funeral home and headed for the car. The doorman called out to him. "Sergeant! Sergeant! You have a phone call."

"Thank you." Spiller slammed the car door and walked back inside. He picked up the phone and said, "Sergeant Spiller."

"This is Pierce, Harry. I have a casualty call for you. Just wounded, just wounded."

"Where at?"

"St. Genevieve."

"Wait a minute." He turned to Mitchell and asked, "Sir, do you have a piece of paper?"

"But of course." Mitchell walked to the back office and returned with a note pad.

"Okay, Gunny, go ahead."

"PFC Tom Bowman, wounded May 14, 1967, stepped on a land mine. Has wounds to both arms, chest, and face. He lost his left leg. Condition: critical. Next of kin, Jesse Bowman, Rt. 2, St. Genevieve. You got it?"

"I got it, Gunny."

"Is everything okay at the funeral home?"

"Everything's okay."

"Good luck on the call."

"Thanks. I'll see you this afternoon."

"Okay."

Spiller hung up the phone. The doorman and funeral director were standing close behind him. He turned facing the two.

"Sergeant, we don't have another?" asked the funeral director.

Spiller interrupted, "No, just wounded. He's in bad shape, but alive."

"May we ask who it is?"

"Tom Bowman, sir. Do you know where the family lives?"

"Yes, sir. Go up to the stop sign going east, take a right, follow that road out of town. About two miles out on the left side of the road, you'll see a red brick home sitting on a hill. The mailbox is located at the edge of the road just before you get to the drive."

"Thank you, sir."

Spiller got into the car and drove until he spotted the mailbox then turned into the driveway. Two middle-aged women stood on each side of a car parked under a carport. Spiller stopped. As he emerged from his car, the woman on the driver's side of the car screamed and ran into the house. The other stood with her hands over her mouth to muffle her cry.

"That was Mrs. Bowman, wasn't it?" Spiller asked, trying to sound casual.

"Yes. Is Tommy dead?"

"Please, I must speak to Mrs. Bowman."

The woman hesitated then said, "Follow me." As they entered the kitchen, Spiller found Mrs. Bowman seated at the table in tears.

"Mrs. Bowman, your son isn't dead. He isn't dead. He's been wounded, but he's alive."

Spiller walked over to her and placed his arm around her shoulders. "He isn't dead," assured Spiller. He held the woman in his arms as she broke down sobbing in relief. Finally the sobs subsided, and she managed to utter, "We were just going to the funeral home to see Jack Simmons. When I saw you. . . ."

"Where's your husband?"

"He should be home any time now. How bad is Tommy?"

"He's in critical condition, ma'am."

"Oh, my God!"

"Now take it easy. He's alive."

Mr. Bowman burst into the room. "Oh, God! Oh, my God!"

"He isn't dead, Mr. Bowman. He isn't dead."

Bowman walked to the table and sat beside his wife.

"How bad is he?"

"Mr. Bowman, he stepped on a land mine. He has wounds to both arms, his face, chest, and he lost his left leg."

"Oh, my God!" Bowman bellowed. Tears rolled down his face.

"His condition is critical and the prognosis is critical," Spiller continued.

Bowman and his wife cried loudly.

"I want a glass casket made so we can see his entire body," sobbed Mr. Bowman.

"Hold on, Mr. Bowman. Your son may be in critical condition, but he isn't dead yet. We have the finest doctors in the world in the military. If there is any possibility of his making it, he has the best chance because he's in good hands."

Bowman wiped his eyes then reached over and took his wife's hand.

"You're telling us everything?"

"Yes, sir. Every bit of information I have. Updates will come from your son's commanding officer. Now, if you don't have any further questions, I'll be leaving."

"I guess we just wait."

"Yes, sir, but remember, your son is in good hands."

Spiller pulled up to the courthouse in St. Genevieve. He took a deep breath then wiped the sweat from his forehead. He reached over the seat, grabbed his briefcase, and headed for the basement of the court-house. Inside he placed his briefcase on a wooden table and slumped down in a chair. He was exhausted. His eyes came to rest on two teen-age boys standing near the table.

"Can I help you, gentlemen?"

"Yes, sir. We want to joint the Marine Corps," replied one boy.

"How old are you?" asked Spiller, looking thoughtfully at the boys.

"We're both 18, sir."

Spiller looked at the boy on his right.

"What's your name?"

"Clyde White."

"And yours?"

"Bill Norman."

"Do either of you know Jack Simmons?"

"Yes, sir. Well, we've heard of him," replied Bill.

"Did you know he was just killed in Vietnam?"

"Yes, sir," they both replied.

Spiller sat on the bench. He stared at the floor for a few seconds, then looked up.

"Do you know where Mitchell Funeral Home is?"

"Yes, sir."

"Well, you walk down to the funeral home and pay Jack a visit. When you're finished, if you still want to join, I'll be here."

"Well, sir, why do you want us to do that?" asked Clyde.

"If you want to join, just do what I tell you. I'll be here, if you still want to join."

"Okay, sir."

A while later the sound of running feet distracted Spiller from his paperwork.

"Sergeant, we're back."

"Well, do you still want to join?" Spiller asked.

"Yes, sir, we do."

"Did you go to the funeral home?"

"Yes, sir."

"And?"

"Sir, he died for his country. We want to fight for our country, too. Die for it if necessary."

"Do you parents know you're down here?"

"Yes, sir."

"They have no objections?"

"Mine said it was up to me," replied Bill.

"Mine weren't thrilled about it, but said they wouldn't stop me if that's what I really wanted to do."

"Sit down, gentlemen. I have some papers for you to sign."

Spiller fumbled through his briefcase. "Guess we'll play a game today," he mumbled as he pulled out the enlistment forms.

"Excuse me, sir?"

"Nothing, nothing. I was just thinking to myself."

For the next half hour, Spiller assisted the two teenagers in filling out the forms. After completing the enlistment kits, Spiller returned to the recruiting office in Cape Girardeau.

"How did the call go?"

"Okay, I guess. The family was pretty upset. They had him dead, but I think I got them settled down. I just hope he doesn't die."

"Me, too."

"I picked up two more, believe it or not. They were waiting for me at the courthouse."

"That's great! If they make it, we'll only need one more for September quota."

"Yeah, just one more."

The next day the two government cars pulled up in front of the funeral home. Once again the recruiters got out of the cars, squared their caps, and put on their white gloves. After walking into the parlor of the funeral home, the Marines lined up, and marched to the front row in the east room.

"Ready, seats," snapped Pierce in a low voice.

The Marines sat at attention as the minister prayed and gave a short sermon. Each row of people passed by the casket as they left the room. The Marines lined up on each side of the casket, lifted the casket, and placed it in the hearse. They moved with the rest of the motorcade across town to the Catholic Church. Once again the Marines lined three on each side at the back of the hearse. Once the family was out of their car, the Marines lifted the casket and carried it into the church and down the long aisle. There they placed it in front of the pulpit. The recruiters sat at attention in the front pew. Spiller sat between Maze and Ledue. The priest began to read from a book in Latin. He then placed something in his mouth. He repeated that same action twice. Maze nudged Spiller.

"We could've brought our lunch if we knew he was going to bring his," he whispered.

You crazy son-of-a-bitch, Spiller thought, trying to keep a straight face.

As the priest conducted the service, the people knelt, then stood, or sat. The Marines, none of whom were Catholic, tried to follow. When the mourners stood, the Marines knelt. When the mourners sat, the Marines stood.

Finally Pierce spoke quietly. "Everyone just sit at attention."

Everyone was red-faced, except Maze, who was snickering at least loudly enough for Spiller to hear. When the services finally ended, everyone filed out. The recruiters marched to the casket and took their positions. They carried the flag-draped casket to the hearse and returned to their cars.

"Gunny, did you hear Maze?"

"No. Why? What did he do?"

"He said the priest brought his lunch so we should've brought ours. That crazy fucker was trying to get me to laugh, and he damned near did!"

Pierce shook his head. "He's crazy!"

The motorcade pulled into the cemetery and came to a stop. The Marines lined up, lifted the casket, and carried it to the burial site. Pierce and Ledue took positions at the ends of the casket. The other Marines hurried back to the car, grabbed their rifles, and took positions for the firing squad.

When the priest was finished, Pierce gave a nod.

"Half right, hau!" ordered Maze.

"Ready! Aim! Fire! Ready! Aim! Fire! Ready! Aim! Fire!"

As the taps sounded, shots echoed across the cemetery.

14

Adventure or Death

For three weeks Pierce and Spiller were kept busy typing out enlistment kits. Pierce was in a good mood. His recruiting time was almost over, and the orders he'd been waiting for finally came. He was to go to Vietnam. That made him happy, and to put the icing on the cake, St. Louis had called to let him know his replacement would be reporting on June 15. Spiller was happy for Pierce. It always seemed to bother him that Harry had been to Vietnam and he hadn't. He'd been in World War II and Korea, so it really shouldn't have bothered him, but he was more like a father to Spiller than the gunny, and Spiller guessed a father could not let his son get ahead of him. Spiller was really sorry to see him leave. Spiller had a lot of respect for Pierce, not just as a Marine, but also as a man. The feelings they had for each other were very special. Pierce always seemed to know when to talk to Spiller and how to give him a lift when he needed one.

It was the first week of June and Pierce was working on an enlistment kit. "Hey, Harry, why don't you go get us a sandwich?"

"You buying, Gunny?"

"Hell, yes. Don't I always buy?"

Spiller laughed. "No, I bought a couple of weeks ago. Besides, you make more money than I do, and I have to go in the rain."

Pierce threw a five dollar bill on the desk.

"Just go get the sandwiches. I'll take a cheeseburger and fries."

"Just one? I'm gonna get two. I'm hungry."

"Hell, yes! Why don't you get three since I'm buying."

Spiller headed for the door. "I would, but you didn't give me enough money," he laughed.

A short time later Spiller walked back into the office carrying two sacks filled with sandwiches and fries.

"Let's eat," said Spiller, placing the sack on the desk.

Pierce sat quietly as Spiller reached in and grabbed a sandwich.

"Guess what?" Pierce mumbled.

"What?" replied Spiller.

"We have two casualty calls."

Spiller looked at Pierce for moment.

"KIAs?" he asked.

"No, wounded. Both are minor."

Spiller took a deep breath.

"I'll be relieved of all this in a month, so I'll make the calls."

"I'll make them, Gunny. You've had your share, and besides they aren't bad." Spiller took a bite of his sandwich, then laughed, "Besides, Gunny, you need to take it easy in your old age."

Pierce, with a warpath look on his face, looked eye to eye at Spiller.

"Listen, youngster, you're getting cocky since I got my orders."

"Now, Gunny take it easy. I was only joking. I'll finish my sandwich and go make the calls, okay?"

Pierce turned and started eating his sandwich.

Spiller finished and threw the sacks in the wastecan. He picked up the casualty cards, and read them. PFC Guy Wilkins, wounded June 6, 1967, Da Nang. Rifle shot to the right shoulder. Condition: good. Prognosis: good. Next of kin: Ralph Wilkins, 207 7th Street, Fredericktown."

"Lance Corporal Benny Smith, wounded June 7, 1967. Fragment wound to the left leg. Condition: good. Prognosis: good. Next of kin: William Smith, Route 4, Ironton, Missouri."

Spiller grabbed his cap and headed for the door. "I'd better get going and get this over with."

"Good luck. If you have a problem, give me a call."

"Okay, Gunny."

Spiller drove to Fredericktown and parked in front of the post office. After receiving directions to 7th Street, he drove to the Wilkinses' home. He parked the car, walked to the front door, and knocked.

A woman in her mid-forties, wearing a full-length short sleeve dress, her hair in rollers, opened the door. Another woman, Mrs. Wilkins, walked into the living room. When she saw Spiller, she bellowed, "Oh, my God!" She then fell to the floor.

"Ma'am? Ma'am?" Spiller said excitedly. He quickly knelt down to feel her pulse, placing two fingers to her throat.

Turning to woman with her hair in rollers, Spiller tensely asked, "Do you know this lady?"

"Yes. Is her son dead?" she inquired in a frantic voice.

"No. No, he isn't. Does she have heart trouble?"

"No, not that I know of."

"Help me get her up."

Spiller lifted the small woman into his arms and carried her to a couch in the living room.

"Get a cold washcloth," Spiller ordered.

Rushing for the bathroom, the woman returned shortly with the cloth. As Spiller placed it on Mrs. Wilkins's forehead, she opened her eyes and moaned.

"Ma'am? Ma'am? Your son isn't dead. He's all right."

It took minutes for the words to sink in. She reached for the cloth and rubbed it over her face, then slowly sat up.

"Are you all right?" Spiller asked.

"What's wrong then if he's okay?" she asked. "Why are you here?"

"He's received a shoulder wound, but he's in good condition. He's okay," he assured her.

"Thank God. Thank God. When I saw you, I thought he was dead."

"He's all right. Are you?"

"Yes, I'm okay," said Mrs. Wilkins, wiping the tears from her cheeks.

"I'm sorry, Sergeant, you must think me a foolish woman but he is all I have."

"No, ma'am. It's understandable. I would've probably done the same. Your son was wounded in Da Nang. His condition is good and the prognosis is good."

The other woman sat down beside Mrs. Wilkins and put her arm around her. "Are you okay?"

"Yes. Yes, I am."

"Mrs. Wilkins, if you have no further questions, I'll be going. You'll get a letter from your son's commanding officer, giving details about your son's condition, and I'm sure you'll be hearing from your son."

"Thank you, Sergeant. Thank you for being so kind."

Spiller smiled. "Thank you, ma'am." He closed the door softly behind him.

Spiller pulled up in front of the post office. A lady was shaking the doorknob of its front door. She mumbled to herself then turned and walked away. Spiller hurried out of the car.

"Ma'am! Ma'am!" Spiller called after her.

The lady turned and looked at Spiller.

"You talking to me?"

"Yes, ma'am. Is the post office closed?"

"Well, they're supposed to be open, but the postmaster's always leaving early." A smile played at the corner of her mouth.

"Could you tell me how to get to William Smith's residence? He lives on Route 4."

"I don't know a William Smith, but Route 4 covers the west side of the county. The highway's over there." She pointed to the highway that ran through the middle of town, and continued. "That's part of Route 4 going west."

"Thank you, ma'am."

"That's just great," he thought as he started the car and headed for the highway.

Driving out of town, he looked at the names on mailboxes, hoping to see the name, Smith. Some ten miles out of town, he spotted a country store.

"Thank God," he whispered as he pulled into the parking lot.

A man in his mid-sixties walked out of the store. The screen door slammed behind him.

"Can I help ya, son?"

"Yes, sir. I'm looking for a William Smith. He lives on Route 4."

The old man glanced around Spiller at the car. "Looks like a government car. Hasn't paid 'ees taxes, huh? Hee, hee."

"No, sir. I mean, I'm not a tax man, sir. I'm in the Marine Corps. I have a message for him about his son."

"Marine Corps, huh? Which way did you come from?"

"Ironton, sir."

"Done passed it. Go back down the road three miles. Road on the left, take it. Two miles or so, you'll come to a crick. He lives on the hill just on the other side."

"Thank you, sir."

"You're welcome, son. Be careful at the crick. The bottom's a little soft this time o' year."

Spiller looked at the old man. "You mean there's no bridge?"

"That's right, sonny. Hee, hee. You in the country now."

Spiller shook his head and drove off. He turned onto the road some three miles from the store. Within a mile the gravel turned into a dirt road with lots of potholes. Finally, he stopped in front of the creek. He got out of the car and looked back and forth at the sandy creek bottom. At the top of the hill about a quarter of a mile away was a log cabin. Beside the cabin was a red 1965 Chevrolet Impala.

"How in the hell did he get that car up there?" Spiller said out loud.

Spiller, afraid to cross the creek in the car for fear of getting stuck, crossed the creek on foot. He was halfway up the hill when a woman, carrying a broom, walked out the front door. As she placed the broom against a pillar on the front porch, she looked up. She spotted Spiller and began screaming.

"Your son's all right! He's all right!" Spiller yelled.

Mr. Smith ran out the front door.

"What's the matter? What's wrong?"

Mrs. Smith kept screaming and pointed to Spiller as he quickly walked toward the cabin.

"Mr. Smith, your son's all right."

Smith grabbed his wife.

"He's all right! Shut up!"

Upon reaching the front porch, Spiller said. "Your son's been wounded, but he's all right. He got hit in the left leg with fragments. His condition and prognosis are both good."

Mrs. Smith, both arms around her husband, sniffled a couple of times and asked, "Are they sending him home?"

"Well, ma'am, I can't answer that. You'll be receiving a letter from his commanding officer giving you full details of the incident. But from what I have here, I don't believe they'll send him home."

"Just going to leave him there until he's killed," she said and started crying again.

"Mr. Smith, I'm sure you'll be hearing from your son soon. If you don't have any questions, I'll be going."

"What good would it do. You don't seem to know anything, just go around scaring people half to death. He turned to his wife, "Come on mother, let's go into the house."

"If I can be of assistance, sir, please call." Spiller shook his head, turned and walked toward his car.

Spiller learned one thing that day. You never knew what to expect when you made a casualty call. He thought everything would be easy since the call was only for a minor wound, but he forgot that while he knew the wound was minor, the family didn't. When applicants saw them, the Marines represented adventure, excitement, and travel. On the other hand, when the parents and families saw Marines, their presence meant death.

For the next month Spiller's office didn't have any casualty calls, just general recruiting duties and filling quotas. On June 15, Pierce's replacement, Gunny Lowery, a gunnery sergeant in the aviation field, arrived. Lowery was to be promoted to first sergeant on August 1. With Pierce getting ready to go on leave, everything was in limbo. Lowery was still on leave, and the two popped in and out of the office occasionally to discuss operations. Spiller pretty much recruited by himself during the month.

The office had been invited to march in the Fourth of July parade in Cape Girardeau. The parade was advertised in the newspaper and people were asked to participate by carrying flags to show their support for the men in Vietnam. The city was expecting a big parade and a big crowd.

Spiller tightened the slings on the M-1 rifles, snapped the keepers then set them on the desk.

"Help me with this harness," ordered Pierce.

Spiller walked over and adjusted the straps on his shoulders, then he checked Lowery's to make sure they were adjusted.

"You both look good."

"What time is it?" asked Pierce.

"0830," replied Lowery.

"We need to be there at 0845. Harry, you need to take your car. We can't get these flags and all of us in one car," said Pierce.

"Okay, Gunny, I'll take the flags and guns with me."

Larry Joyner, a PFC home on leave, walked in.

"Hi, Larry," said Pierce.

"Hi, Gunny."

"Larry, this is Gunny Lowery and Sergeant Spiller. This is Larry Joyner, one of my enlistees about eight months ago."

"Larry, you wanna give me a hand?" asked Spiller.

"Sure, Sarge."

"Take these rifles, and I'll get the flags."

Spiller started out the door.

"Gunny, we'll go on down. Meet you there in a few minutes."

Spiller and Joyner loaded the car and headed down to the waterfront. After parking the car, Spiller looked around. Three antique cars were parked bumper to bumper. Aside from the drivers standing by them, the streets were empty.

"Damn! Where's everybody at? The parade starts in 15 minutes."

"I don't know," replied Joyner.

Spiller stepped out of the car and walked back to Pierce and Lowery, who had just pulled up behind him.

"Gunny, we at the right place? There's nobody here."

"This is it. Go see if you can find out what's going on."

Spiller walked over to the drivers who were standing in a huddle.

"Where's everybody at?"

"This is it," replied a driver.

"Guess everybody's busy, it being a holiday," replied another.

Spiller walked back to the car. Pierce and Lowery had now mounted their flags.

"You believe this shit? We're the parade."

"Well, let's get up there and line up," ordered Pierce.

The Marines led the parade that day and were followed by the lady that ran the draft office and her grandson. Both carried American flags. Directly behind them were the three antique cars. They marched a mile from the waterfront down Broadway to Capa Hall Park. Thirty people came to watch the parade. That number included at least ten who were related to those in the parade. At Capa Hall Park, a small ceremony was held for the war dead. The Vietnam War was an unpopular war, and those few who participated in the ceremony were part of that unpopularity. It was as if they were the enemy, as if the war was all their doing. It was a lonely time for all of them.

A week later, Gunny Pierce left for Vietnam. Spiller felt badly about his leaving, but not for long. He was planning to get married on August 6, 1967. Most of his free time was spent looking for a mobile home. He and his fiancée looked at every trailer sale in Southern Illinois and Southeast Missouri. Those they really liked required more of a down payment than they had. When they finally picked a trailer that they could afford, it was set up at the Star View Trailer Park in Cape Girardeau. Their wedding ceremony was held at the Second Baptist Church in Marion. The reception was at their mobile home. When the reception was over, they threw all the dirty paper plates in a cardboard box and put them under the trailer because they had forgotten to buy a wastecan. Since they could not afford a TV, they listened to records and swatted flies until 2 A.M.

Spiller's wife got broken into military life right away. Harry didn't get any time off from work for a honeymoon. The day after his wedding, he had to go back to work. He was up at 6 A.M. and had to take applications in Cairo. He didn't get home until 8 P.M. that night. The next day he had to attend a funeral in Poplar Bluff. Again, he got home late, only to have to leave early the next morning for St. Louis.

He had to get the colors for a rodeo parade in Sikeston the same day. At 5 A.M. he left home, returned at 3 P.M., and left again for Sikeston at 3:30 P.M. The parade was to start at 6:00 P.M., and they were supposed to line up for it at 5:50 P.M. Maze, Roberts, and Ledue were to meet Spiller there. When Spiller got to Sikeston and met up with them, Maze told him to give him his keys, and he'd park the car at the end of the parade. That way they'd be able to drive back to the starting point rather than walk. Spiller gave Maze the keys, and he parked the car at the ending point. The recruiter brought him back to the starting point. Spiller just wanted to get the parade over with and go home, but as usual, the parade started late. They were right behind the horses and marched for what seemed to be forever. Finally, they got to the end of the parade and jumped into the car. When they got back to Maze's car, he gave his keys to Roberts and told him to follow. But, Maze wouldn't give Harry his keys. He said Harry had to have a beer with them before he could leave. Spiller really got mad, but it didn't do any good. They just laughed. Maze pulled up in front of a local tavern and walked in. Spiller followed, yelling at Maze to give him his keys. Maze just laughed and ordered everybody a beer. Finally, after Spiller drank a beer, Maze gave him his keys. He got home at 10:00 P.M. that night.

15
Memorial Service

Filling quotas was going well, but Spiller was having trouble with First Sergeant Lowery. He let his position go to his head. Spiller had to go on the road every day now because Lowery decided that first sergeant shouldn't have to do that type of thing. He sat around smoking his cigars, and when Spiller was there, gave him orders. It was the beginning of September. Lowery hadn't recruited a single person, and acted as though he had no intention of doing any recruiting.

Lowery sat puffing on a cigar and fumbled through a leatherneck magazine. Spiller sat at the other desk typing up an enlistment kit.

The phone rang, Lowery leaned over to pick up the receiver.

"United States Marine Corps Recruiting Station, First Sergeant Lowery."

He paused for a moment.

"Hi, Sergeant Major, how are you today? Oh. Oh!"

Lowery dropped his cigar.

"Just a minute. Let me get a casualty card."

Spiller pulled the desk drawer open, picked up a card, and handed it to Lowery. Lowery, with the phone in one hand and pencil in the other, gave an occasional uh-huh as he wrote. He looked at Spiller when he finished the call.

"We have a casualty call. The guy was crossing a creek, fell off a rope bridge, and drowned."

Spiller paused for a moment.

"Damn! Where at?"

"Da Nang."

"I mean, where does his family live?"

"Oh, Charleston, Missouri. He's black. PFC Leroy Jenkins."

"First Sergeant Lowery, you'd better get your cigar."

Lowery looked quickly at the floor.

"Oh!" Reaching down to pick it up, he said, "Let's go."

The two men drove into Charleston.

"How do we get to Mississippi Street?" asked Lowery as they entered the town.

"It's on the east side of town, but we need to find a minister before we go to the house."

"Where do we find one?"

"There's a church in the black district. We can stop there."

Spiller directed Lowery to the black district of Charleston. Lowery, dodging potholes in the street, weaved back and forth. Eventually, they came to a small white church in the middle of the block. The two got out of the car and walked to the front door. Spiller opened the wooden, paint-peeled door and walked in. Lowery followed.

"No one here," said Spiller.

"I wonder where he lives," said Lowery.

"Don't know, but maybe we can ask around."

Spiller and Lowery walked out of the church. They came face to face with a small black man wearing a white shirt and gray, loose, suit pants, held up with wide, red suspenders.

"May I help ya?"

"Yes, sir, we're looking for the minister," said Spiller.

"I'm Reverend Rollins. What can I do for you gentlemen today?"

"Sir, do you know Leroy Jenkins?" Spiller asked.

"Yes. Yes. His mother comes to church every Sunday. How's the boy doing?"

"He's dead, sir. He drowned crossing a bridge."

"Oh my, oh my," said Reverend Rollins, rubbing the top of his bald head.

"We were hoping you'd go with us to tell the family."

"Be glad to. Be glad to. Let me go tell the wife I'll be gone a while."

Reverend Rollins walked to the small house next to the church. He returned shortly and climbed into the back seat of the car.

"Do you know where the family lives?" asked Spiller.

"Yes, sir. Just go down two blocks and turn left."

Lowery drove again swerving and turning in the road.

"It's the fifth house on the left."

"Is this it?" Lowery asked.

"Sure is."

"First Sergeant, do you want me to tell the family?" asked Spiller.

"No. I need to handle this one."

The three started toward the front door. A tall black man in his early twenties walked out the door with a beer in one hand and a cigarette in the other. He looked at the reverend with a frown.

"Reverend? What's wrong?"

"It's Leroy. He's dead. Is Mrs. Jenkins here?"

"She's in the house," he said, lowering his beer can.

"Let's go. These gentlemen need to give her the news."

The young man walked in first. Two other men sat on a couch with a black woman. All held a can of beer in their hands. The woman looked up at Lowery with a look of half-shock.

"What's the matter? Something happen to Leroy? What is it?"

Lowery stood for a minute then spoke. "Ma'am your son has drowned. He's dead."

The woman bellowed, "Oh, my God, not my baby! Not my baby!"

Spiller looked at the floor as he thought about the way Lowery had said, "Your son has drowned. He's dead."

"Good God, he didn't use any tact," thought Spiller.

The reverend looked up, raising both arms in the air.

"Sweet Jesus. Oh sweet Jesus! Bless this family. Bless them all through this tragedy."

Lowery and Spiller stepped outside. The young man that met them at the door followed them out into the yard.

"Sir, is Leroy your brother?" asked Spiller.

"Yes, yes, sir."

"Sir, your brother will be sent back within 10 to 14 days to whatever funeral home you request. We'll give full military honors, if you request. We'll send a telegram tomorrow, so we'll get back in touch with you in the morning, if that will be okay."

"That'll be okay, Sergeant. Could you tell me what happened?"

"Sir, the only thing I can tell you is that he was in the Da Nang area. His unit was crossing a bridge. He fell into the water and drowned. You'll be receiving a letter from his commanding officer, who will give you full details."

"Thank you, Sergeant," he replied quietly, looking sadly at the ground.

"We'll be in contact with you in the morning, sir."

Spiller turned and walked toward the car. Lowery was pacing back and forth beside the car.

"Ready to go, First Sergeant?"

They both got into the car and Lowery drove off. This time he hit every pothole in the street. Just outside of town, Lowery looked over at Spiller.

"How did I do?"

"Well, First Sergeant, they never told us what to say to the families in recruiters school. As a matter of fact, they just didn't mention casualty calls, but what I've always done is say, 'As a Representative of the President of the United States and the Commandant of the Marine Corps, it is my duty to inform you that your son has been killed in action in the Republic of South Vietnam in defense of the United States of America.' I don't know if that's the best way to tell them. I don't know if there is a best way, but I can tell you this, the casualty calls don't get any easier to make. The more you make, the worse they get. You'll never get used to making them. Never."

A week later Spiller and Lowery were in the office getting ready to go to Jenkins's funeral.

"Hey, Lowery, is there any place we can change uniforms when we get to Charleston? If we put these blouses on in this heat, we'll be soaked by the time we get down there," said Maze.

"Not that I know of."

"Great. It's 110 in the shade, and we're going to drive 40 miles in full dress before the funeral. Damn, my nuts itch."

"If the Marine Corps wasn't so cheap, they'd put air conditioners in the cars," snapped Roberts.

The recruiters put their blouses on and drove to Charleston. Both cars turned onto the block where the church was located. Both cars, dodging potholes and weaving back and forth in the street, finally came to a halt in front of the church. Cars were lined to each end of the block on both sides of the street. The small churchyard was filled with people dressed in a multitude of colors. They were laughing, smoking, shaking hands, and reminiscing.

The recruiters climbed out of the cars, squared their hats, and pulled their gloves on. They lined up and marched into the church. Every seat was taken except the front row. Those six seats were left vacant for the pall bearers. Mourners, standing in all the aisles, stepped to the side as the recruiters marched to the front row and sat at attention. The temperature was at least 130 degrees inside the church. The crowd fanned themselves with the programs handed to them. The Marines, at attention, perspired heavily, as everyone waited for the Reverend Rollins.

Piano music echoed throughout the church. The Marines stood for the Marine Corps hymn and, when the music ended, took their seats again.

"My baby has done went and left me," screamed Jenkins's mother. "Uh, uh, uh!"

"No greater a man than a man that lays down his life for a friend," yelled the Reverend Rollins. "Did ya hear me? No greater a man than a man that lays down his life for a friend. That's what Jesus said."

"My baby has done gone and left me! Uh! Uh!"

"Uh, uh, uh," Maze mocked in a low voice.

"He drowned. Yes, he did! Uh! Uh!"

"Uh, uh, uh," mocked Maze once again.

Spiller elbowed Maze.

"Knock it off," he whispered out of the corner of his mouth.

Maze smirked then sat quietly.

The reverend finished his sermon. The people in the aisle passed and viewed the body. Several let out screams, others sobbed uncontrollably. Finally, all but the immediate family had left.

As two men helped Mrs. Jenkins up, she screamed out, "My baby has left me! Uh! Uh!"

"Uh, uh, uh," mocked Maze.

Mrs. Jenkins fainted and fell to the floor.

"Maze, Spiller, go help them with her," ordered Ledue.

They hurried to Mrs. Jenkins. Each placed an arm around her shoulders and carried her to the car. Once she was safely inside the car, Spiller and Maze hurried back inside the church. Taking their places on each side of the casket, the Marines walked into the churchyard and then to the back of the hearse. They placed the casket inside the hearse, saluted, then returned to their cars.

The Marines quickly rolled the windows down as the motorcade pulled out.

"Damn! It must have been 150 degrees in that church," complained Lowery.

"My t-shirt's soaked," snarled Spiller.

"No wonder! That woman must have weighed 200 pounds, and we had to carry her to the car. I'm not only hot, my nuts itch," replied Maze.

"Maze, you better quit pulling that shit in the middle of these funerals," snapped Spiller. "It's hard to keep a straight face."

"Plant one, enlist one, that's the name of the game. And when you play the game, it never hurts to have a little humor. Uh! Uh! I'm not a racist and you know it. Shit, man."

Spiller looked out the window and shook his head. The motorcade turned onto a dirt road which the Marines followed for a couple of miles. After stopping in front of a small, unkempt cemetery on the left side of the road, the recruiters walked to the back of the hearse and lined up three on each side. Spiller stood directly across from Maze. The hot, muggy weather brought swarms of mosquitoes. One landed on Maze's cheek. He reached up and slapped the mosquito.

"That son-of-a-bitch could've stood flat footed and fucked a turkey," Maze whispered.

Spiller and Lowery snickered. Looking at the ground, both attempted to regain a straight face. The funeral director opened the back door of the hearse, and the Marines took the casket to the gravesite. Two-by-fours were laid across the open grave. The Marines placed the casket on the boards. Ledue and Maze took positions at each end of the casket. Spiller and the other Marines walked back to the cars, picked up the rifles, and took positions a couple of hundred feet from the gravesite. The reverend prayed, and Ledue gave the nod to the firing squad.

"Half right, hau!" ordered First Sergeant Lowery. "Ready! Aim! Fire!"

The shots rang out. Screams came from the crowd, and one woman fell to the ground.

"Ready! Aim! Fire!"

Once again shots rang out, and another woman fell.

"Ready! Aim! Fire!"

As usual, taps were played by a high school volunteer then the flag was folded and presented to Mrs. Jenkins.

Spiller and the rest of the firing squad laid their rifles on the ground and rushed to the two women lying on the ground. Both had come to. The Marines helped them to their feet and to their cars.

All the way back to Cape Girardeau, Spiller thought about the gravesite. A 19-year-old boy joins the Marines, is killed in action, and all he gets is a two-by-four to hold his casket up in the middle of a swamp area. It sure made Spiller think about all the freedom and equality he was taught about in school. Then there was Maze and his funny comments. They were really his way of covering up his true feelings. Spiller would look at him when he didn't know it, and he could see the hurt in his eyes. All of them felt the pain and helplessness. At the burial sites, the families looked at the Marines as if to say, "Please do something!" They could see it in their eyes. They could feel it inside themselves, yet there was nothing they could say or do.

The Marines returned to Cape Girardeau in the afternoon, only to prepare for another funeral in Sikeston the following day. This time they were to meet the other recruiters at the funeral home.

It was another record-temperature day of 107 degrees. The Marines pulled up to the funeral home. They were met in the front lobby by the funeral director.

"I'm Tom Martin, gentlemen," he said, extending his right hand.

"First Sergeant Lowery, sir."

"Harry Spiller, sir," Harry said as they shook hands.

"The other gentlemen are in the basement getting dressed, if you care to go down."

Spiller and Lowery followed the director to the stairwell.

"Thank you, sir," replied Spiller. He and Lowery made their way down the steps.

Spiller walked into the basement. He stopped suddenly and looked around. The floor was covered with red carpet, and at least 25 caskets of all sizes and colors were on display throughout the room. The top of each casket was open. The price tags were placed on the pillows. Maze and the other recruiters were getting dressed. Maze cracked one joke after another.

"Hey, Harry, why don't you crawl into one of those caskets and try it on for size?" said Maze when he caught a glimpse of the two.

"Hell, no! Let's get dressed and get out of here."

Spiller turned and looked back. A young girl in her twenties, seven or eight months pregnant, dressed in black, walked down the aisle holding the hand of her five-year-old daughter who wore a full-length white dress. The little girl looked around inquisitively. The red swollen face of the pregnant woman could easily be seen underneath the black veil she wore.

"Mommy, where is Daddy? You said Daddy would be here. Mommy you promised. I wore his favorite dress."

The woman attempted to keep her composure as she tried to quiet her daughter. The girl was pointing to the casket and whispering back to her mother, "Is Daddy in there? Mommy, why don't Daddy talk to us? I want him to tell me he likes my dress like he did before he went bye-bye."

As taps sounded Lowery and Maze folded the flag. The first sergeant stepped in front of the pregnant widow who looked straight ahead. The young daughter looked up at Lowery with a frown.

"As a representative of the President of the United States and the Commandant of the Marine Corps, we would like to present you with our nation's colors in recognition of your husband who laid down his life for his country."

The woman, motionless except for the tears streaming down her face, stared into space. As Lowery carefully laid the flag in the woman's hands, the little girl spoke up.

"I don't like you. You make my Mommy cry. What did you do with my Daddy?"

Lowery stepped back quickly. A combination of shock and pain showed on his face, he turned and walked away.

In early September 1967, Spiller had his October quotas to fill. Those were always the tough months because everyone wanted to stay home for the holidays. Lowery still wasn't making much of an effort to recruit, and that wasn't helping. He'd lost his big head. Spiller thought the funerals had taken care of that. It had been a week since the last funeral, and Spiller had just gotten back to the office after being on the road all day.

The phone rang and Spiller lifted the receiver. "Marine Recruiting, Sergeant Spiller."

"Sergeant Spiller, this is the Sergeant Major."

"How are you today, sir?"

"Fine, yourself?"

"Busy, trying to make quota."

"Sergeant Spiller, I have a KIA for you."

"Yes, sir, let me get a casualty card," Spiller said, taking a deep breath.

Spiller turned to Lowery. "First Sergeant, would you hand me a casualty card? We have a call."

Lowery opened the desk, then walked over to Spiller and handed him the card.

"Okay, Sergeant Major, go ahead."

"PFC Bradford Sinks, KIA, September 6, 1967, Da Nang area. Next of kin: Mr. and Mrs. Ralph Sinks, 306 Fairfield Street, Anna, Illinois. You got that?"

"Yes, sir."

"There's one other thing."

"What's that, sir?"

The Sergeant Major paused for a moment.

"He was hit directly by a rocket. There are no remains."

"My God!"

"It's going to be a tough one. You let them know that we'll give a memorial service if they request."

"Yes, sir."

"Good luck."

"Another KIA?" asked Lowery.

"Yes, but you won't believe this one. The guy got a direct hit by a rocket. There are no remains."

"Jesus! Oh shit! Where are the next of kin?"

"Anna."

"Fuck! Well, let's go get this one over with. I'm gonna get orders out of this fucking place," said Lowery.

They drove to Anna, neither saying a word.

"Got any idea where Fairfield Street is?" asked Lowery.

"Not the slightest. I guess we'd better stop at the police station and ask. The post office is closed by now."

"Where's the police station?"

"It's on this street about three blocks down."

Lowery parked in front of the station. Spiller went inside to get directions to Fairfield Street and returned shortly to the car.

"We've got to go back down the street about six blocks. Remember the used car lot we passed?"

"Yeah."

"We turn left there and go two blocks. We'll run right onto it."

Lowery made a U-turn in the street and followed the directions. Finally they were at the stop sign adjacent to Fairfield Street.

"Which way do we turn?"

"They didn't say. Let's go right."

Lowery turned and drove slowly as Spiller attempted to read the house numbers.

"Six-0-eight. We're in the six hundred block."

Lowery continued to drive slowly into the next block.

"We need to turn around. This is the seven hundred block. We're going the wrong way," said Spiller.

Lowery pulled into a driveway and turned around.

"If the house numbers are right, we need to go back about four blocks," said Spiller.

Lowery drove back four blocks. Spiller watched the numbers.

"Three-ten, this is the block. No house number. Three-0-six; there it is."

Lowery pulled up and parked the car. Both Spiller and Lowery slowly got out of the car and walked up to the front porch. Spiller carried the casualty card. He knocked on the door. Pausing for a moment, he knocked again.

"I don't believe anyone's at home."

"I can't hear any movement in the house," replied Lowery.

"Me either."

Spiller knocked once more, and still, there was no response. They turned to walk off the porch. At the bottom of the steps watching them was a middle-aged man.

"Looking for the Sinkses?"

"Yes, sir," said Spiller.

"They're both at work. Down at the glove factory."

"Do they both work there?"

"Yes, sir. Sure do."

"Well, thank you, sir. Oh, one more thing. Could you please tell us how to get to the glove factory?"

Lowery pulled into the factory parking lot. He and Spiller left the car and walked into the plant. Spiller opened the door to the first office they came to, where he found a receptionist.

"Ma'am, could you tell me where I can find the plant manager?"

The girl, in her twenties, quit typing.

"I can call him on the phone, sir. Your name?"

"Sergeant Spiller."

"May I tell him the nature of the call?"

"Just tell him it's an emergency."

"Yes, sir."

The secretary picked up the phone and dialed two numbers.

"Mr. Burton, there's a Sergeant Spiller from the Marine Corps here to see you. He says he has an emergency. Yes, sir. Okay." Turning to Spiller, she said, "Mr. Burton will be right here."

"Thank you, ma'am."

Spiller and Lowery stood in the hallway for only a short time when the manager appeared.

"What's the problem?" he asked, looking quite concerned.

"Do you have a Mr. and Mrs. Ralph Sinks working here?"

"Yes, sir. I believe we do."

"Well, sir, we need to speak with them. Their son has been killed in action."

"My God! I'll get them."

"Oh, Mr. Burton, do you have a vacant office or room we could use to talk with the family?"

"Yes, follow me."

They followed the manager down the hall through a set of double doors into a large room. Several rows of benches were wall to wall. Men and women were busy working. As Spiller and Lowery walked through the room, several of the workers snickered and pointed at the Marines. The manager opened a door. Lowery and Spiller followed him into the small room. Except for some chairs, the room was empty.

"Will this be all right, gentlemen?"

"Fine, sir."

Spiller and Lowery stood staring silently, wondering if it would be Mr. or Mrs. Sinks who got the bad news first. The door opened and a small-framed, grey-headed man entered the room. A puzzled look came to his face, then sudden shock.

"Oh, no! No!"

Spiller snapped to attention.

"Sir, as a Representative of the President of the United States and the Commandant of the Marine Corps, it is my duty to inform you that your son, Bradford Sinks, has been killed in action, in the Republic of South Vietnam in the defense of the United States of America."

Mr. Sinks plopped into a chair and cried. He drew his knees to his chest and put both arms around his legs.

"Oh, my God! Oh, my God!"

The door opened again, and Mrs. Sinks, dressed in work slacks and a sweatshirt, entered. She looked down at her husband.

"Ralph, what is it?"

She then looked up with the same expression of shock.

"Oh, no! He isn't dead, is he?"

"Yes, ma'am. I'm afraid he is."

She cried uproariously as she walked to her husband. She fell to her knees, putting both arms around him. A few minutes passed.

"When will they send him home?" asked Mr. Sinks.

"Sir, sir, your son received a direct hit by a rocket. Sir, there are no remains."

Mrs. Sinks screamed uncontrollably. Mr. Sinks, crying loudly, fell from his chair and lay in the floor with his hands over his face. Ten minutes passed. Spiller and Lowery helped both Mr. and Mrs. Sinks off the floor and into the chairs.

"Why don't we go to your home, Mr. Sinks?" Spiller suggested, trying to keep his composure.

"Yes, we need to get in touch with the rest of the family," replied Mr. Sinks.

Spiller and Lowery followed Mr. and Mrs. Sinks out of the room. The people in the room snickered and pointed at Spiller. Spiller, noticing a cup of coffee on a table, grabbed the cup and poured the coffee on one of the men's head.

"Present for ya from the U.S. Marine Corps, asshole."

The man fell back off his stool and shook his shirt. Mr. and Mrs. Sinks had already gone through the double doors. Lowery looked back. The room was filled with silence.

"Harry, what are you doing? Come on! Come on!"

"I'm coming, First Sergeant."

Then Spiller turned and addressed the workers. "As I leave this room, if I see one smile, just one, I'll have your ass."

Spiller walked backwards to the double doors looking left to right at the stone-faced men and women. He turned, when he got to the double doors and slammed the doors against the walls.

"Take it easy, Harry. Take it easy."

"Take it easy, hell! Did you see them laughing at Mr. and Mrs.

Sinks and us as we went through. What the fuck is the matter with people?"

"Take it easy. Come on. We have to help the family."

Spiller and Lowery walked to the front door where Mr. and Mrs. Sinks stood waiting.

"Do you have a car?" asked Lowery.

"Yes," replied Mr. Sinks.

"If you'll show Spiller where it is, he'll drive it home for you, and you can ride with me."

Mr. Sinks gave Spiller the keys and pointed to an old 1936 pick-up. Spiller walked to the truck and opened the door. A set of springs with a thick piece of cardboard on the driver's side was all that consisted of the seat. Spiller climbed in and pushed the starter and gas pedal until the truck started. Shifting half-a-dozen gears, Spiller finally found reverse and backed up. Another half dozen shifts, and he pulled forward and followed the government car to the Sinkses' residence.

Lowery and Spiller arrived at the cemetery early. The cemetery was located two miles into the country off a gravel road. A large steep hill was on one side. The grass had been freshly cut, and it had rained the night before. Ledue, Maze, and Roberts had finally arrived.

"First Sergeant, I'm going to climb the hill and play from there. That way no one can see me while I play."

"Okay, Harry."

Spiller got the coronet out of the car and started up the hill. Halfway up the hill, he slipped and fell. His cap fell off and rolled down the hill like a saucer.

"Damn!" Spiller yelled as he went back down the hill and finally reached the cap.

He laid the horn down and tried to clean the grass and mud off his cap and gloves. He then squared his cap and put the gloves back on.

A motorcade of cars pulled up in front of the cemetery, this time without a hearse. Family and friends walked to the burial site, where only a memorial stone was placed. The minister gave a short sermon and a prayer. Ledue gave the firing squad a nod.

"Half right, hau! Ready! Aim! Fire! Ready! Aim! Fire!"

Spiller raised the coronet to his lips and blew into the horn.

"Bert, bert...."

He jerked the horn down quickly and looked at it.

"What the hell?" Spiller thought as he raised the horn and sloppily played taps.

Ledue gave the family a flag, and the service was over. Spiller climbed down the hill with his head hanging.

As he reached the bottom of the hill, the first sergeant asked, "What happened?"

"Shit, First Sergeant, I'm sorry I screwed everything up. This fucking horn has a hole in it. I must have done it when I fell. I had to stick my finger in the hole to get it to play. I'm sorry."

16

The Parade

A couple of weeks had gone by since Sinks's funeral and Lowery was unusually jolly. Spiller knew something was up, but he couldn't figure out what, until one day when he came in off the road. Lowery, as usual, was sitting behind the desk puffing on a cigar. He had a big smile on his face. He told Spiller he'd just received orders for Cherry Point, North Carolina. Spiller was surprised. He didn't expect him to last his full tour, but he didn't expect him to leave so quickly either. Later, Spiller found out he'd been calling St. Louis two or three times a week for at least a month, asking to be transferred. Gunnery Sgt. John Liss, also an aviation specialist, was coming to replace him. Liss was due to arrive in one week. Because Lowery had been no help at all, Spiller was greatly relieved that he was leaving. Harry couldn't help wondering if this new gunny sergeant would be any better.

After completing an enlistment kit, Spiller sat at his desk putting forms in order. The door opened and a small man, five feet four, weighing about 120 pounds, walked in. The man, wearing levis and a t-shirt, approached Spiller's desk.

"May I help you, sir?"

"You must be Sergeant Spiller."

"Yes, sir, I am."

Extending his hand, he said, "I'm Gunnery Sergeant Liss."

"Glad to meet you, Gunny. Welcome aboard," Spiller said as he shook hands with Liss.

"Where's the first sergeant?"

"He took the day off. I can get him, if you like."

"That isn't necessary. Just wanted to let him know I was in town.

We have a house to look at today. From the rent ad, I think we'll probably take it. I'll be back in a few days. Just let Sergeant Lowery know."

"Yes, sir. I sure will."

Liss looked Spiller up and down, then turned and walked out of the office.

Spiller sat down in his chair as he watched Liss walk across the street to his pick-up truck. The phone rang. Spiller reached for the receiver.

"U.S. Marine Corps Recruiting Station, Sergeant Spiller. May I help you?"

"Sergeant Spiller, this is Sergeant Major. I have a casualty call for you."

Spiller jotted down the information. Corporal Walter Cockrum, wounded September 26, Da Nang area, stepped on a land mine, received wounds to both legs, stomach and face. He's lost his right eye, and right arm. Condition: Critical. Prognosis: Critical. Next of kin: Thelma Cockrum, 1207 N. 5th Street, Farmington, Missouri.

Spiller finished his coffee, grabbed the casualty card, and left.

He arrived in Farmington about an hour later and drove slowly until he found 1207 N. 5th Street. Taking a deep breath, he grabbed the card and got out of the car. A woman, who lived next door to the Cockrum home, was working in her flowerbed.

Looking up, she smiled and said, "She isn't home. She's working today."

"Do you know where she works?"

"Yes, sir. Farmington State Hospital."

"Thank you, ma'am," Spiller replied as he turned and walked for the car. "You have a good day."

"Thank you, young man. You do the same."

Spiller drove to the state hospital just outside of Farmington. He parked the car, and walked into the administration building. He stopped at the reception desk. A short, stocky man dressed in white stood looking at Spiller with a sort of half grin.

"Good morning, Sergeant. May I help you?"

"Yes, sir. Does Thelma Cockrum work here?"

"She sure does."

"Well, sir, I need to talk with her. I have a message about her son."

Turning and pointing out a window, the man replied, "She works in that building over there."

Looking out the window from left to right, Spiller saw several buildings sitting on a huge, dark green lawn.

"Just ring the bell and a nurse will let you in," the gentleman continued.

"Thank you, sir," Spiller replied as he turned to leave the building.

Spiller walked across the lawn in search of Mrs. Cockrum. When he reached her building, he was surprised to find the door standing wide open. Inside the room, patients walked about, while others watched TV or read magazines. A tall, thin man, dressed in a suit, spotted Spiller standing just outside the door.

"Good morning, Sergeant. Come in."

Spiller stepped into the room and looked around at the patients.

"Can I help you, Sergeant."

"Yes, sir. I'm looking for Thelma Cockrum. Is she here?"

"She certainly is. Follow me, Sergeant."

Spiller started across the room. A rather disheveled man ran to Spiller, grabbing at his coat.

"Boy, this is a pretty suit, a pretty suit. I want one," said the patient.

Spiller pulled his arm back. Another patient appeared.

"Mrs. Cockrum is here. She's here. Back in the office. What do you want with her, huh? What?"

"I need to talk to her," Spiller replied.

Spiller stopped in the hallway in front of the door. On both sides of the entrance were two large windows. Three patients surrounded Spiller as he gazed upon the backs of two nurses, who were busy shuffling papers. Another patient was busy mopping in the corner of the office.

"Mrs. Cockrum, there's a Sergeant here to see you," said the man who met him at the door.

Mrs. Cockrum turned quickly looking eye to eye with Spiller.

"Oh, no!"

"He isn't dead, ma'am. He isn't dead."

"What's wrong?" she asked, walking up to Spiller.

"Your son's been wounded, ma'am. He stepped on a land mine."

"Oh, God!" she said as tears streamed down her face.

"He has wounds to both legs, his chest, his face... Ma'am, your son's lost his right arm and right eye."

"Oh, God, no!"

"His condition is critical and the prognosis is critical."

Mrs. Cockrum wept loudly. The patient, mopping the office floor, walked in a threatening manner toward Spiller.

"I'll kill you! I'll kill you!" the patient said as he swung the mop at Spiller. "You hurt Mrs. Cockrum."

Just as the patient swung, Spiller grabbed the end of the mop. One of the patients, standing behind Spiller, jumped on his back. Spiller swung the man off. The patient with the mop grabbed Spiller.

"No, no! Leave him alone!" yelled Mrs. Cockrum. "He's my friend. He isn't trying to hurt me."

Mrs. Cockrum grabbed the patient with the mop and pulled him back. Spiller pushed the patient that jumped him from behind.

"You stay back, ma'am. If you want to talk, we're going to have to leave this building," Spiller yelled to Mrs. Cockrum.

"Yes, Sergeant, come with me. I'm sorry to put you through this, but they think because I'm crying, you were trying to hurt me."

"Yes, ma'am, I figured that out," Spiller replied nervously.

Spiller and Mrs. Cockrum walked outside. As Spiller took a deep breath, Mrs. Cockrum started crying. She put her arms around Spiller.

"I'm sorry to put you through that. I know it scared you. You're my son's age. I just hope he'll be all right," she said in a shaky voice as she buried her face in Spiller's arms.

"We have the best doctors, ma'am. He'll make it."

Spiller didn't know what else to tell her. Even as he told her her son would be okay, he knew he'd have to come back and tell her he hadn't survived. From the information he already had, Spiller didn't think her son would make it, but he had to give her some hope, something to hang onto.

As for the casualty call, it was probably the first and only time the family's reaction wasn't Spiller's first concern. He was frightened by the patients from the moment he walked in until he left. Spiller was scared to death, and all he could think of was getting out of there.

The next day both Lowery and Liss were in the office. As Spiller told them about the incident with the mental patients, Lowery gave that dumb look he was so famous for, and Liss laughed. Spiller didn't say anything when Liss laughed because he knew he wouldn't be laughing long.

Lowery left and for almost a month there were no casualty calls. Liss and Spiller got along very well. Harry did suspect, however, that

Liss had a drinking problem. Sometimes Spiller could smell beer on his breath when he came into the office in the morning. He wasn't sure if it was from the night before or not, but he did know Liss was drinking at lunch time.

After about a month, Liss received a call from the C.O. Maze was being transferred to Quincy, Illinois, to take over that recruiting station. Liss and Spiller were to cover the Poplar Bluff area until a new recruiter reported in, probably within two months. They had to handle casualty calls and recruiting for the additional 18 counties. While Spiller held their office down, Liss made two and three trips a week to Poplar Bluff. Liss had just returned from Poplar Bluff one late afternoon when the phone rang.

"U.S. Marine Corps Recruiting, Sergeant Spiller."

"Sergeant Spiller, this is the Sergeant Major. I have a casualty call for you."

L/CPL James Allen had been killed in action on October 26, 1967, near Da Nang. He'd been hit by a booby trap. He was black, and next of kin was Janice Allen, 805 Courtney Street, Caruthersville, Missouri.

"We got a KIA, Gunny," Spiller said.

"Where at?"

"Caruthersville, Missouri."

"Shit, that's a two-hour drive!"

"I know, but we'll have to go tonight. They're releasing the telegram at 0800 in the morning."

Spiller and Liss drove for two-and-a-half hours to Caruthersville.

"What time is it?" asked Liss.

"Seven-thirty."

"Let's get a cup of coffee before we make the call."

"Sounds good. Maybe we can get directions in the restaurant."

Spiller and Liss walked into a coffee shop in downtown Caruthersville and sat in a booth just inside the door.

"May I help you, sirs?" asked the waitress.

"Two coffees, ma'am," said Spiller.

The waitress returned shortly with two cups of coffee.

"Ma'am, could you tell us where Courtney Street is?" asked Spiller.

"Yes, sir. Go three blocks north. Turn left at the stop sign, and you'll run right into it. It's about ten blocks after you make your turn."

"Thank you, ma'am."

Spiller and Liss sat sipping their coffee. Liss bellowed, "I'll handle the call."

"Okay."

"Is there any particular thing you tell them?"

"I just tell them I'm a Representative of the President of the United States and the Commandant of the Marine Corps. Then tell them—"

"What then?" Liss interrupted.

"You wait for a while until they settle down, and explain the details about the funeral arrangements."

"After that?"

"After that you offer your services, if needed, and leave."

"That shouldn't be too hard. It'll take a couple of times to get used to it, and then I'll have it down pat."

"Wrong, Gunny. You never get used to it. The more you make, the worse they get. But you have to play the game."

"What game?"

"It's the game Gunny Maze told me about. You enlist one, and you plant one. We'll plant this one and tomorrow enlist one to replace him. If we plant more than we enlist, we lose."

Liss laughed, "You're crazy. You've been on recruiting duty too long."

"Maybe, Gunny, but we're playing the game right now."

Liss swallowed his coffee and put the cup down. "We'd better get going."

Spiller grabbed his cap and scooted out of the booth.

They soon found Courtney Street.

"We'd better find a minister before we go to the house," said Spiller.

"The hell with a minister. It's going to be midnight before we get home now."

"It helps the family, Gunny."

"We can handle it."

Liss stopped in front of the residence. Eight or ten children were playing in the front yard. Spiller and Liss got out of the car and headed for the front door. The children ran up to the two Marines.

"Man, look at them uniforms! Look at those shoes! My brother's a Marine," said voices from the crowd.

Spiller knocked on the door.

"I'll get my mom," said a boy about ten years old.

He opened the door and ran inside.

"Mommy, Mommy, there's Marines here to see you!"

The woman walked into the living room and, looking very frightened, stared through the screen door. Opening the door slightly, she looked at Liss.

"May I help you?" she asked in a shaky voice.

"Yes, ma'am. Are you Mrs. Allen?" Liss asked.

"Yes, sir. I am. Is James all right?"

"No, ma'am. I'm afraid he isn't. He's been killed in action."

Mrs. Allen squealed loudly and fell to the floor. Liss simply stared at her.

"Let's get in there," yelled Spiller as he quickly opened the door. "Get her feet, Gunny."

Spiller and Liss picked Mrs. Allen up and carried her to the couch. She moaned. Spiller turned to the young boy who was crying. Spiller put his arm around the youngster.

"Your mother will be all right but we need a cold washcloth for her. Hurry and get one, okay?"

The youngster ran for the bathroom. He returned with the cloth, and Spiller placed it on Mrs. Allen's forehead. For a couple of minutes she lay moaning, then she opened her eyes.

"Oh, God! My baby! Bring him back!"

Two large black women burst through the door.

"Oh, sweet Jesus! What's happened, Janet? What's happened?" one woman yelled.

"James is dead! Oh, dear God, bring him back!"

The children that had been playing in the yard were now standing in the living room.

"Bring my baby, dear God!" yelled Mrs. Allen.

"Oh, sweet Jesus, bring James back to us!" yelled one of the women.

The children began running around the house.

"Bring him back! Please, Jesus, bring him back!"

Liss, wide-eyed, looked around.

"What do we do now?"

"We should've gotten a minister, Gunny. It would've helped. There isn't anything we can do, but wait 'til they calm down then tell them about the funeral arrangements."

Spiller and Liss were there for two hours before they got everything settled down and could give them information about the services. By the time they left the house was packed with men, women, and children from all over the neighborhood.

Liss and Spiller left the mourning family three hours after they had broken the news. Spiller sat quietly, his insides in knots. Liss stared out the window on the way back. He wasn't laughing anymore.

Ten days later Spiller and Liss pulled up in front of a gym and parked in front of the hearse. As they approached the gym, Spiller and Liss were met by a woman, dressed in white, who handed them a program.

"Gentlemen, you have seats reserved in the front row."

The gym floor was filled with folding chairs. The open casket lay directly in front of the first row of chairs. Behind the casket was a stage filled with band equipment. On the stage, were a couple of men tuning electric guitars. Women, dressed in white, milled around the crowd handing out programs. Everyone in the crowd acted as though they were attending a family reunion, not a funeral. They shook hands and laughed. Spiller and Liss walked to the front row. Spiller sat down by Maze.

"Hi, Gunny."

"Don't talk so loud. I have a hell of a hangover. Fuck, man, I got here last night, started drinking, walked out of the bar, and fell in the grass. I held on for an hour-and-a-half. Man, I thought I was sliding off the face of the earth."

Spiller snickered, then tried to regain his composure.

The band was set up. Everyone was seated and waiting for the minister. Ten minutes passed and still no minister. The crowd was getting restless. The band began to play a tune unknown to Spiller. He watched as a band member picked his guitar. Two strings were missing. A woman grabbed a cymbal and a flat piece of tin can and in time with the music, banged them together. She stood at the end of the row beside Maze, clanging the instruments in his ears. The song finally ended.

Maze looked up at the woman.

"Lady, you trying to drive off the pall bearers?"

Spiller snickered but tried desperately to keep from laughing.

"She starts that shit again, and I'm leaving," Maze said in a low voice. "A fucking can and cymbal."

At last the minister walked into the gym and up the side steps of the stage. Behind the pulpit, he smiled and waved at the crowd. Wearing loose trousers, wide suspenders, and a white shirt, the minister looked like Amos, on the "Amos and Andy Show."

He spoke at the microphone. "Forgive me for being late. Let us have a prayer."

The minister prayed, then the band started playing. The woman, standing beside Maze, banged loudly on the cymbal and tin can again. The crowd stomped their feet to the beat of the music.

"Well, fuck! If you can't beat 'em, you might as well join 'em," said Maze as he stomped his feet and clapped his hands along with the rest of the crowd.

Spiller could hold back no longer and started to laugh. He bowed his head, trying to hide his laughter. Liss and Ledue snickered. The band finished the song and the minister gave his sermon. The Marines regained their composure and sat quietly listening to the minister, who patted the podium as he spoke. The crowd tapped their feet to his rhythm and so did Maze. The tapping continued, until the sermon was finished. The band played again, and once again, the woman beside Maze banged her cymbals.

"Oh, fuck! Not again," snapped Maze.

The song ended and the minister gave a closing prayer. The crowd passed for one last viewing. For the first time it seemed like a funeral. The people cried and screamed as they passed the casket. The family viewed James Allen one last time then waited for the Marines to move the casket to the hearse. As Spiller and the other recruiters took their places on each side of the casket, a man walked up to Liss.

"We moved the hearse around to the side of the gym so we can go through this door over here."

The Marines walked slowly to the door. The family followed close behind. Because the door was only wide enough to get the casket through, Liss and three others walked just outside the door, while Ledue held one end of the casket, and Spiller the other. As they started through the door with the casket, Spiller heard a scream from behind him. Suddenly a woman jumped on his back.

"Bring him back! Oh, sweet Jesus, bring him back!"

Spiller struggled to hold the casket and to maintain his balance.

"Go with it, First Sergeant. I'm going to drop it."

Ledue pulled quickly as Spiller pushed to get the casket through the door with the woman still pawing at him. Once through the door the other Marines grabbed the casket as Spiller reached around attempting to get the woman off his back.

"Ma'am, ma'am! Take it easy," he urged.

Family members grabbed her and pulled her back. Spiller ran to the casket and helped place it in the hearse. Liss and Spiller returned to their car.

"What the hell was she doing?" asked Liss.

"She was trying to get to the casket. She got me instead. Let's go. The hearse is pulling out."

Liss pulled around the school, stopped behind a police car, and waited for the government car to pull out. A black policeman got out of the car and walked back to Liss and Spiller.

"Gentlemen, my battery's gone dead. You'll have to go around."

"You'll have to get the hearse to go in front of us, sir. We don't know where the cemetery is."

"Yes, sir. Yes, sir."

The policeman stood back and with a smile directed the hearse, the Marines, and the rest of the motorcade around the stalled car.

James Allen was buried in a cemetery in the middle of a swampy area. Cemeteries for the blacks always seemed to be in a less than desirable place. It seemed such a shame that they didn't have much of a choice.

Sad as the situation was, thinking about Maze made Spiller laugh all the way back to Cape Girardeau. The funeral didn't bother him like the others had, in part because it didn't seem to bother the friends and relatives, at least not until they viewed the deceased for the last time. Spiller had never seen a funeral like it before.

For the next three days Spiller held down the office and Liss went to Poplar Bluff. They had both met in the office early on the fourth day. The phone rang.

"Marine Corps Recruiting Station, Gunny Sergeant Liss."

"Good morning, Sergeant Major. . . . Yes, sir. Just a minute."

As the sergeant major dictated over the phone, Liss filled out the card.

Liss hung up the phone and said, "We have another KIA. Kennett, Missouri, this time. There went the quotas for today."

"Who was it?"

"L/Cpl Charles Rector, killed in the Chu Li area, a booby trap."

"Well, let's get it over with."

"The sooner the better," said Liss.

Liss and Spiller drove for an hour and a half.

"Let's stop at the police station and ask directions," Spiller suggested.

Liss pulled up in front of the police station.

"I'll be back in a minute," said Spiller.

Spiller approached two police officers who were talking in the hallway.

"Good morning, Sergeant," the policemen said.

"Good morning, sirs. Could you tell me how to get to 7th Street?"

"Who are you looking for, Sergeant?"

"A Harry Rector, 402 North 7th Street."

The policeman narrowed his eyes.

"Isn't his son in the Marine Corps? He isn't dead, is he?"

"Yes, sir. I'm afraid he is."

"Damn! This town's been hit hard with casualties. This makes the fifth. Well, come on. You can follow me."

"Thank you, sir."

Spiller walked to the car.

"He's going to show us the way," he said to Liss.

Liss followed the police car to the residence on 7th Street. Spiller and Liss got out of the car. The officer pointed to the house.

"That's it."

Spiller and Liss started up the walk. A woman in her mid-fifties stood looking out the glass front door. With both hands over her mouth, she began to cry. Liss and Spiller stood at the front door. Mrs. Rector just stood there crying. Spiller reached for the door, pulling it open. Liss stepped inside.

"Mrs. Rector, your son...."

She grabbed Liss on the outside of each arm and started screaming.

"Mrs. Rector! Mrs. Rector, your son...."

She kept screaming, and holding Liss by the arms with a death grip. Liss tried to pull away, but was unable to.

"Mrs. Rector!"

She kept screaming and pulling Liss until they were standing in the middle of the living room. The police officer walked in along with a man dressed in carpenter clothes.

Mrs. Rector looked over. "Oh, Harry!"
The two embraced.

When Spiller and Liss got back to Cape Girardeau, Liss had red marks on both arms. He didn't have to say anything, Spiller could tell it bothered him a lot.

Two weeks later the Marines buried Mr. and Mrs. Rector's only son. When the funeral ended, Mrs. Rector had to be pulled off the casket. It took three people to subdue her.

For the next two months the office didn't get a single casualty. A new recruiter took over the Poplar Bluff recruiting station, so Spiller and Liss were back to working their own area. By that time Liss was beginning to drink pretty heavily. He took days off during the week. Several times Spiller had to cover for him when the sergeant major called. He wasn't enlisting many people, generally just walk-ins.

One day Spiller had come back to the office from off the road and was sipping a cup of coffee when the phone rang.

"Marine Corps Recruiting Station, Sergeant Spiller."

"Sergeant Spiller, this is the Sergeant Major. I have a KIA for you."

Spiller wrote down the information. PFC John Finney, killed in action December 6, 1968, Da Nang area, stepped on a booby trap. Next of kin: Mr. and Mrs. John Finney, Sr., 1111 Texas Avenue, Sikeston, Missouri. Religion: Protestant.

"I hate to hurry, but I have two more to give out. I'll call you later," said the sergeant major.

"Yes, sir."

Liss looking at Spiller, asked, "Another one?"

"Yeah, another one. I guess we're winning though. I picked up two applicants today. Enlist two, plant one. Yeah, I guess we're winning the fucking game."

Spiller threw his cap down on the desk. Liss sat quietly.

"I'll call the pastor at the First Baptist Church. He's always been pretty responsive. I'll see if he'll go with us," said Spiller.

"All right," replied Liss.

Spiller looked up the number and called the pastor.

"Mr. Watson, this is Sergeant Spiller. We have a KIA in Sikeston, and I was wondering if you could go with us to make the call."

"Sure, Harry, I'd be glad to. When are you leaving?"

"As soon as you're ready, sir."

"Give me ten minutes."

"Okay, we'll pick you up."

"See you then."

"Thank you, sir."

Spiller hung up the phone.

Spiller and Liss stopped at the service station, then picked the minister up and drove to Sikeston.

"We'd better stop at the police station and get directions," said Liss.

"I know where the street is, Gunny."

Spiller drove slowly on Texas Street. All three watched for the house number.

"We're in the eight hundred block," Mr. Watson said.

Creeping into the eleven hundred block, Spiller looked to the left.

"Here it is," replied Watson.

Spiller stopped the car and pulled over to the curb. All three got out of the car. As they did, Liss doubled over.

"Oh, shit, my stomach."

"What's wrong, Gunny?"

"Got a hell of a pain in my stomach. I feel like I'm gonna throw up."

"You want us to wait for a few minutes? You can't go up there like this."

"No, you'd better go on and tell them, Harry. They may see us out here, and we don't need to be making casualty calls in the middle of the street."

"Okay, Gunny. Come on, Mr. Watson."

Spiller and the pastor walked up on the front porch. Spiller knocked on the door. A short, thin middle-aged man answered the door on the first knock.

He smiled as he asked, "May I help you, Sergeant?"

"Yes, sir. Are you John Finney?"

"Sure am."

Spiller snapped to attention. "Sir, as a Representative of the President of the United States of America and the Commandant of the Marine Corps, it is my duty to inform you that your son, PFC John Finney, has been killed in action in the Republic of South Vietnam in the defense of the United States of America."

"Oh, no!" screamed Mr. Finney as he turned and ran into the house.

Spiller and the pastor followed him into the living room. A woman entered the room from the hallway.

"What's wrong, John?"

"Johnny's dead! He's dead!"

Suddenly, Mr. Finney turned and looked at Spiller.

"God damn you! You son-of-a-bitch! I'll get you for this!"

Mr. Finney dashed from the hallway.

"John, John, calm down. It isn't his fault."

Mrs. Finney ran down the hall. Spiller looked at Mr. Watson.

"If he's going after a gun, we're getting the hell out of here!"

"Let me talk to him. Maybe we can have a prayer and calm him down."

"We'll pray later!" said Spiller.

"John, John, put that down right now!"

"I'll kill that son-of-a-bitch!"

"Give it to me! Give it to me! All right now settle down."

Mr. and Mrs. Finney returned to the living room. Mrs. Finney had a .38 pistol in her hand. She handed it to Spiller. "Unload this thing. I don't know anything about guns."

Spiller took the gun, opened the chamber, and dropped six .38 caliber shells into his hand. Spiller stared at them for a moment then looked over at Mr. Watson. Mr. Watson, with tear-filled eyes, stood staring at Spiller.

Spiller looked back at Mr. Finney who said, "You're a no good son-of-a-bitch for being in that uniform. I should've shot you."

Mr. Finney paced back and forth.

"Fucking senseless war! Senseless shit! And look at our pretty, little sergeant all dressed up in his uniform. Why the fuck don't they send you over there? I'll bet your sweet little ass wouldn't look so pretty then."

Mr. Finney, face to face with Spiller, asked bitterly, "What are you sweating for, Sergeant, am I hitting home?" Then looking at Mr. Watson, he charged, "And who the fuck are you, mister? I'll bet you're going to pray for my son, aren't you?"

Mr. Finney looked at Spiller.

"Still sweating, huh, Sergeant? You son-of-a-bitch."

Mr. Finney turned and continued to pace back and forth across the room.

"Dead! Oh, my God!"

Again, Mr. Finney walked over to Spiller.

"You know how old my son was? Do you, Sergeant?"

"No, sir."

"He was twenty-one. Twenty-one, Sergeant! How old are you? Huh, Sergeant? How old are you?"

"Twenty-two, sir."

For a moment Mr. Finney looked at Spiller with a glare then turned and silently walked over to a chair and sat down.

"May we have a prayer before we leave, sir?" asked Mr. Watson.

"No," said Mr. Finney. "We're not ready for prayer."

Spiller handed Mrs. Finney the gun and a business card. As he started out the door, he looked back at Mr. Finney, who was staring into space.

Spiller and Watson left the house and walked out to the car, where they found Liss had quickly recovered from his stomach pains. Smoking a cigarette, he stood up against the car. Being called everything in the world, almost shot, and then finding Liss had faked his stomach ache to get out of making the call made Spiller feel depressed. He didn't have any support, and he really felt alone. The pastor cried and hugged him. Spiller thought that it bothered the pastor as much as it did him.

The Marines didn't have a funeral for John Finney. His family was originally from Florida, so the funeral was held there.

During the next three months, Liss enlisted three walk-ins and Spiller got the rest. They made their quota without any problem. Their pool, which was to have half of their quotas filled three months ahead of time, was filled too. At that time, Liss made a bad decision. The quota for the month of March for the St. Louis station was short. The C.O. called all the recruiting stations and asked them to call the applicants in the pool to see if any of them would be willing to go in March. Liss figured out what it would take to win the quarterly award for outstanding recruiting station, so he drained their entire pool just for that award. Liss and Spiller went to St. Louis, where both of them received a pen set and one large plaque for outstanding recruiting station.

During the same three months, they only received three casualty calls, and they had all been wounded in action. Since Liss was always conveniently busy, Spiller made all three of the calls.

In May 1968 Ledue called to ask them to participate in a color guard for a Memorial Day parade to begin at the Southern Illinois University Campus.

Spiller tightened the sling on the M-1 rifle, while Ledue and Liss adjusted their harnesses to carry the flags. The color guard stood on the curb near the football field waiting for the parade to begin. Across the campus a group of hippies had gathered to demonstrate. One hippie carried a Vietcong flag. The group started to run with the lead man carrying the flag.

"Ho, Ho, Ho Chi Minh. Ho, Ho, Ho Chi Minh," they chanted.

The group ran around the side of a building and were suddenly silent.

"Wonder what happened to them?" asked Spiller.

"Don't know," said Ledue.

Soon a police officer came around the corner of the building carrying the Vietcong flag. Right behind him came three officers, carrying the hippies by their hands and feet.

"All right!" said Spiller.

"Way to go!" said Liss.

"That's the end of that demonstration," said Ledue.

17
Enough Is Enough

Because the summer months were the easy months, Spiller and Liss filled their quota quite easily. They'd received nine casualty calls during the summer. Eight were wounded in action and one was a KIA. Spiller made eight of the nine calls and was by now doing all the recruiting. Liss was taking off two and three days a week. He would show up at the office early in the morning, tell Spiller he wasn't coming in, and Spiller wouldn't see him sometimes for two days. Spiller would cover for him, but now the sergeant major was getting suspicious. Liss finally made a big mistake.

Spiller was on the road almost five days a week, in and out of air-conditioning. He had caught a bad cold. He called Liss at the office one morning and asked if he could take the day off. When Liss asked what the problem was, Spiller told him. Liss told Spiller to take the day off, so Spiller went back to bed. Early that afternoon, Liss called to ask how Spiller was doing. Spiller's wife told him that Harry was doing okay, but was running a temperature of 102 degrees. Liss demanded that Harry go to the hospital immediately. Spiller's wife and Liss argued for ten minutes. He finally hung up. She told Harry that Liss was drunk and that he was coming to the house. Harry couldn't believe he was making such a big deal out of a cold. When Liss got to the house, he was so drunk he could hardly walk. He and Spiller's wife began to argue again.

Liss later called the sergeant major and told him Spiller had a temperature of 106 and was so sick he couldn't get out of bed. To make matters worse, he said Spiller's wife wouldn't send him to the hospital. The sergeant major called the house and ordered Spiller's wife to take him to the hospital. She told him she wasn't in the Marine Corps, didn't take orders from anybody, and hung up. Spiller was sure he was going to be court-martialed, but he couldn't believe it was going to be over a common cold.

Later that afternoon Spiller called the sergeant major and told him he wasn't dying, but that he did have a cold and temperature of 102. The sergeant major wanted to know why Liss was making such a big deal out of it, so Spiller told him the whole story about his drinking and everything he'd been doing. The sergeant major went wild.

The following week Liss made his biggest mistake. The C.O. came down for inspection. Instead of being there for inspection, Liss went on the road and left Spiller to meet the captain. Liss was relieved from recruiting duty, and the captain put Spiller in charge of the station. There was to be no replacement for Liss.

It was September 1968, and Spiller had his work cut out for him. The tough months were ahead, and he didn't have a single enlistment for October, November, or December. In addition, the captain left the quota the same, just as if Spiller were a two-man recruiting station.

For the next two months, Spiller worked day and night trying to make quota. His wife went to the recruiting station with him and helped by doing the paperwork. They spent many long nights at the office. They not only made the quotas, but shipped two over quota in December. Spiller won the outstanding recruiting station for the quarter and received a plaque. He and his wife continued in January, February, and March working day and night. Spiller not only made quota for those months, he shipped 200 percent. He'd been lucky. In six months, he'd made only two casualty calls, and both were wounded in action. Spiller won outstanding recruiting station again, and the captain came down to present a special award to his wife for helping him in the office.

All too soon, it was time for high school career days, and Spiller was preparing for a presentation at Fredericktown High School.

Spiller parked in the lot behind the Fredericktown High School gym, picked up his briefcase, and walked into the gym. The scene was the same as the year before. Chairs were lined up in front and a podium in the middle. Spiller walked to his table and neatly stacked Marine Corps literature. Jack Palmer, the school's guidance counselor, walked up to the table.

"Good morning, Sergeant Spiller. How are you, today?"

"Great. How are you?"

"I'm fine. We're going to do this one like last year, a five-minute presentation each, then the students interested can come to your table. There is one request however."

Spiller stopped stacking literature and looked up. "What's that?"

"The other recruiters have requested that you go first."

Spiller laughed, "Oh! All right, Mr. Palmer. I don't mind going first."

"Good, good. I just didn't want any problems."

"No problem at all."

Spiller walked to the stage and sat erect in his chair, watching the students file into the gym. Mr. Palmer walked to the podium.

"I'd like to thank our guests from the Armed Forces today for participating in our career day. Students, each representative will give a five-minute presentation, then they'll go to their tables. If you're interested in talking with them, do so at that time. Our first speaker is from the United States Marine Corps, Sergeant Spiller."

Mr. Palmer turned, "Sergeant."

Spiller walked to the podium and looked left to right across the entire student body.

"The United States Marine Corps is the greatest fighting force in the world. We serve on land, at sea, and in the air. We have every job occupation that the rest of the services have, except for one thing. We don't promise you anything. If you want a certain job, then you have to earn it. We have two-, three-, or four-year enlistments, and you can sign up for our 120-day delay program. If you want to be part of the elite, and you have the guts to try, I'll be in the far corner at the table. If you want promises, then go to some other table."

Spiller turned and walked back to his chair. The other branches of the service made their presentations, and the students were dismissed. Spiller walked to his table. Students flocked, grabbing at the literature. A well-built senior in levis and a t-shirt stood to the side of the crowd talking with four other students. When the crowd cleared, he walked toward Spiller. The others followed.

"We want to join the Marine Corps, sir," said the senior with a smile.

"All five of you?"

"Yes, sir."

Spiller smiled. "You've made a good choice, gentlemen. Grab some of those chairs and bring them over. We'll get started."

Spiller was really happy. Recruits seemed to flock to him everywhere he went. Even with the same quota that a two-man station was assigned, he was over quota almost every month. These five recruits were from Marquand, Missouri. Spiller filled out their enlistment kits that day.

The next morning as he was typing out enlistment kits on the five recruits, the phone rang.

"Marine Corps Recruiting Station, Sergeant Spiller."

"Sergeant Spiller, this is Bill Avery from Marquand. I enlisted yesterday at school."

"Yeah, Bill. What can I do for you?"

"We have four more of our buddies that want to sign up."

"Really? How old are they?"

"They're all 18, sir. They're serious, too."

"Could they meet with me today?"

"Yes, sir."

"Okay. Let's see . . . ."

Spiller looked at the clock. It was 9 A.M.

"How about if I meet you in front of the J.C. Penney store at 12:00 noon?"

"That'll be fine, sir."

Spiller laughed, "See you then, Bill."

Spiller drove for a little over an hour until he hit the blacktop that led to Marquand. As Spiller approached the town that spring day in 1969, he noticed just how beautiful the small country town was. A bridge crossed a stream at the town's edge. Bluish-gray water ran over the rocky stream bed. Redbuds on both sides of the stream were in bloom. A small, quiet, country church sat visibly on a hilltop at the far edge of town.

"It's everything you could possibly picture in your mind. What a beautiful little town," Spiller thought, as he read the sign, Marquand, Missouri – Population 98.

Spiller stopped in front of the J.C. Penney store. Standing in front of the store was Bill Avery and four other young men. Spiller stepped out of the car and walked up to them.

"Good morning, men! I understand you're interested in becoming Marines."

"Yes, sir," replied the four teenagers excitedly.

"Okay, let me get the forms, and we'll get started. Is there some place we can go to get this paperwork done?"

"We can go to my house," replied Bill.

"Sure your parents won't mind?"

"No. As a matter of fact, they want to meet you."

Spiller laughed.

"Okay. You got a car?"

"Yes, sir."

"I'll follow you."

The teenagers ran for Bill's car.

Spiller followed the potential applicants across town. Bill pulled into the driveway, and Spiller parked near the curb in front of the house.

Picking up his briefcase, Spiller followed Bill into the living room, where a middle-aged woman stood smiling.

"Sergeant Spiller, I'd like you to meet my mother."

"Mrs. Avery, it's nice to meet you."

"I feel like I already know you, Sergeant Spiller. All I've heard is Sergeant Spiller said this or that," replied Mrs. Avery.

"Mom, we want to use the table in the kitchen, so Sergeant Spiller can fill out the forms for these guys."

Spiller and the five teenagers went into the kitchen and seated themselves at the table. Spiller spent the next hour asking questions, filling out forms, and getting signatures.

"Okay, gentlemen, I'll send all nine of you together next Thursday. I'll bring your bus tickets on Wednesday. You'll leave Thursday, spend the night in St. Louis, and take your physical and written test on Friday. That sound okay?" Spiller asked with a grin.

"Yes, sir!" said the applicants.

As Spiller walked out the door, the five boys and Mrs. Avery were all smiles. So was Spiller. A town with 98 population, and he'd just enlisted nine of them. He was excited. He couldn't wait to get them on that bus. He went back the following Wednesday and gave them the bus tickets for St. Louis. He met with four other parents. They thought Spiller was great, too. He'd helped their sons' careers, their futures. Mrs. Avery even thanked him for making such an impression on her son. All nine passed their physicals and left for boot camp in June 1969.

It was September, and the phone rang.

"Marine Corps Recruiting Station, Staff Sergeant Spiller."

"Sergeant Spiller, this is the Sergeant Major. How are you today?"

"Doing fine. I have a casualty notification for you, Harry."

"Okay, Sergeant Major. Let me get a card."

Spiller pulled a card from the drawer and placed it in front of him.

"Go ahead, Sergeant Major."

"PFC Bill Avery, KIA, September 1969, Da Nang area. Stepped on a booby trap. Religion: Protestant, Next of Kin: Mr. and Mrs. Bill Avery, Rt. 1, Marquand, Missouri. Got it?"

"Yes, yes, I've got the information, Sergeant Major."

"Okay, I'll talk to you later. I have three more of these. Things must be breaking loose over there."

"Yes, sir."

Spiller hung up the phone and just sat back in his chair. A short time later, he picked up his cap and the casualty card and headed for Marquand.

All the casualty calls Spiller had made in the past bothered him, but this was the first KIA he had to make on a Marine that he had enlisted. All the way to Marquand, he kept thinking about Avery, the other seniors he had enlisted, and how excited they were. One thing that really bothered Spiller was Bill's parents. He remembered the day Mrs. Avery thanked him for making such a good impression on her son and said he had helped set his future. Over and over those words kept going through Spiller's mind.... "He helped set his future...."

Spiller pushed into Marquand, drove across town, and parked in front of the Avery house. He hesitated for a moment, picked up the casualty card, and hopped out of the car. He headed toward the house. Mrs. Avery heard the car door slam and came to the front door. Spiller looked up at Mrs. Avery. As he walked closer to the house, Mrs. Avery's smile changed to a frown.

When Spiller came face to face with her, she asked, "Sergeant Spiller, what's wrong?"

Spiller's lip quivered as he looked Mrs. Avery in the eye.

"Ma'am, I'm afraid I have some bad news."

"Oh, no! Oh, no! Bill isn't dead, is he?"

Spiller took a deep breath and looked to the ground. Tears welled in his eyes.

Looking back up at Mrs. Avery, he replied, "Yes, ma'am, I'm afraid he is."

Mrs. Avery fell into Spiller's arms and cried. This time Spiller cried too.

Spiller felt responsible for Avery's death. He'd helped him plan his future. Death to an 18-year-old, fighting an unpopular war. The Averys treated Spiller like he was part of their family. He did not know what he would have done if the Averys had blamed him for their son's death. Spiller and the Avery family planned a military funeral. Upon his return to Cape Girardeau, Spiller went to the hotel bar across the street from the office and had a couple of beers.

For the next ten days he had four wounded-in-action calls to make and one funeral to attend in Carbondale. The casualties were pouring in to all the recruiting stations. Ten days after the casualty notification, the recruiters met in Marquand for Avery's funeral. Unlike most of the caskets, Avery's was open. The government had an air-tight, see-through shield placed on the casket so that when the lid was opened, the body could be viewed. They did that on all open caskets from Vietnam. The funeral was held at the country church on the hill at the edge of town.

The Marines lined up just outside of the church and marched down the aisle to the front pew, where they sat at attention. All eyes were on the Marines as they stood at attention while the organist played the Marine Corps hymn.

"No greater a man than a man that lays down his life for a friend," said the minister.

They said that at every funeral Spiller attended, but as the minister spoke those words, Spiller wondered what kind of friend he had been. In desperation, he tried to blank out as much of the funeral as he could. He felt guilty and blamed himself for Avery's death. He tried not to recall, but his attempt to forget, to block out, was all in vain. Flowing through his mind was the image of Bill Avery on the day he enlisted. His eyes were alive with excitement. To him and his parents, Spiller represented a bright future, a future full of excitement, but the excitement was short-lived.

When the funeral was over, everyone in the church passed by the casket to view the body one last time. As Spiller walked by, he looked straight ahead. He couldn't make himself look at the still body that was once so full of life. The funeral director wheeled the casket to the pall bearers as they waited at the front door.

The Marines took positions on each side of the casket, then walked down the steps and into the church cemetery. Placing the casket at the grave, Spiller took the position at the head of the casket. Ledue was at the other end. The remainder of the Marines lined up for the firing squad. The minister prayed, and Spiller gave the nod to the firing squad. The shots echoed across the cemetery and hills in Marquand. Spiller then took one end of the flag. Ledue folded toward Spiller. Having tucked the flag Ledue handed it to Spiller. Spiller, with flag in hand, walked to Mr. and Mrs. Avery.

"Mr. and Mrs. Avery, we'd like to present our nation's colors to you in recognition of your son's giving of his life in the Republic of South Vietnam in the defense of the United States of America."

Spiller bent over and laid the flag in Mrs. Avery's lap. As he did, Mrs. Avery looked at him and laid her hand on top of his. Tears streamed down her face.

"We love you too, son. Thank you for being so kind."

Tears rushed to Spiller's eyes as he pulled away. He stood erect and saluted the family. He then did a right face and walked away....

Driving back to Cape Girardeau that day, Spiller was haunted by Mrs. Avery's words. "We love you too, son. Thank you for being so kind." The other KIAs had been tough, but this was by far the toughest. The war, the KIAs, they'd become very personal to him. When Spiller returned to Cape Girardeau, he stopped at the hotel bar again and had a few beers.

During the next month, Spiller didn't do much recruiting. He was really depressed. In those two months, he'd attended two funerals, one in Marion, the other in Poplar Bluff. Of the three wounded-in-action calls, two were his enlistees.

Before long, Spiller was spending more and more time in bars – a few beers at lunchtime, then a few after work. Just as he returned from the post office one morning, the phone rang.

"Marine Corps Recruiting Station, Staff Sergeant Spiller."

"Harry, this is the Sergeant Major. I have a KIA for you."

Spiller took a deep breath.

"Just a minute, Sergeant Major," he said, reaching for a card. "Go ahead, Sergeant Major."

"L/CPL Dale Smith, Quang Tri, KIA, October 10, 1969, Religion: Protestant; Next of Kin: Mr. and Mrs. Jesse Smith, Rt. 1, Marquand, Missouri. Got it, Harry?"

"Yeah, I got it, Sergeant Major."

"Harry, I know you've been hit hard with casualties, but so have other areas. You're a Marine. Keep your helmet on. Understand? Understand?"

"Yes, sir. Yes, sir. I understand."

"That a boy. *Semper fidelis.* Let's hear you say it."

"*Semper fidelis. Semper fidelis,* sir," Spiller repeated unenthusiastically.

"That a boy. I'll see you."

Once again, Spiller drove to Marquand. He couldn't believe it. Two KIAs in a little over a month and both from Marquand. And what did the sergeant major say? *"Semper fidelis"*? Now that he thought about it, there really wasn't anything else he could have said. At the time Spiller wondered just how faithful he had been to the families in Marquand, and furthermore, how faithful would they be to him?

Spiller passed the sign to Marquand. He drove the route across town to the Smith's residence.

Taking a deep breath, he reached for the card and his cap, and then slowly got out of the car. Spiller squared his cap, walked slowly to the front door. He hesitated for a moment, then knocked. Mrs. Smith opened the door, looked up at Spiller, then stepped back.

"Oh, God! No! Dale! Please, Sergeant Spiller!"

"Ma'am, your son's been killed in action."

The Smith family treated Spiller just as the Averys had – as if he were part of the family. The funeral was held in the same country church.

Upon returning to the office that day, Spiller found he had another casualty call to make. The sergeant major had given the information to the Navy recruiter. While it was only a wounded-in-action, the Marine from Jackson, Missouri, was also one of his enlistees.

For the next two weeks, Spiller was on the road, but he made no effort to enlist anyone. He was burned out, depressed, and to be truthful, he wasn't sure he was doing the right thing anymore.

He blamed himself for every killed in action he had enlisted, just as if he had pulled the trigger. He was too proud to admit that it was getting to him. After all, Spiller was a Marine. He was supposed to "always be faithful." He was brainwashed and just too stupid to admit it. It was like surrendering, and a Marine would never surrender. He was trapped. His drinking became more and more frequent, and more and more often, he was staying out late at night. This caused a good deal of trouble between he and his wife. It had been difficult for her to begin with. Military life always is. They would never have enough money to do anything, and with his extra responsibilities, he was gone all the time. To make matters worse, one night Spiller got into a fight.

Spiller walked into the hotel bar across from the recruiting station and took a seat at the bar. To Spiller's left, at the far end of the bar, were three men in their early twenties, sipping beer. They all had beards and shoulder-length hair. One wore a gold earring. As Spiller sat sipping his beer, the men looked down the bar at Spiller, laughed, and then whispered to themselves.

"Hey, Marine," the man closest to Spiller yelled. "You look real pretty sitting there."

Spiller, taking a sip of beer, sat quietly.

"Hey, Marine, you too good to talk to us? You some kind of hero or what?"

Spiller was silent.

The three whispered among themselves. The two men farthest from Spiller got up and walked past him into the restroom. The one remaining smiled devilishly, as he sat at the bar looking at Spiller. The bathroom door opened, and the two men stepped out. As they stood there, the one at the bar got off the bar stool and proceeded to walk toward Spiller. Spiller looked slightly to his left and noticed the other two walking slowly toward him. The other man stopped a couple of feet from him.

"Look, Mister, I'm not bothering you. Just leave me alone."

"Well, looky here. Our pretty little Marine can talk. We thought maybe you were too damned good to talk to us."

Spiller watched the man out of the corner of his eye.

"Look at all them medals. Why, he's a hero! Don't want to admit you're a hero, Marine?"

"Mister, please, just leave me alone."

"What's the matter? Does it bring back memories, Marine? Want to forget it? Just how many babies and women did you murder to get those?"

"Ooooooh!" Spiller yelled as he swung his left arm back, hitting the man in the throat.

The guy directly behind Spiller put a choke hold on Spiller, as the other drew back to hit him. Spiller threw his body up and kicked the second man in the face. The first man, still bent over holding his throat was making a gurgling sound. The second man, holding his face, lay on the floor. Spiller threw the third man across his shoulder. When he hit the floor, Spiller kicked him in his privates. Spiller stepped back, trying to catch his breath.

"I called the police!" said the bartender excitedly.

"Damn! I'll get in trouble for this."

"No, you won't. They started it, and I'm a witness."

A short time later, two police officers arrived. Spiller stood silently watching the three men. One stood rubbing his throat, the second held a handkerchief over his bloody nose, and the third, in great pain, still holding his privates, sat moaning on the floor.

"What happened here?" asked Officer Robbins.

"That son-of-a-bitch hit me in the throat!"

"Yeah, he attacked us."

"Is that right, Sergeant?" asked Officer Robbins.

"Well, sir, not exactly. I did hit them, but they called me a murderer, sir."

"That's right, officer. The sarge was sitting here minding his own business, and these guys kept picking at him."

With a slight grin, Officer Robbins looked at Spiller.

"Sarge, I haven't seen you at the police station for a while. Did you quit enlisting, or have they stopped the police checks?"

"Neither, sir. Things have been a little slow."

"We want him arrested," said the man rubbing his throat.

"Shut up, hippie, and get up against the bar. All of you up against the bar and spread 'em."

"What are we being arrested for?" asked the man with the bloody nose.

"Disorderly conduct."

The police took all three of them away, and Spiller had another beer. "Murderer," that was a typical statement during that time. Marines were labeled warmongers and murderers. Though there were those who supported the Marines; few come forward. It made those in the service feel as though they'd been abandoned by their own country.

By then Spiller and his wife were having serious troubles. Spiller would go home drunk, and if his wife said anything about it, Spiller would just get up and leave. If she tried to talk to him, he'd yell at her or throw something across the room. Finally, she left him.

The sergeant major, sensing that something was wrong, came down. While he knew the casualty calls were getting to Spiller, he didn't know the rest. He was an observant man. Spiller had a lot of respect for him. Spiller told him about the drinking and about his wife leaving. The sergeant major gave Spiller a lecture he couldn't believe. What really got to Spiller was when the sergeant major told him he could get as drunk as he wanted every day and every night and crawl in the gutter in dress blues, but sooner or later, he'd keep running and he'd hit a dead end, alone, and with nowhere else to run. The people that cared about him wouldn't be there anymore. He was right. The casualty calls had been tough, and Spiller had begun to take the war personally. It was like it was his war, just his.

While Spiller was trying to run from all that, he was chasing away the very people that cared most about him. The sergeant major gave him two weeks to straighten up. Spiller went to his mother-in-law's home in Vienna and pleaded with his wife to come home. It took a little persuasion, but she came back.

Before long Spiller was filling his quotas, though not as eagerly as he once had. His heart was no longer in it.

On a Sunday in March 1970, Spiller and his wife were at home watching TV, when the phone rang.

"Hello," Spiller answered.

"Harry, this is the Sergeant Major. I have a casualty call for you."

"Okay, Sergeant Major. Let me find a casualty card."

Spiller opened a kitchen drawer and shuffled through papers until he found a card.

"Okay, go ahead."

"L/Cpl Scott Pennington, killed in action, March 7, 1970, Quang Tri, land mine. Religion: Protestant; Next of kin: Harold Pennington, Route 2, Marquand, Missouri. "You got it?"

"Yes, sir."

"Okay, gotta go. I have another call to make."

"Yes, sir."

Spiller turned to his wife and said, "I've got another KIA."

"Where at?"

"Marquand. Will you go with me?"

"Sure. I'll go."

Spiller and his wife drove for a little over an hour, finally reaching Marquand.

"I don't know how I'm going to find Route 2. The post office is closed."

"Didn't you enlist him?"

"Yeah, but I was never at his house. I enlisted him at the high school. Let me ask that guy over there."

"Sir, sir," he called out to a man walking across the street.

The man looked back. "You calling me?"

"Yes, sir. Could you tell me how to get on Route 2? I'm looking for the Penningtons."

"Best I know, Route 2 covers all the roads north of town. Heard of that Pennington fellow. I just don't know where he lives."

"Thank you, sir."

Spiller crawled back into the car.

"What did he say?"

"He didn't know where the Penningtons lived, but Route 2 covers the whole northern end of Marquand."

Spiller drove through town and onto a blacktop road. About a half-mile out of town Spiller pulled into a driveway.

"I'll be back in a minute."

"Okay, be careful."

Spiller walked to the front of the house and knocked. A large collie in the yard barked at Spiller.

A man in his sixties, wearing bib overalls and a t-shirt underneath, came to the door.

"Can I help ya?"

"Yes, sir. I'm looking for the Pennington residence, sir."

"Pennington? Pennington? Heard that name, but don't know where they live."

"Is this Route 2?"

"Surely is, son."

"Thank you, sir."

As Spiller turned to walk back to the car, the collie snapped.

"Ouch! Shit!"

Spiller ran for the car, the dog right on his heels. Quickly, he opened the door and jumped in.

"Ouch! Shit! That son-of-a-bitch bit me on the ass!"

"Well, honey, let's see. Did he break the skin?"

"Wait 'til we get down the road a little."

Spiller pulled out of the driveway, drove about a quarter of a mile down the road, and stopped. He opened the car door and stepped out.

"Did the son-of-a-bitch rip my pants?"

"No, they're okay."

Spiller plopped back into the seat and drove another half-mile. They stopped at two more houses, and finally, the people at the last house gave Spiller directions.

"Well, did they know them?" his wife asked.

"Sure did. We're supposed to take the first road to the right and follow it for about a mile. The house is on the left side of the road."

Spiller drove about an eighth of a mile and came to a narrow road.

"Is that it?"

"I guess. They said the first road."

Spiller turned and drove down the road. The further he drove, the narrower the road got. It was getting dark and Spiller was in the middle of the woods. The road was getting muddier.

"This is a log road."

"You'd better turn around. We're gonna get stuck."

"I can't. It's too dark, and we've gone too far."

"Oh, Harry, we're going to get stuck."

"We'll get out of here."

Spiller drove another quarter of a mile and ran into a gravel road.

"I didn't think a gravel road could look so good."

"Me either."

"I don't know where we are. Guess I'll stop at the first house we come to and start over."

Spiller drove for almost a mile, where he spotted several cars parked in the road ahead.

"Wonder what's going on up there?"

"I don't know," said Spiller, "but we should be able to find out where we are."

Spiller pulled behind a car and as he parked, looked up at the people standing in the yard.

"I don't believe it!" he said.

Spiller and his wife had been all over the country asking for the Penningtons, and no one knew them, except the people at the last house. But standing in the yard were the three different men that Spiller had asked for directions. They'd already told the family their son was dead. Spiller had not said a word to either of them, but they knew. Spiller guessed his very presence spelled death to them. The Penningtons never did ask if there had been a mistake or if he had just been wounded. They just accepted that their son was dead.

Two weeks later, they had the funeral.

Spiller and the other Marines walked slowly to the gravesite and set the casket in position. Spiller took the position at the head of the casket. Ledue stood at the opposite end. The minister began, "He maketh me to lie down in green pastures...."

Harry drifted back to Vietnam, 1965. Spiller and Smith each grabbed the end of a body bag. As they ran for the truck, blood oozed from beneath the bag. Both Spiller and Smith laughed and yelled. So did the rest of the Marines that carried bodies to the truck. One Marine, with a camera, took pictures of the entire incident. Spiller looked across the runway as the truck pulled away. The passengers from the civilian airline lined the edge of the airfield watching the Marines. Men, women, and children looked horrified. Two six-bys pulled up to a Vietnamese cemetery just outside Phu Bai village. A Vietnamese, sitting on a back hoe, was parked beside a large hole, soon to be a mass grave for the dead VC.

Spiller and Smith stood up.

"Let's take this one first," said Spiller. "He has an arm missing."

"Okay," said Smith. "Let's see how high we can throw him."

Smith grabbed the arm. Spiller grabbed the legs. Back and forth they swung the body.

"Are you ready?" asked Spiller. "Here we go. One, two, three!"

Spiller and Smith tossed the body into the air. The corpse hit with a thud. Both laughed and grabbed for another body.

Shots rang out. Spiller looked at Ledue, wondering if the first sergeant had given the nod to the firing squad. Spiller and Ledue folded the flag and Spiller walked to the family.

"Mr. and Mrs. Pennington, I'd like to present you with our nation's

Mound City National Cemetery (courtesy of Marilyn Mick Blatter).

colors in recognition of your son who gave his life in the Republic of South Vietnam in the defense of the United States of America."

Spiller laid the flag in Mrs. Pennington's lap, stood, saluted the family, did a right face, and walked off.

Spiller's routine continued, on the road one day and in the office the next. When the sergeant major called one day and told him he had another recruiter coming in, Spiller was thrilled and relieved. He knew he'd be getting orders soon.

Mound City National Cemetery (courtesy of Marilyn Mick Blatter).

It was that time of year again for high school career days, and Spiller pulled into the parking lot of Farmington High School.

Spiller walked into the gym. The bleachers were pulled out on one side of the gym floor. A podium sat a few feet in front of the bleachers. Several chairs were placed in a straight line behind the podium. On the opposite side of the gym were tables tagged with labels for each branch of service. Spiller took a seat. A tall, thin man walked up to Spiller.

"Good morning, Sergeant. I'm Mr. Wilson. We'll be getting started shortly. I'll introduce each of you, and you can make your presentation. If you could please hold it to ten minutes."

"Thank you, sir."

Spiller watched the students laughing as they entered the gym and took seats on the bleachers. Mr. Wilson walked to the podium.

"Let me have your attention, please. We have members of all the Armed Forces with us today. Each one will speak to you for five to ten minutes, then you'll have a chance to ask questions afterwards. I would like to introduce Staff Sergeant Harry Spiller from the United States Marine Corps.

Spiller, walking to the podium, looked from left to right. He glanced at the young faces, energetic, so full of life. He thought back. . . .

"We want to join the Marine Corps, sir."

"All five of you?"

"Yes, sir!"

"You've made a good choice, gentlemen...."

"Mrs. Avery, it's nice to meet you."

"I feel like I already know you, Sergeant Spiller. That's all I've heard is Sergeant Spiller said this or that.... Thank you for making such a good impression on my son."

Spiller looked back across the crowd of high school students. Mr. Wilson, obviously puzzled by Spiller's strange behavior, looked at Spiller.

"Sergeant Spiller, what's wrong?"

...Spiller's lip quivered, as he looked Mrs. Avery in the eye.

"Ma'am, I'm afraid I have some bad news."

"Oh no! Oh no! Bill isn't dead, is he?"

Tears welled in his eyes. He looked back up at Mrs. Avery.

"Yes, ma'am. I'm afraid he is...."

Spiller, still silent, with tear-filled eyes, looked over at Mr. Wilson.

"Thank you, sir, for having invited me." He turned, picked up his briefcase, and walked out of the gym. As the recruiter disappeared through the door, giggles and whispers from the young students filled the air with energy, innocence, and life.

Index